THE DEFENDERS

DIAMONDS ARE FOREVER

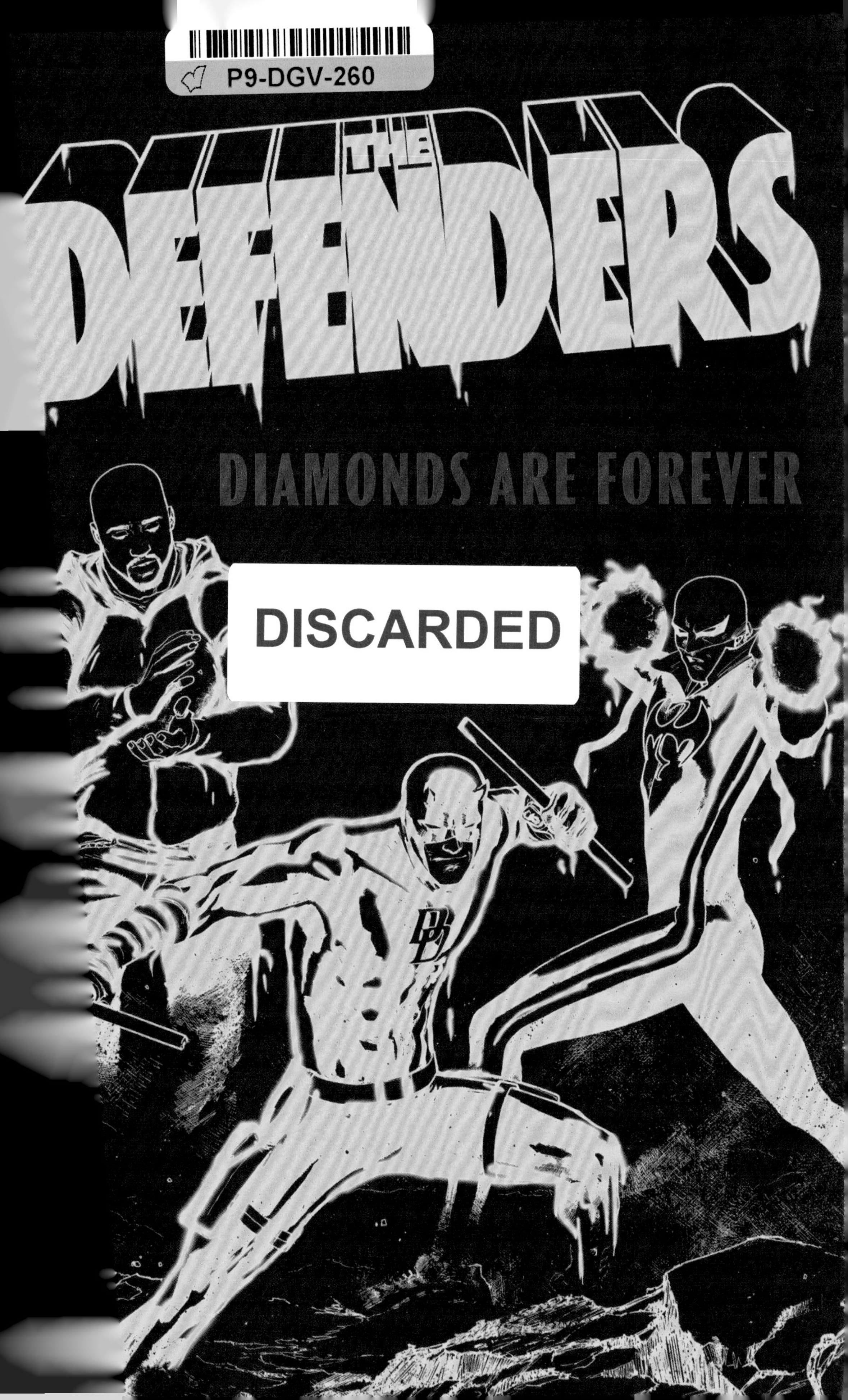

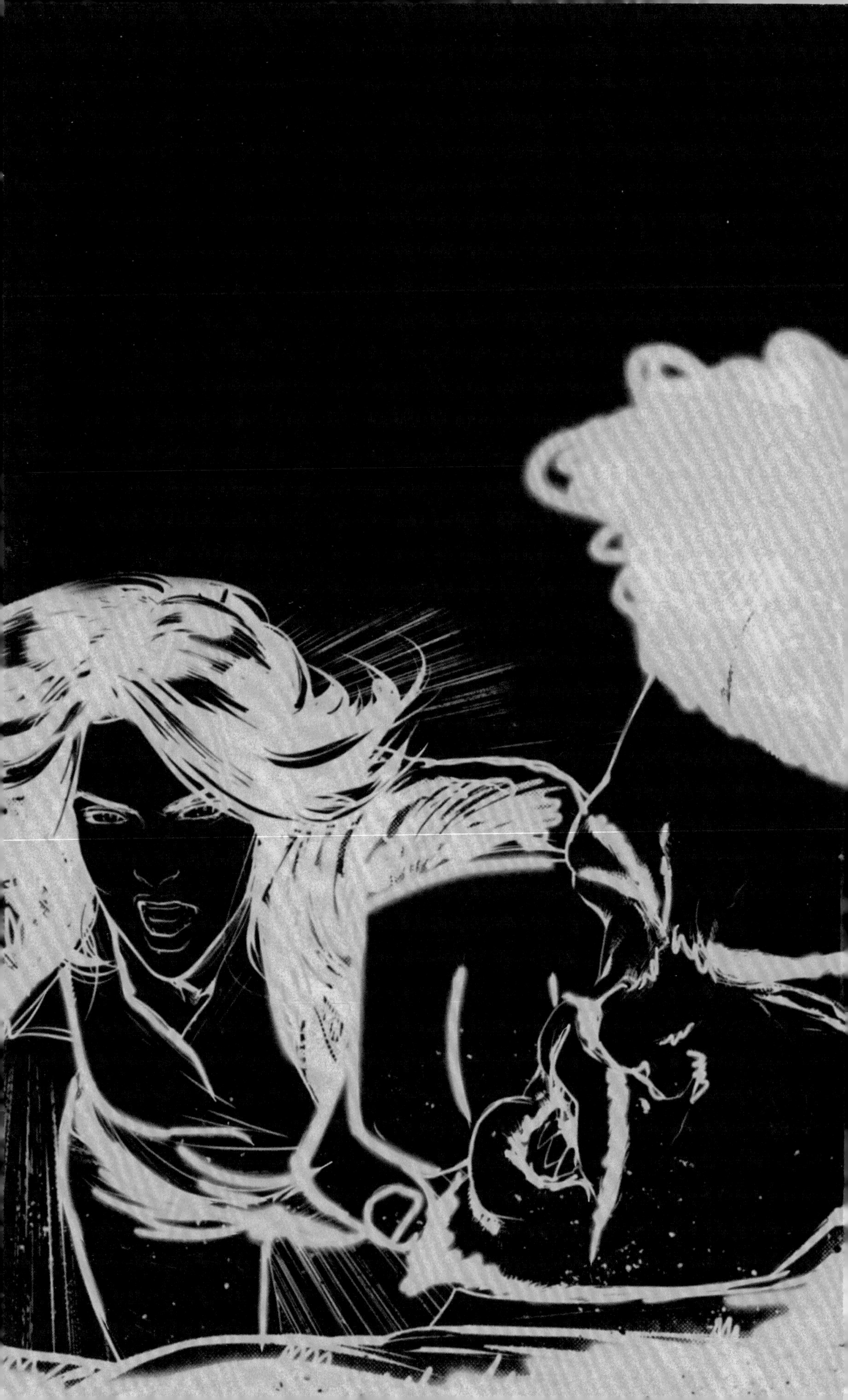

THE DEFENDERS

DIAMONDS ARE FOREVER

BRIAN MICHAEL BENDIS
WRITER

DAVID MARQUEZ
ARTIST

JUSTIN PONSOR
COLOR ARTIST

VC's CORY PETIT
LETTERER

**DAVID MARQUEZ &
JUSTIN PONSOR**
COVER ART

ALANNA SMITH
ASSISTANT EDITOR

TOM BREVOORT
EDITOR

COLLECTION EDITOR: **JENNIFER GRÜNWALD**   VP PRODUCTION & SPECIAL PROJECTS: **JEFF YOUNGQUIST**   EDITOR IN CHIEF: **AXEL ALONSO**
ASSISTANT EDITOR: **CAITLIN O'CONNELL**   SVP PRINT, SALES & MARKETING: **DAVID GABRIEL**   CHIEF CREATIVE OFFICER: **JOE QUESADA**
ASSOCIATE MANAGING EDITOR: **KATERI WOODY**   BOOK DESIGNER: **ADAM DEL RE**   PRESIDENT: **DAN BUCKLEY**
EDITOR, SPECIAL PROJECTS: **MARK D. BEAZLEY**   EXECUTIVE PRODUCER: **ALAN FINE**

DEFENDERS VOL. 1: DIAMONDS ARE FOREVER. Contains material originally published in magazine form as FREE COMIC BOOK DAY 2017 (ALL-NEW GUARDIANS OF THE GALAXY) #1 and DEFENDERS #1-5. First printing 2017. ISBN# 978-1-302-90746-4. Published by MARVEL WORLDWIDE, INC., a subsidiary of MARVEL ENTERTAINMENT, LLC. OFFICE OF PUBLICATION: 135 West 50th Street, New York, NY 10020. Copyright © 2017 MARVEL. No similarity between any of the names, characters, persons, and/or institutions in this magazine with those of any living or dead person or institution is intended, and any such similarity which may exist is purely coincidental. **Printed in Canada.** DAN BUCKLEY, President, Marvel Entertainment; JOE QUESADA, Chief Creative Officer; TOM BREVOORT, SVP of Publishing; DAVID BOGART, SVP of Business Affairs & Operations, Publishing & Partnership; C.B. CEBULSKI, VP of Brand Management & Development, Asia; DAVID GABRIEL, SVP of Sales & Marketing, Publishing; JEFF YOUNGQUIST, VP of Production & Special Projects; DAN CARR, Executive Director of Publishing Technology; ALEX MORALES, Director of Publishing Operations; SUSAN CRESPI, Production Manager; STAN LEE, Chairman Emeritus. For information regarding advertising in Marvel Comics or on Marvel.com, please contact Vit DeBellis, Integrated Sales Manager, at vdebellis@marvel.com. For Marvel subscription inquiries, please call 888-511-5480. **Manufactured between 10/20/2017 and 11/21/2017 by SOLISCO PRINTERS, SCOTT, QC, CANADA.**

10 9 8 7 6 5 4 3 2 1

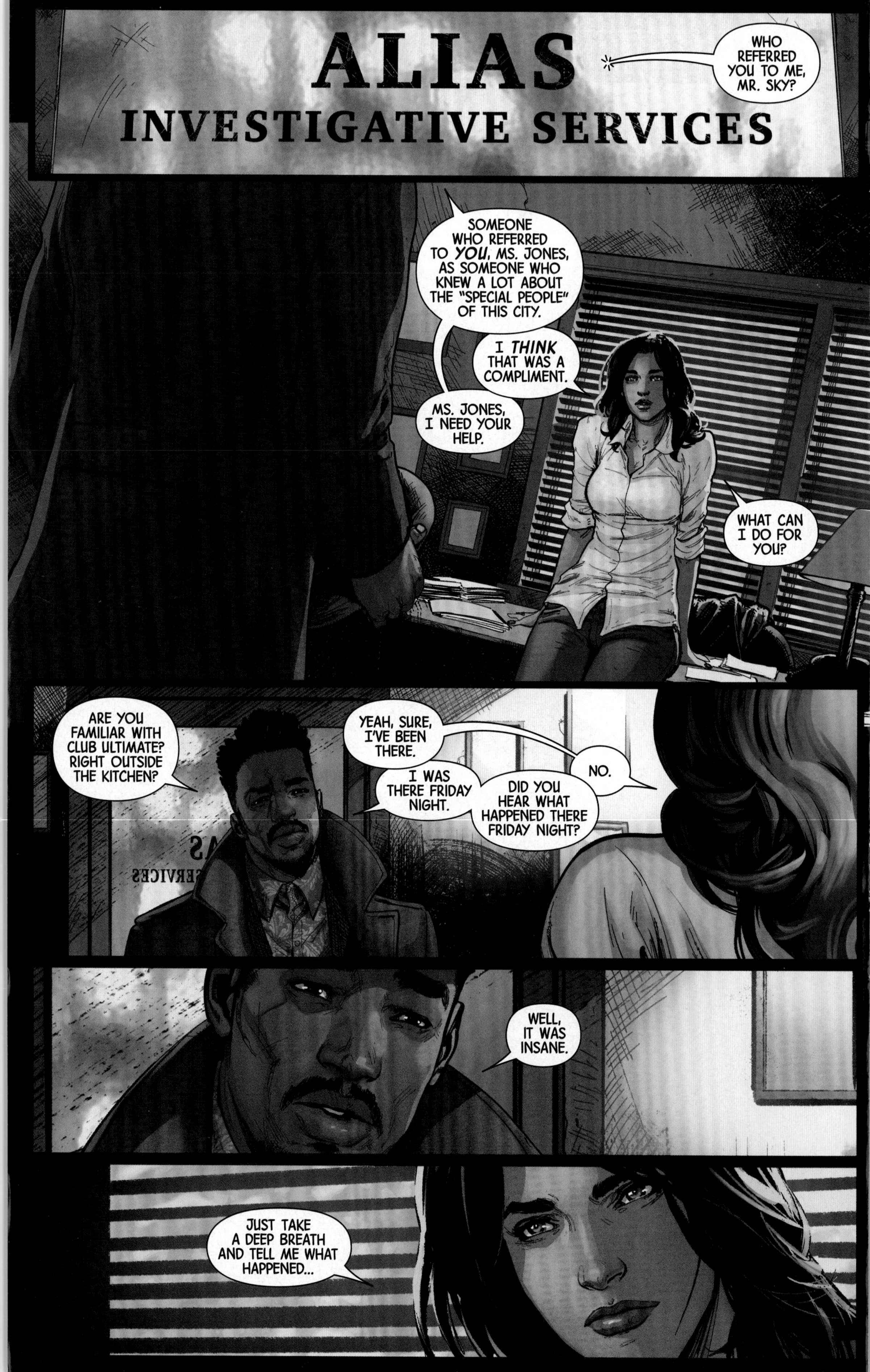
ALIAS
INVESTIGATIVE SERVICES
WHO REFERRED YOU TO ME, MR. SKY?
SOMEONE WHO REFERRED TO YOU, MS. JONES, AS SOMEONE WHO KNEW A LOT ABOUT THE "SPECIAL PEOPLE" OF THIS CITY.
I THINK THAT WAS A COMPLIMENT.
MS. JONES, I NEED YOUR HELP.
WHAT CAN I DO FOR YOU?
ARE YOU FAMILIAR WITH CLUB ULTIMATE? RIGHT OUTSIDE THE KITCHEN?
YEAH, SURE, I'VE BEEN THERE.
I WAS THERE FRIDAY NIGHT.
DID YOU HEAR WHAT HAPPENED THERE FRIDAY NIGHT?
NO.
WELL, IT WAS INSANE.
JUST TAKE A DEEP BREATH AND TELL ME WHAT HAPPENED...

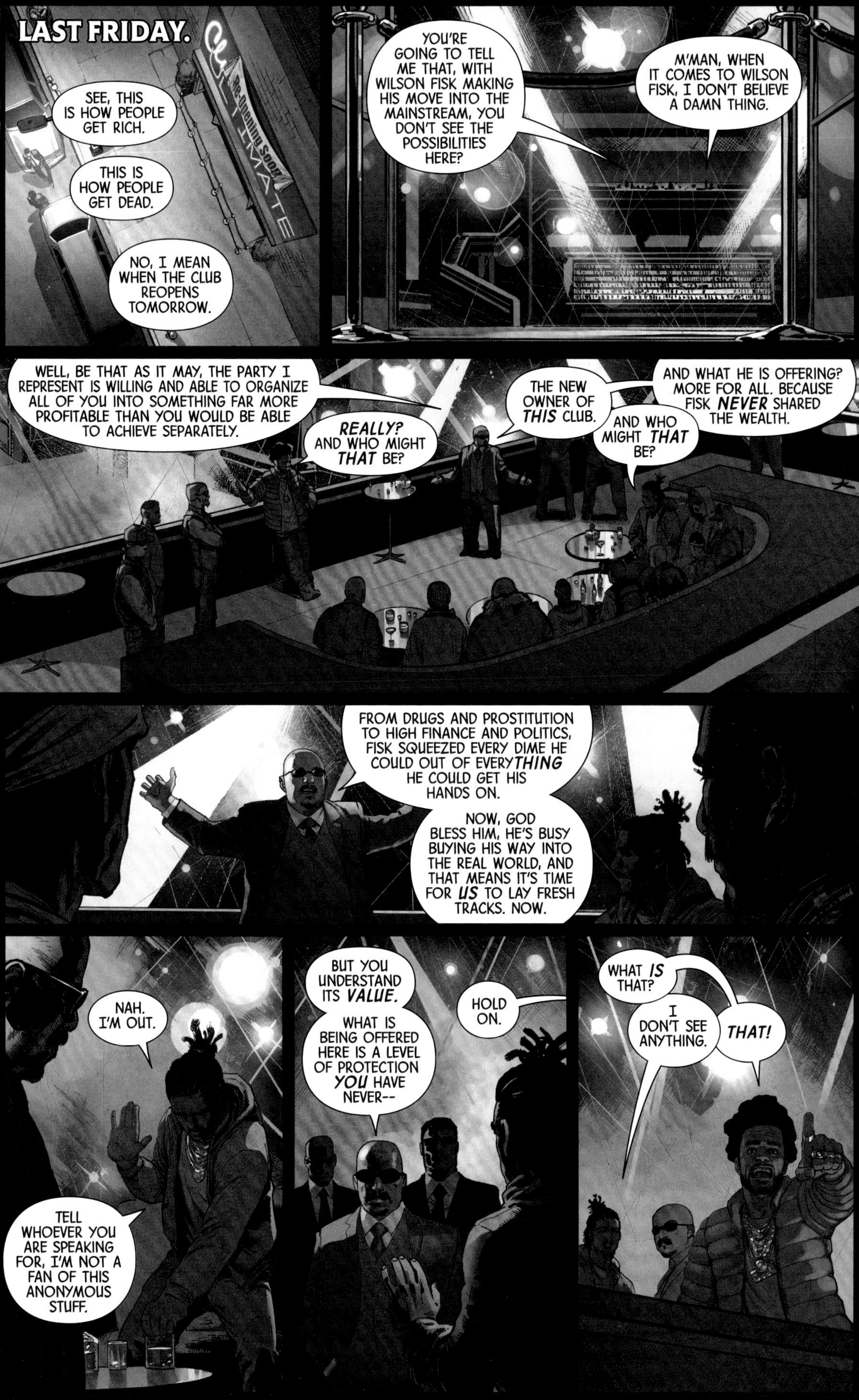

LAST FRIDAY.
SEE, THIS IS HOW PEOPLE GET RICH.
THIS IS HOW PEOPLE GET DEAD.
NO, I MEAN WHEN THE CLUB REOPENS TOMORROW.
YOU'RE GOING TO TELL ME THAT, WITH WILSON FISK MAKING HIS MOVE INTO THE MAINSTREAM, YOU DON'T SEE THE POSSIBILITIES HERE?
M'MAN, WHEN IT COMES TO WILSON FISK, I DON'T BELIEVE A DAMN THING.
WELL, BE THAT AS IT MAY, THE PARTY I REPRESENT IS WILLING AND ABLE TO ORGANIZE ALL OF YOU INTO SOMETHING FAR MORE PROFITABLE THAN YOU WOULD BE ABLE TO ACHIEVE SEPARATELY.
REALLY? AND WHO MIGHT THAT BE?
THE NEW OWNER OF THIS CLUB.
AND WHO MIGHT THAT BE?
AND WHAT HE IS OFFERING? MORE FOR ALL. BECAUSE FISK NEVER SHARED THE WEALTH.
FROM DRUGS AND PROSTITUTION TO HIGH FINANCE AND POLITICS, FISK SQUEEZED EVERY DIME HE COULD OUT OF EVERYTHING HE COULD GET HIS HANDS ON.
NOW, GOD BLESS HIM, HE'S BUSY BUYING HIS WAY INTO THE REAL WORLD, AND THAT MEANS IT'S TIME FOR US TO LAY FRESH TRACKS. NOW.
NAH. I'M OUT.
TELL WHOEVER YOU ARE SPEAKING FOR, I'M NOT A FAN OF THIS ANONYMOUS STUFF.
BUT YOU UNDERSTAND ITS VALUE.
WHAT IS BEING OFFERED HERE IS A LEVEL OF PROTECTION YOU HAVE NEVER--
HOLD ON.
WHAT IS THAT?
I DON'T SEE ANYTHING.
THAT!

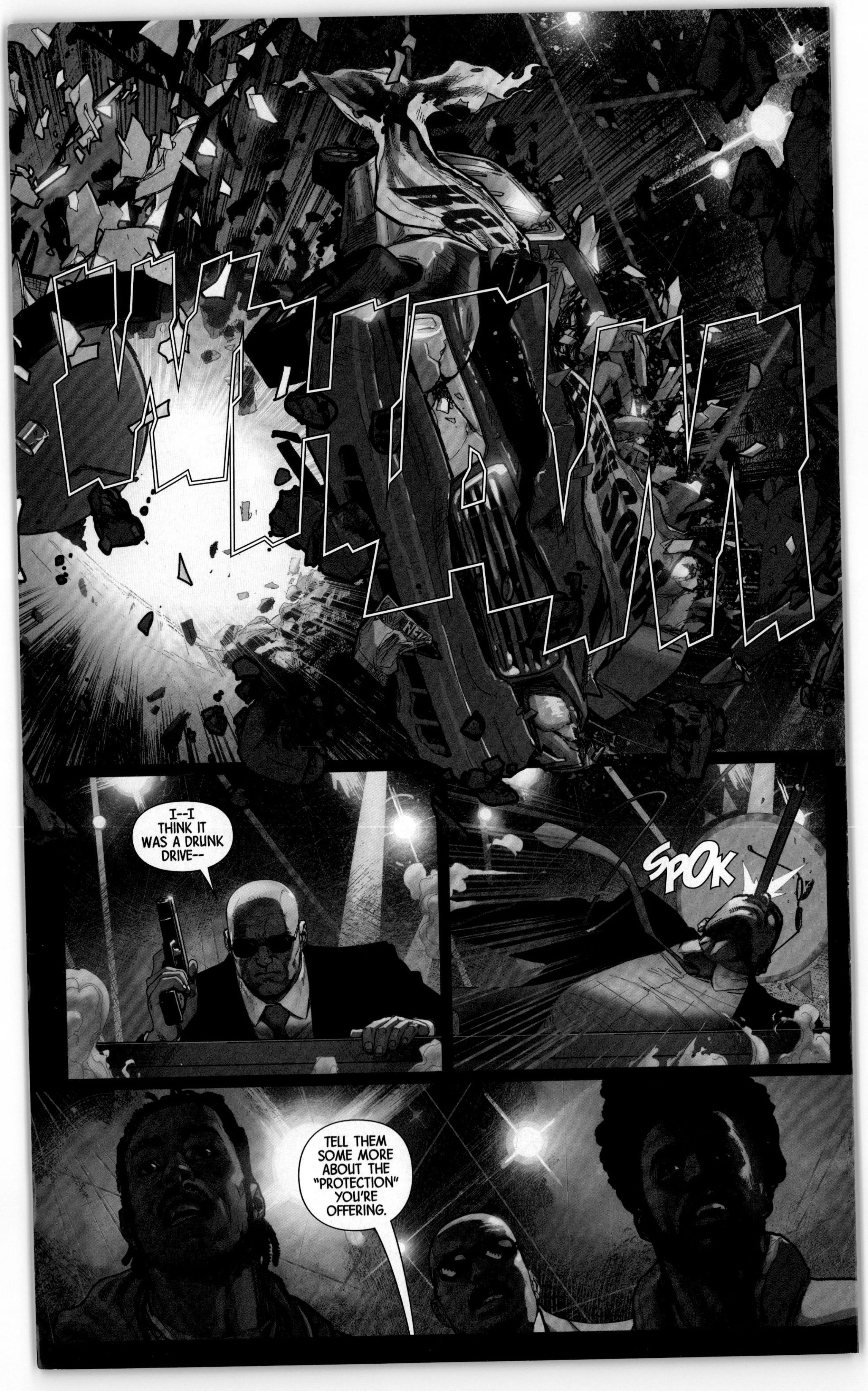
WHAAM
I--I THINK IT WAS A DRUNK DRIVE--
SPOK
TELL THEM SOME MORE ABOUT THE "PROTECTION" YOU'RE OFFERING.

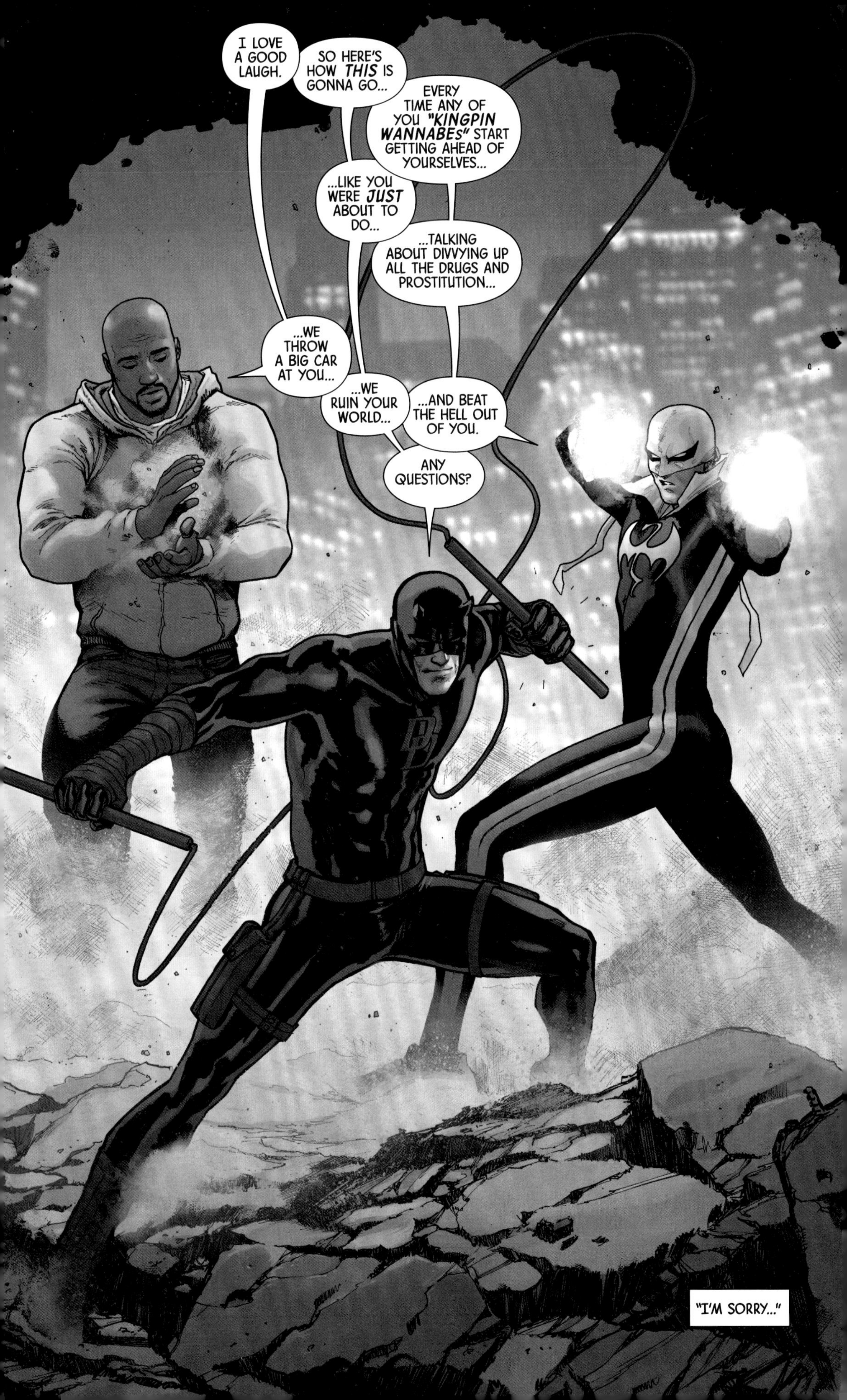
I LOVE A GOOD LAUGH.
SO HERE'S HOW THIS IS GONNA GO...
EVERY TIME ANY OF YOU "KINGPIN WANNABEs" START GETTING AHEAD OF YOURSELVES...
...LIKE YOU WERE JUST ABOUT TO DO...
...TALKING ABOUT DIVVYING UP ALL THE DRUGS AND PROSTITUTION...
...WE THROW A BIG CAR AT YOU...
...WE RUIN YOUR WORLD...
...AND BEAT THE HELL OUT OF YOU.
ANY QUESTIONS?
"I'M SORRY..."

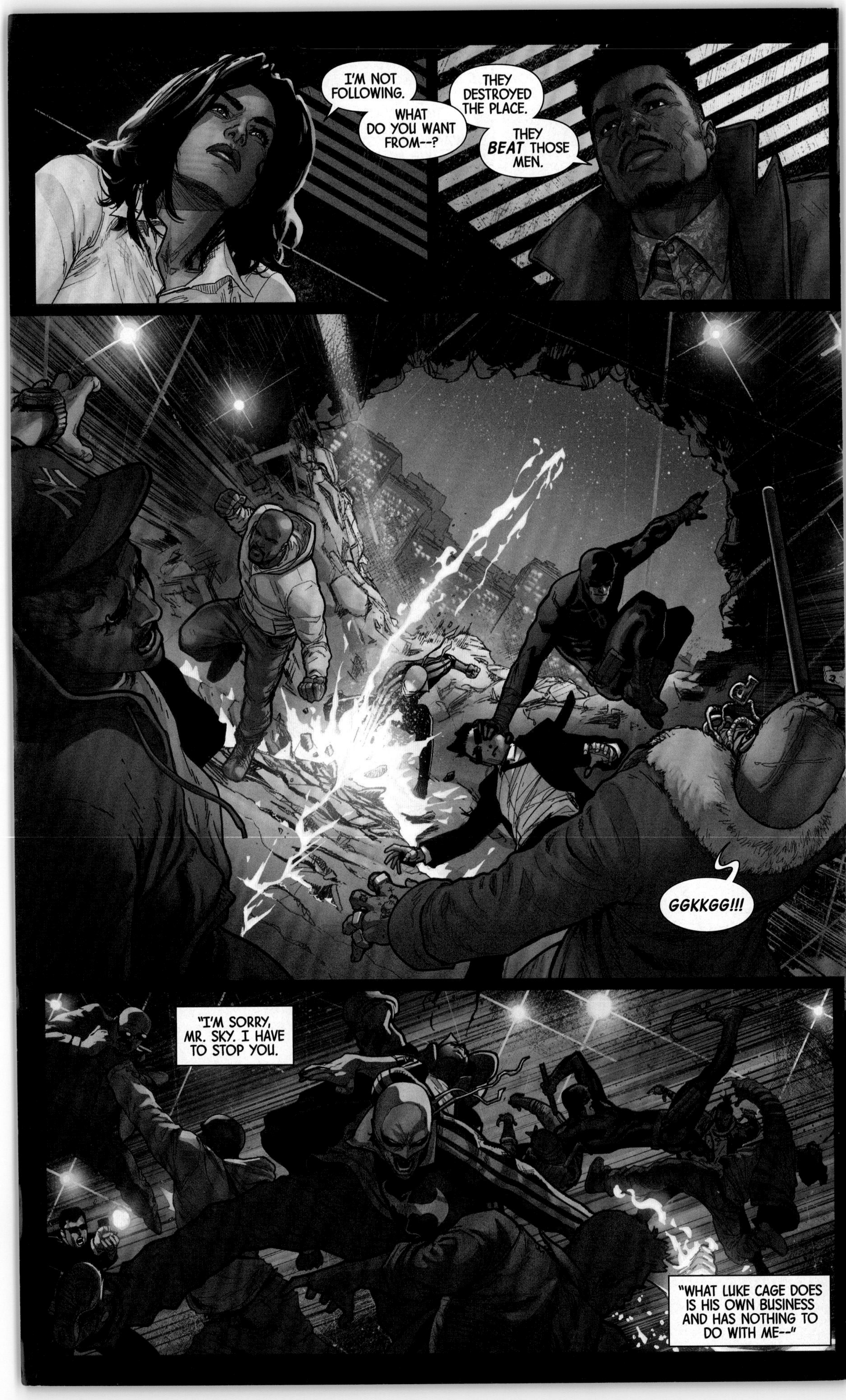

I'M NOT FOLLOWING.
WHAT DO YOU WANT FROM--?
THEY DESTROYED THE PLACE.
THEY *BEAT* THOSE MEN.
GGKKGG!!!
"I'M SORRY, MR. SKY. I HAVE TO STOP YOU.
"WHAT LUKE CAGE DOES IS HIS OWN BUSINESS AND HAS NOTHING TO DO WITH ME--"

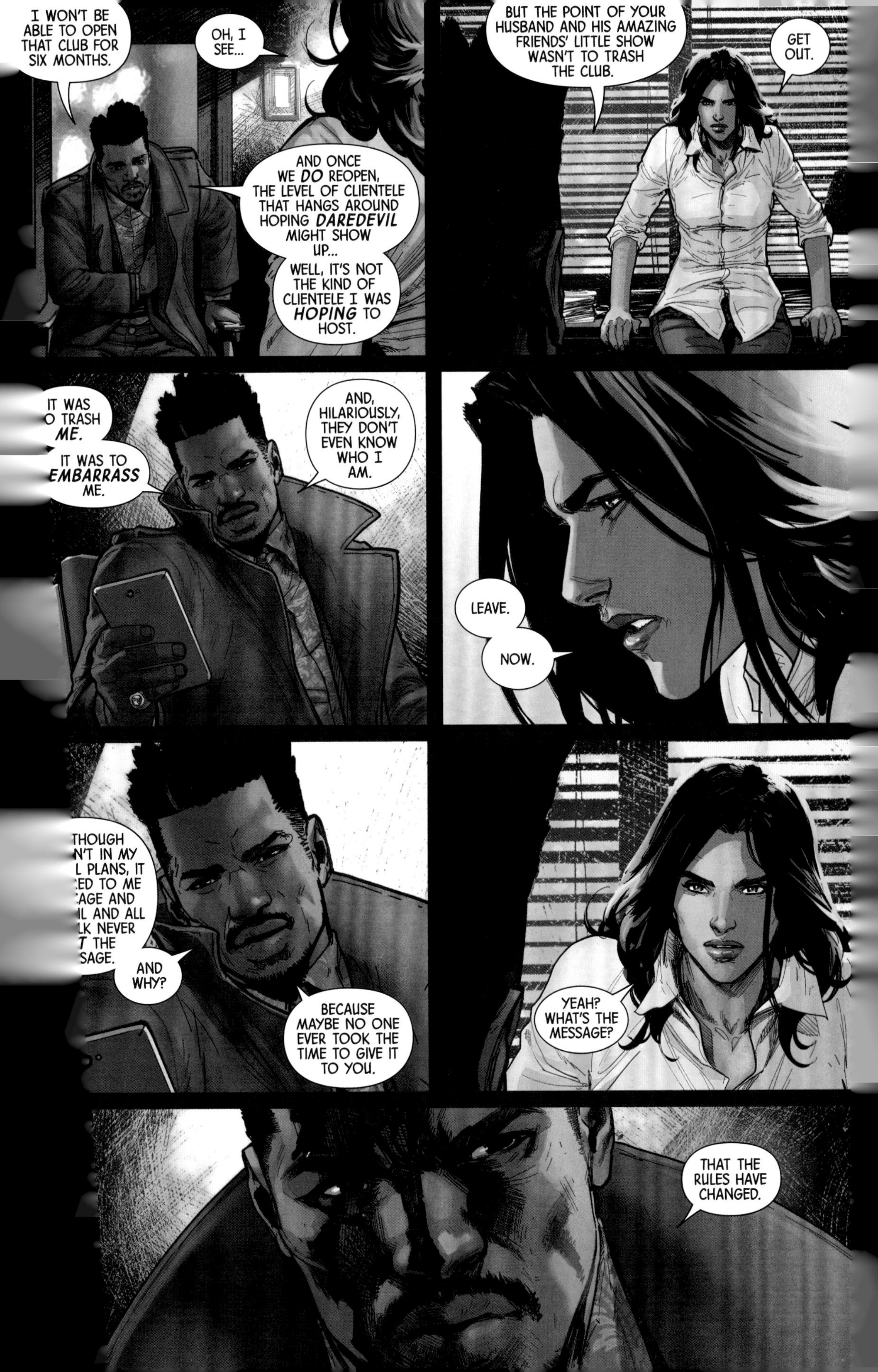

I WON'T BE ABLE TO OPEN THAT CLUB FOR SIX MONTHS.
OH, I SEE...
AND ONCE WE DO REOPEN, THE LEVEL OF CLIENTELE THAT HANGS AROUND HOPING DAREDEVIL MIGHT SHOW UP...
WELL, IT'S NOT THE KIND OF CLIENTELE I WAS HOPING TO HOST.
BUT THE POINT OF YOUR HUSBAND AND HIS AMAZING FRIENDS' LITTLE SHOW WASN'T TO TRASH THE CLUB.
GET OUT.
IT WAS O TRASH ME.
IT WAS TO EMBARRASS ME.
AND, HILARIOUSLY, THEY DON'T EVEN KNOW WHO I AM.
LEAVE.
NOW.
THOUGH N'T IN MY L PLANS, IT ED TO ME AGE AND L AND ALL K NEVER T THE SAGE.
AND WHY?
BECAUSE MAYBE NO ONE EVER TOOK THE TIME TO GIVE IT TO YOU.
YEAH? WHAT'S THE MESSAGE?
THAT THE RULES HAVE CHANGED.

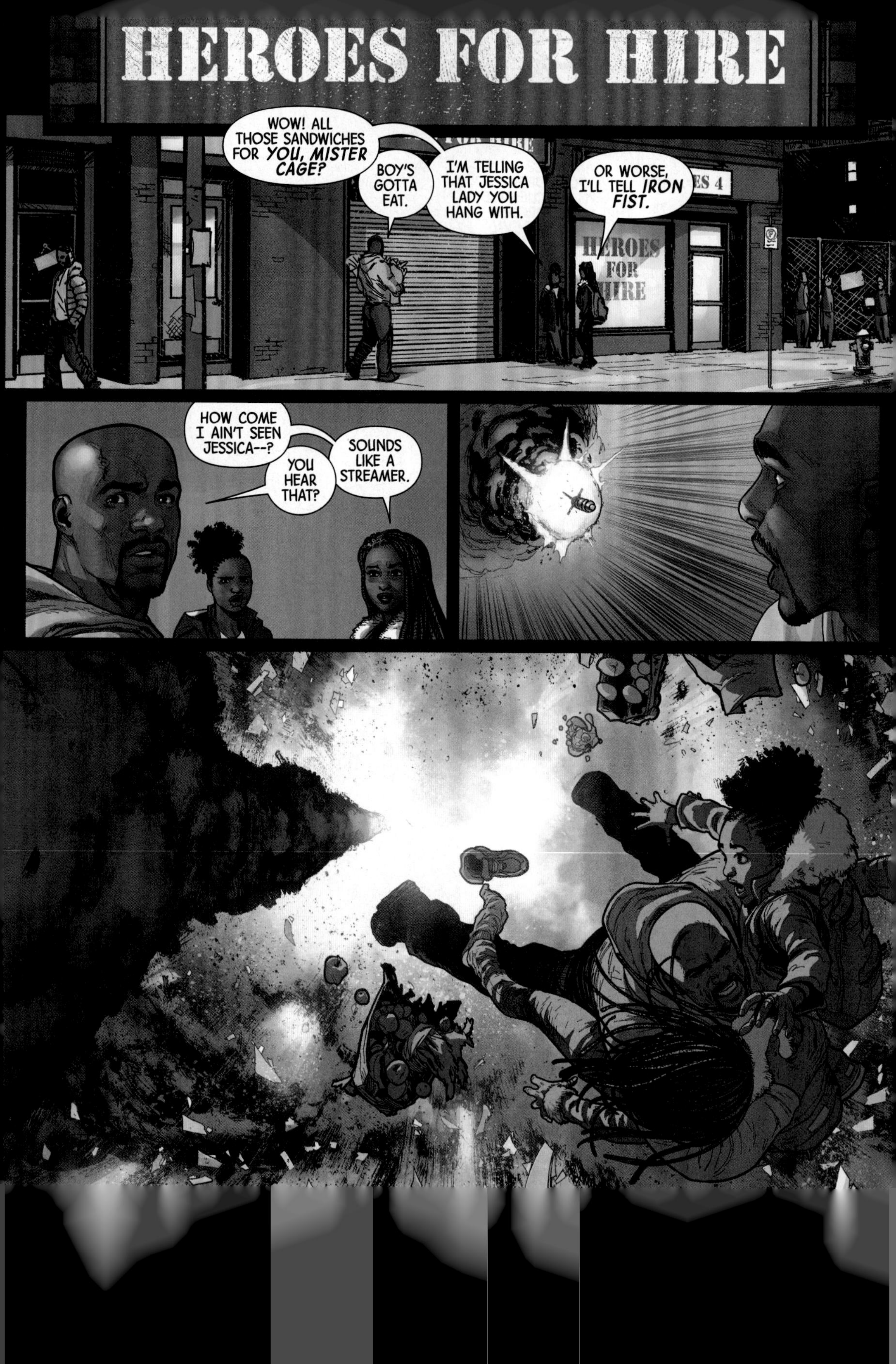
HEROES FOR HIRE
WOW! ALL THOSE SANDWICHES FOR YOU, MISTER CAGE?
BOY'S GOTTA EAT.
I'M TELLING THAT JESSICA LADY YOU HANG WITH.
OR WORSE, I'LL TELL IRON FIST.
HEROES FOR HIRE
HOW COME I AIN'T SEEN JESSICA--?
YOU HEAR THAT?
SOUNDS LIKE A STREAMER.

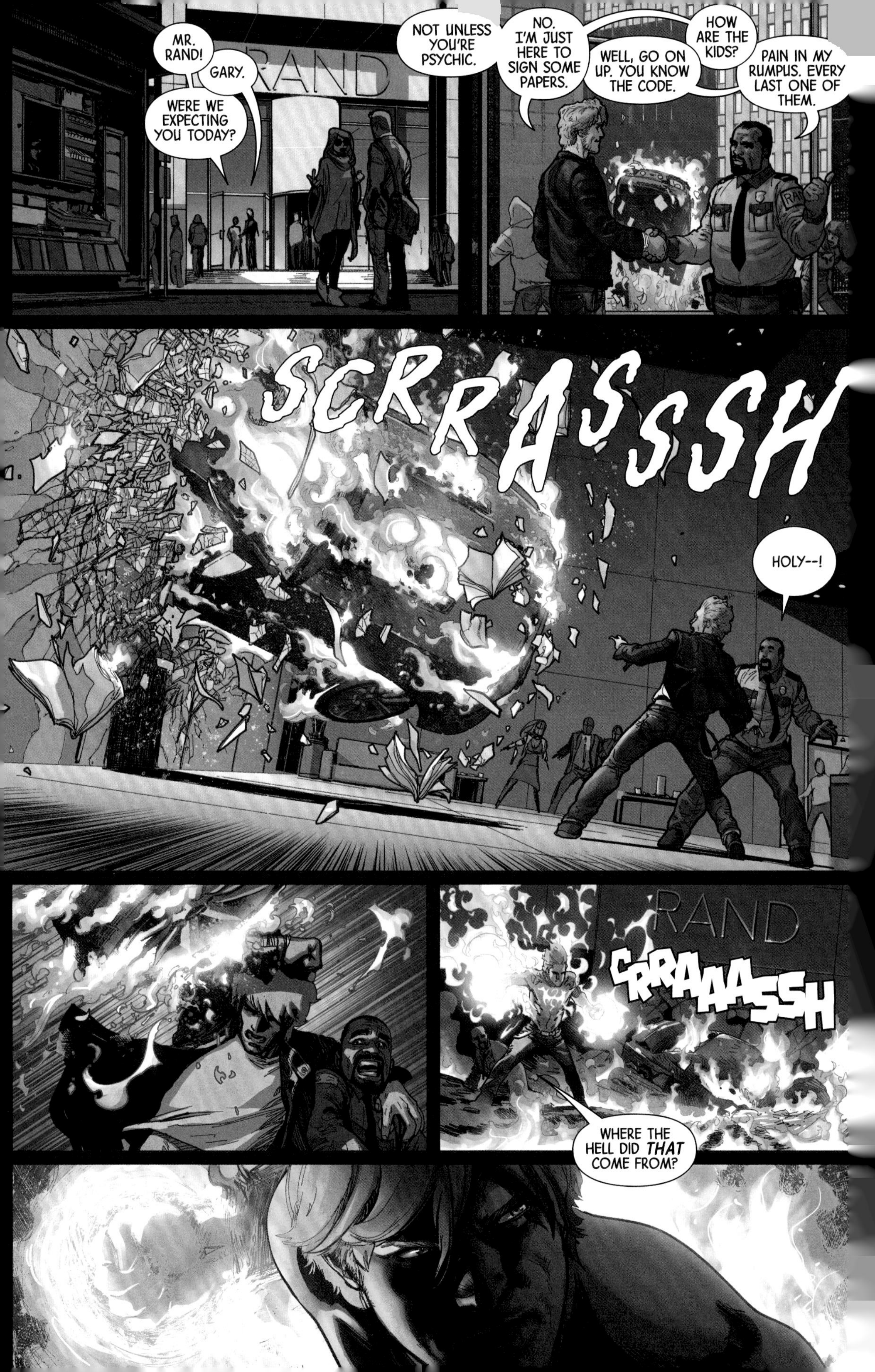
MR. RAND!
GARY.
WERE WE EXPECTING YOU TODAY?
NOT UNLESS YOU'RE PSYCHIC.
NO. I'M JUST HERE TO SIGN SOME PAPERS.
HOW ARE THE KIDS?
WELL, GO ON UP. YOU KNOW THE CODE.
PAIN IN MY RUMPUS. EVERY LAST ONE OF THEM.
RAND
SCRRASSSH
HOLY--!
RAND
CRRAAAASSH
WHERE THE HELL DID *THAT* COME FROM?

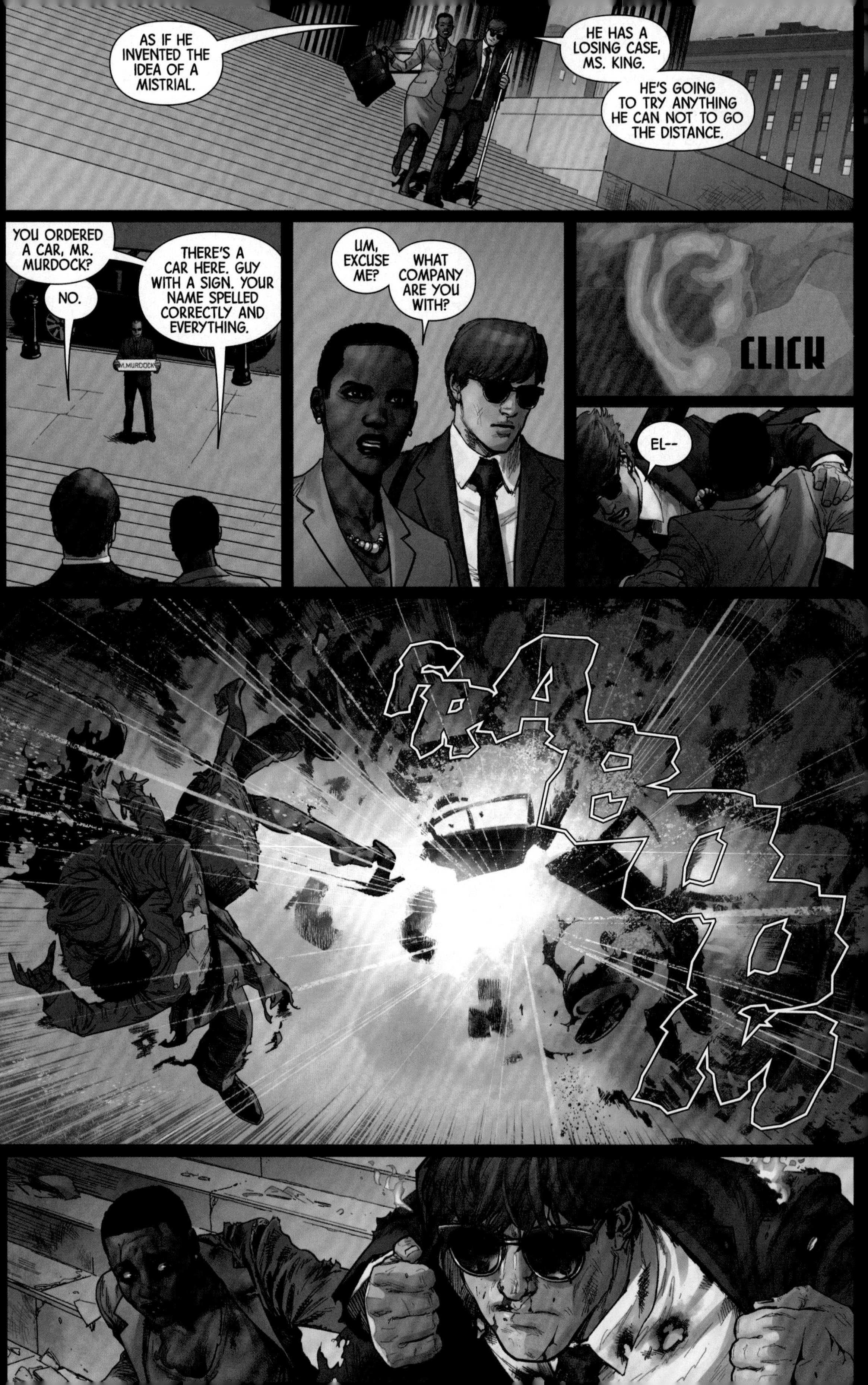
AS IF HE INVENTED THE IDEA OF A MISTRIAL.
HE HAS A LOSING CASE, MS. KING.
HE'S GOING TO TRY ANYTHING HE CAN NOT TO GO THE DISTANCE.
YOU ORDERED A CAR, MR. MURDOCK?
NO.
THERE'S A CAR HERE. GUY WITH A SIGN. YOUR NAME SPELLED CORRECTLY AND EVERYTHING.
M.MURDOCK
UM, EXCUSE ME?
WHAT COMPANY ARE YOU WITH?
CLICK
EL--
KA-BOOM

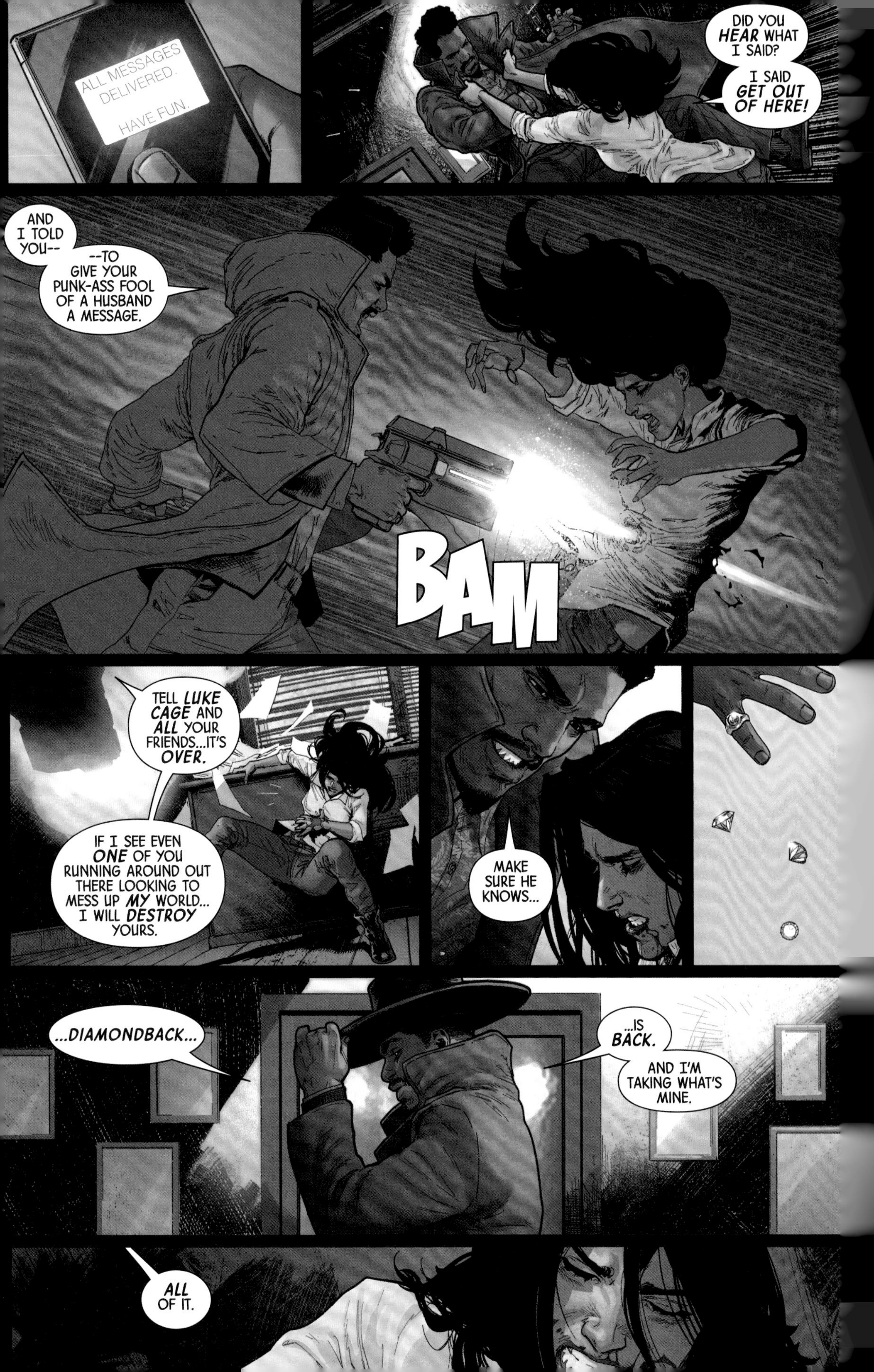
ALL MESSAGES DELIVERED. HAVE FUN.
DID YOU HEAR WHAT I SAID?
I SAID GET OUT OF HERE!
AND I TOLD YOU--
--TO GIVE YOUR PUNK-ASS FOOL OF A HUSBAND A MESSAGE.
BAM
TELL LUKE CAGE AND ALL YOUR FRIENDS...IT'S OVER.
IF I SEE EVEN ONE OF YOU RUNNING AROUND OUT THERE LOOKING TO MESS UP MY WORLD... I WILL DESTROY YOURS.
MAKE SURE HE KNOWS...
...DIAMONDBACK...
...IS BACK.
AND I'M TAKING WHAT'S MINE.
ALL OF IT.

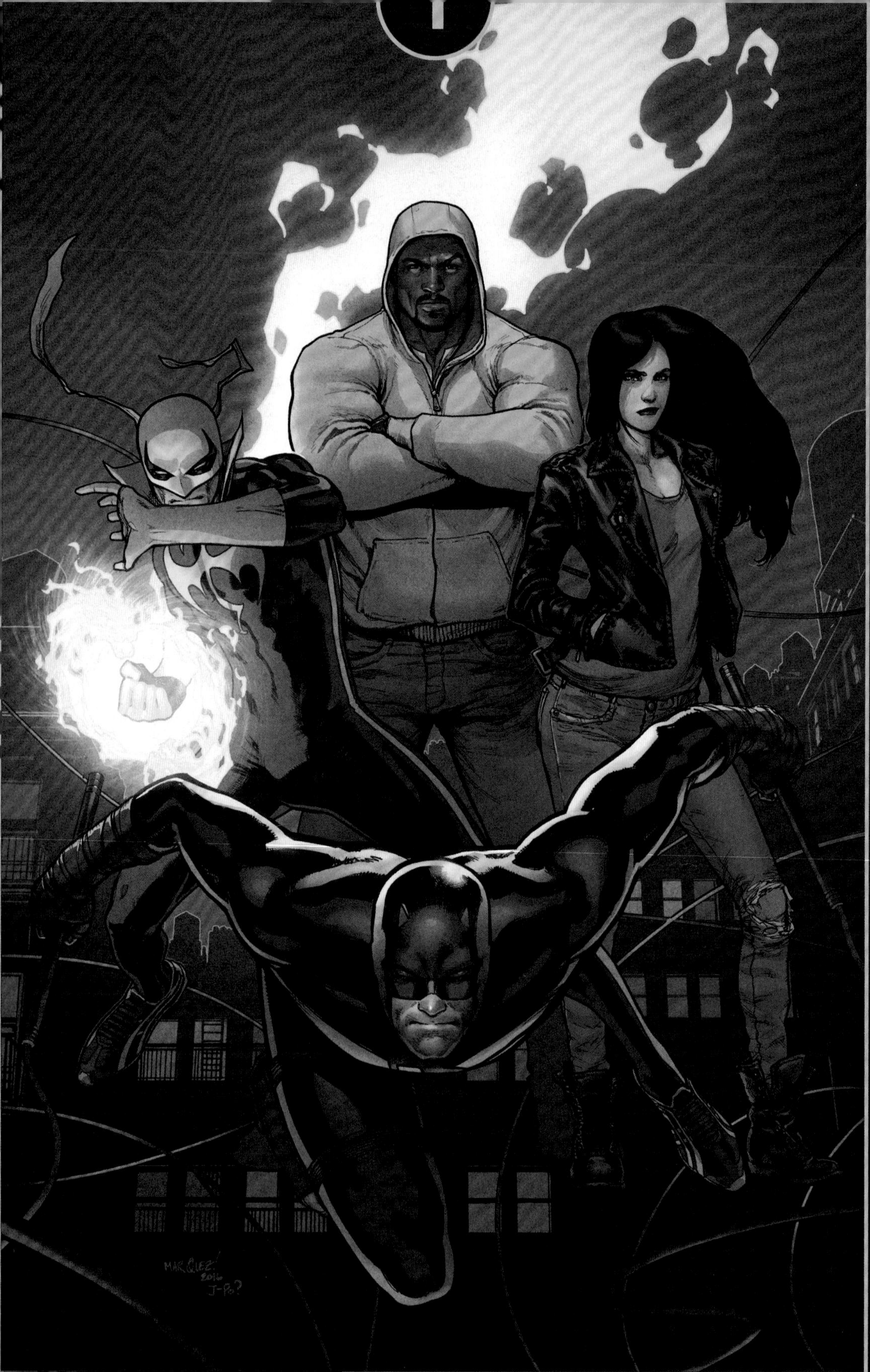

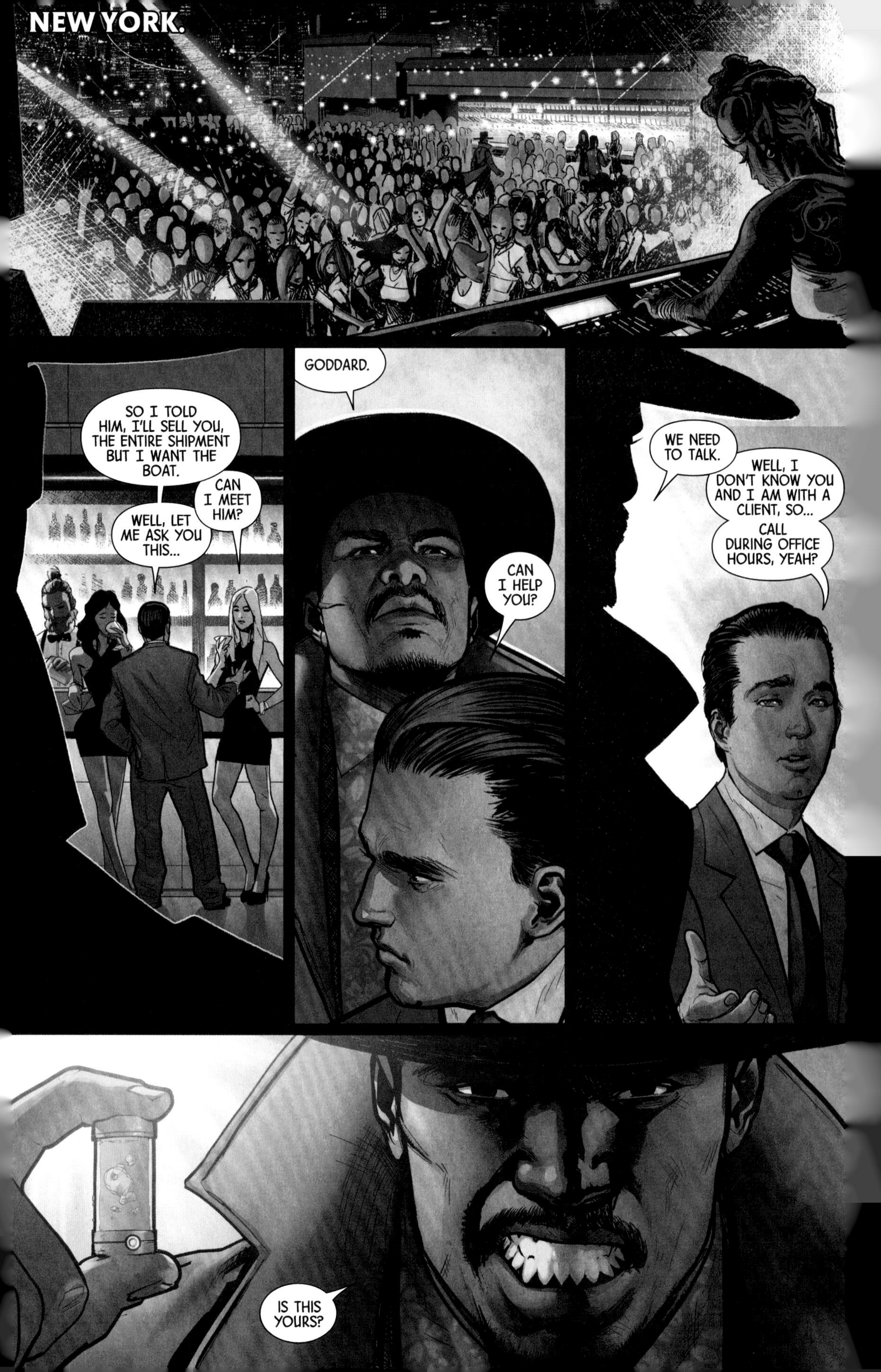
NEW YORK.
SO I TOLD HIM, I'LL SELL YOU, THE ENTIRE SHIPMENT BUT I WANT THE BOAT.
CAN I MEET HIM?
WELL, LET ME ASK YOU THIS...
GODDARD.
CAN I HELP YOU?
WE NEED TO TALK.
WELL, I DON'T KNOW YOU AND I AM WITH A CLIENT, SO...
CALL DURING OFFICE HOURS, YEAH?
IS THIS YOURS?

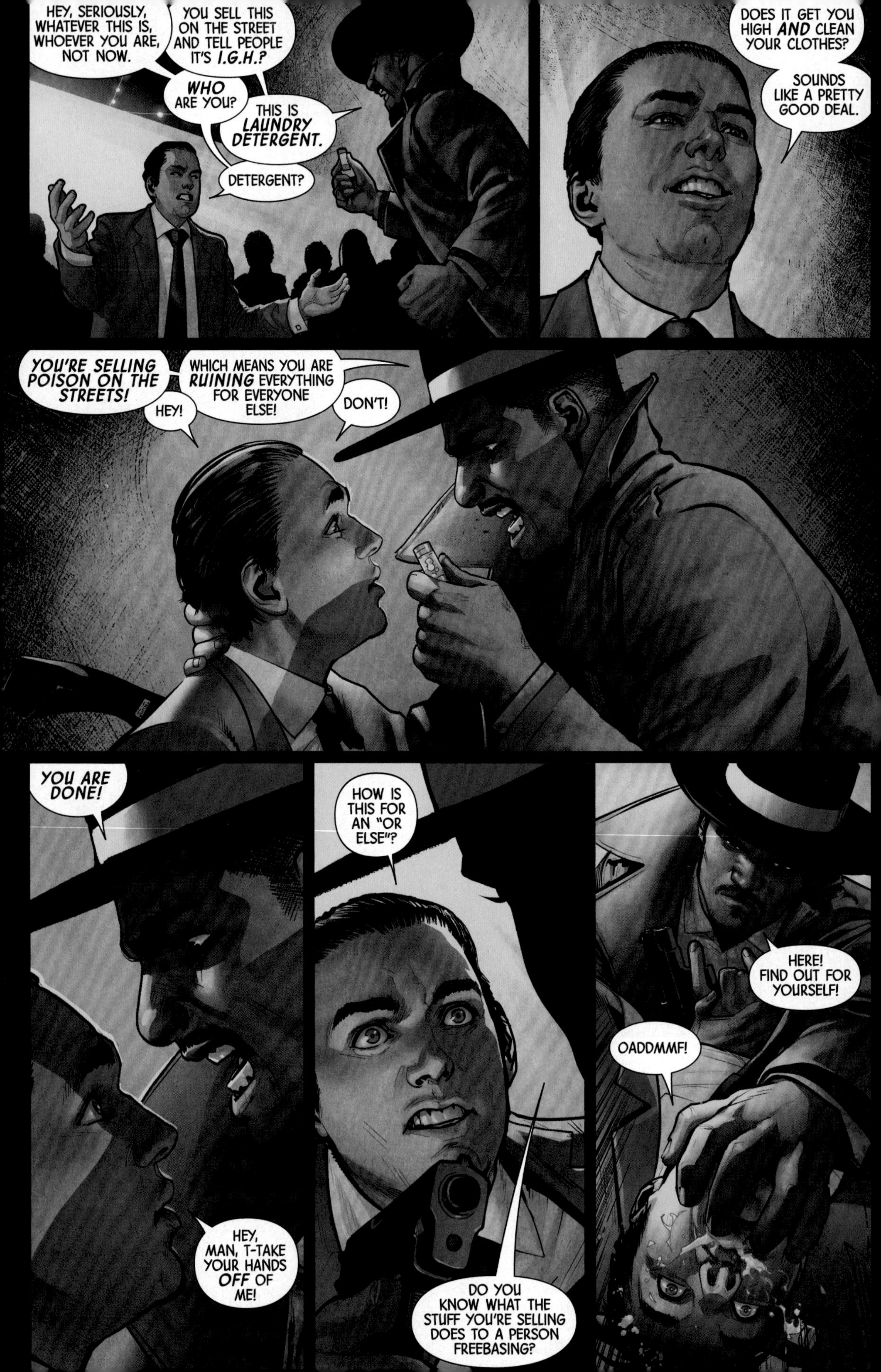
HEY, SERIOUSLY, WHATEVER THIS IS, WHOEVER YOU ARE, NOT NOW.
YOU SELL THIS ON THE STREET AND TELL PEOPLE IT'S I.G.H.?
WHO ARE YOU?
THIS IS LAUNDRY DETERGENT.
DETERGENT?
DOES IT GET YOU HIGH AND CLEAN YOUR CLOTHES?
SOUNDS LIKE A PRETTY GOOD DEAL.
YOU'RE SELLING POISON ON THE STREETS!
WHICH MEANS YOU ARE RUINING EVERYTHING FOR EVERYONE ELSE!
HEY!
DON'T!
YOU ARE DONE!
HEY, MAN, T-TAKE YOUR HANDS OFF OF ME!
HOW IS THIS FOR AN "OR ELSE"?
DO YOU KNOW WHAT THE STUFF YOU'RE SELLING DOES TO A PERSON FREEBASING?
HERE! FIND OUT FOR YOURSELF!
OADDMMF!

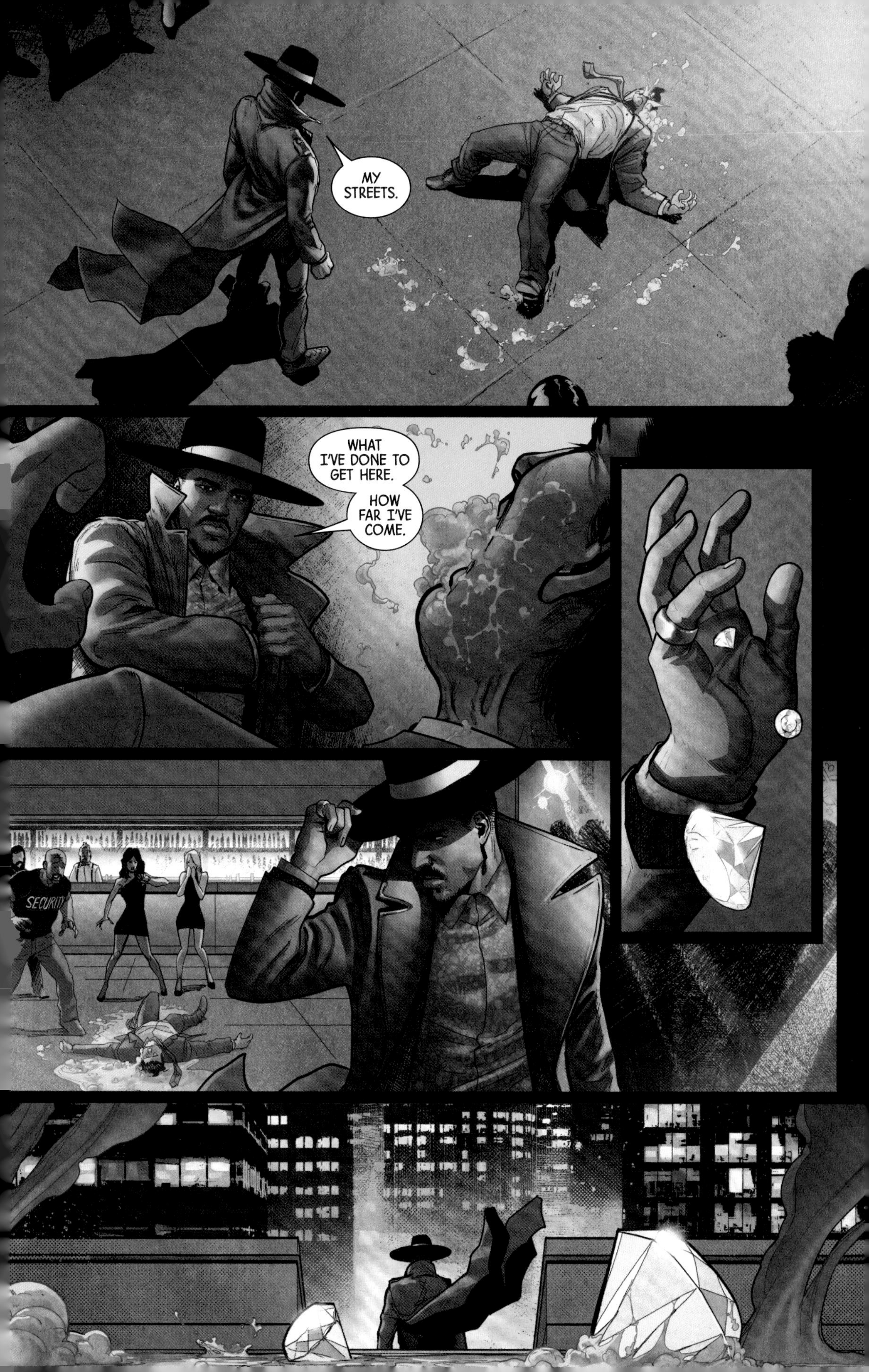
MY STREETS.
WHAT I'VE DONE TO GET HERE.
HOW FAR I'VE COME.
SECURITY

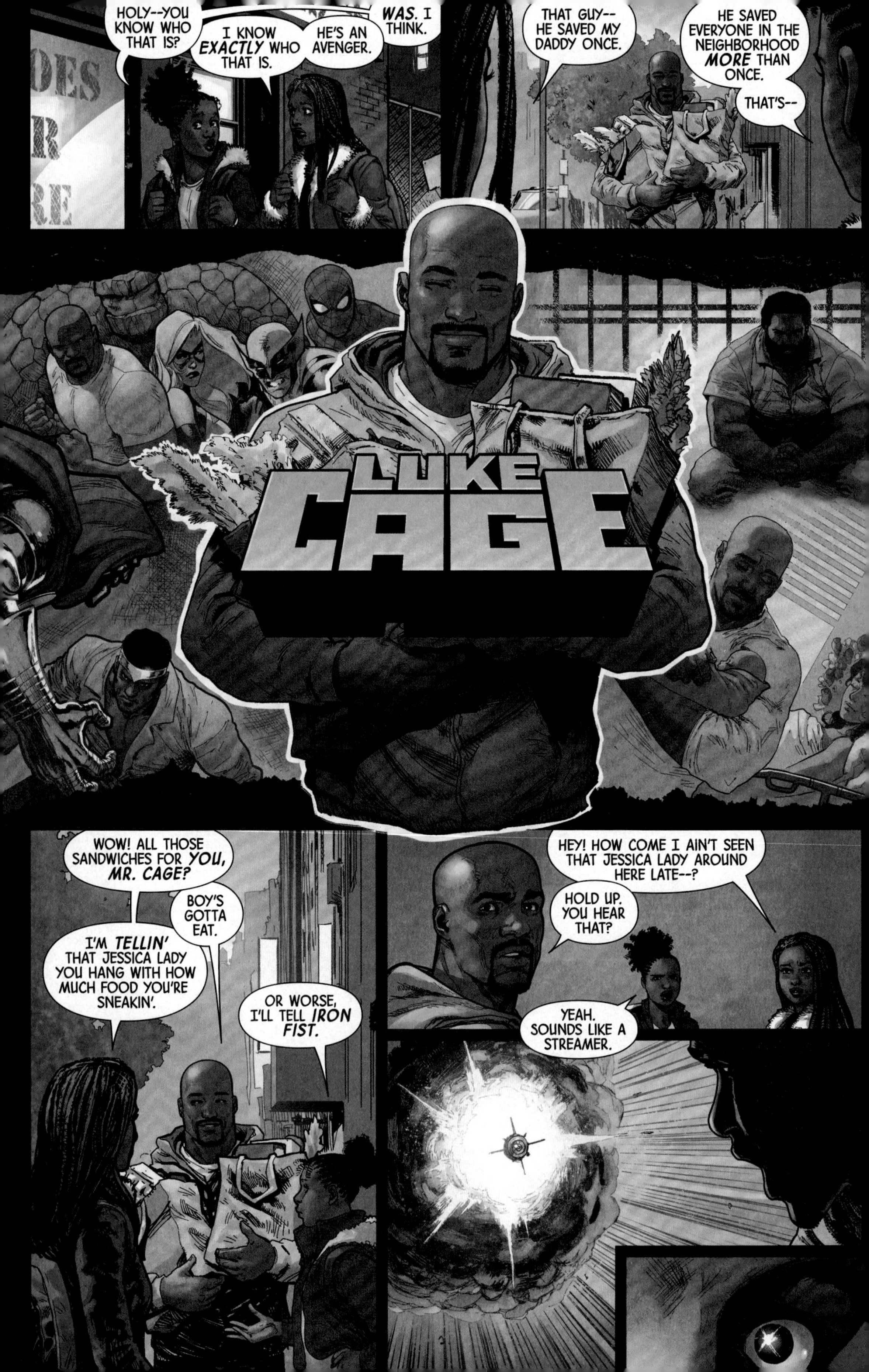
HOLY--YOU KNOW WHO THAT IS?
I KNOW EXACTLY WHO THAT IS.
HE'S AN AVENGER.
WAS. I THINK.
THAT GUY-- HE SAVED MY DADDY ONCE.
HE SAVED EVERYONE IN THE NEIGHBORHOOD MORE THAN ONCE.
THAT'S--
LUKE CAGE
WOW! ALL THOSE SANDWICHES FOR YOU, MR. CAGE?
BOY'S GOTTA EAT.
I'M TELLIN' THAT JESSICA LADY YOU HANG WITH HOW MUCH FOOD YOU'RE SNEAKIN'.
OR WORSE, I'LL TELL IRON FIST.
HEY! HOW COME I AIN'T SEEN THAT JESSICA LADY AROUND HERE LATE--?
HOLD UP. YOU HEAR THAT?
YEAH. SOUNDS LIKE A STREAMER.

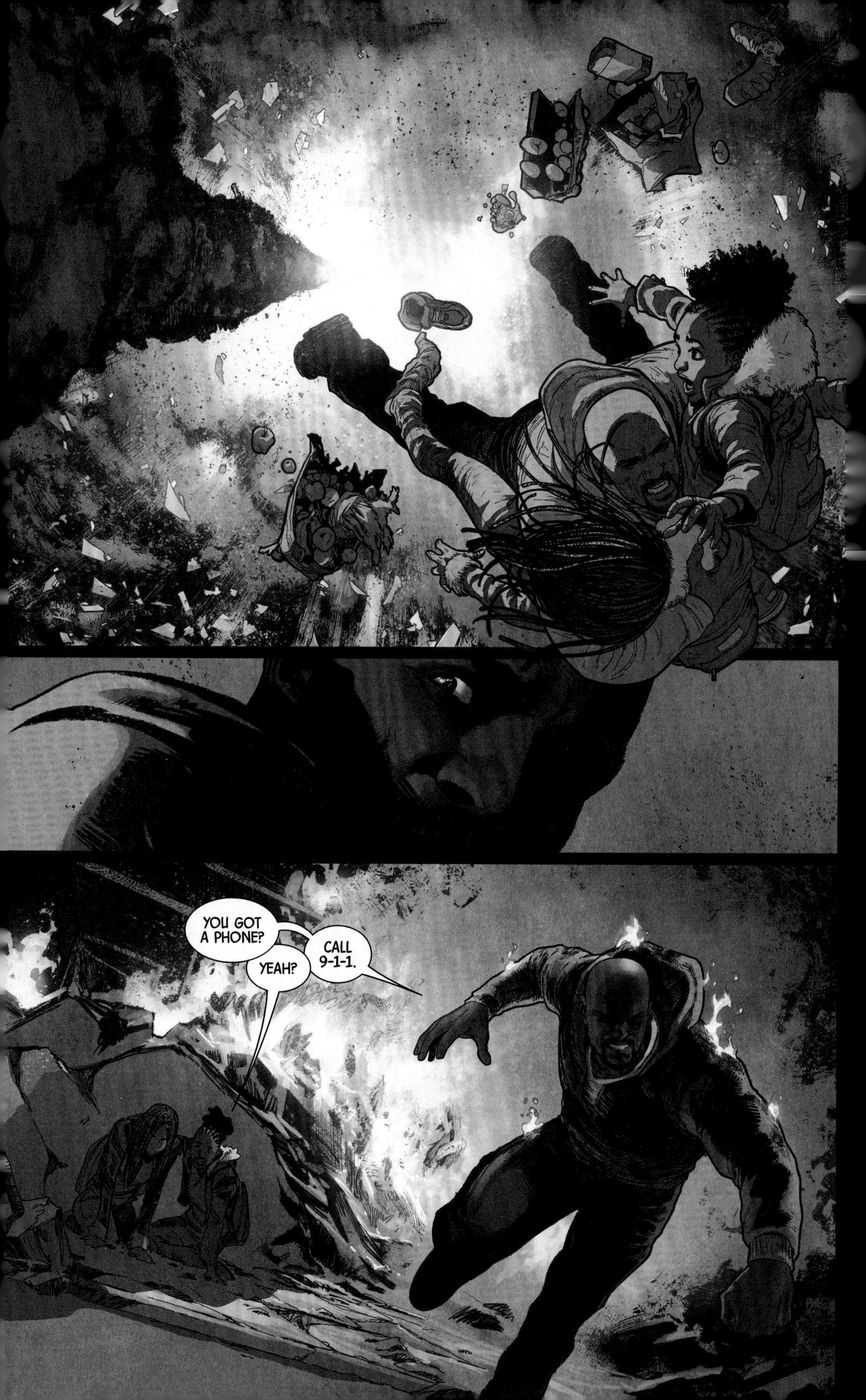
YOU GOT A PHONE?
YEAH?
CALL 9-1-1.

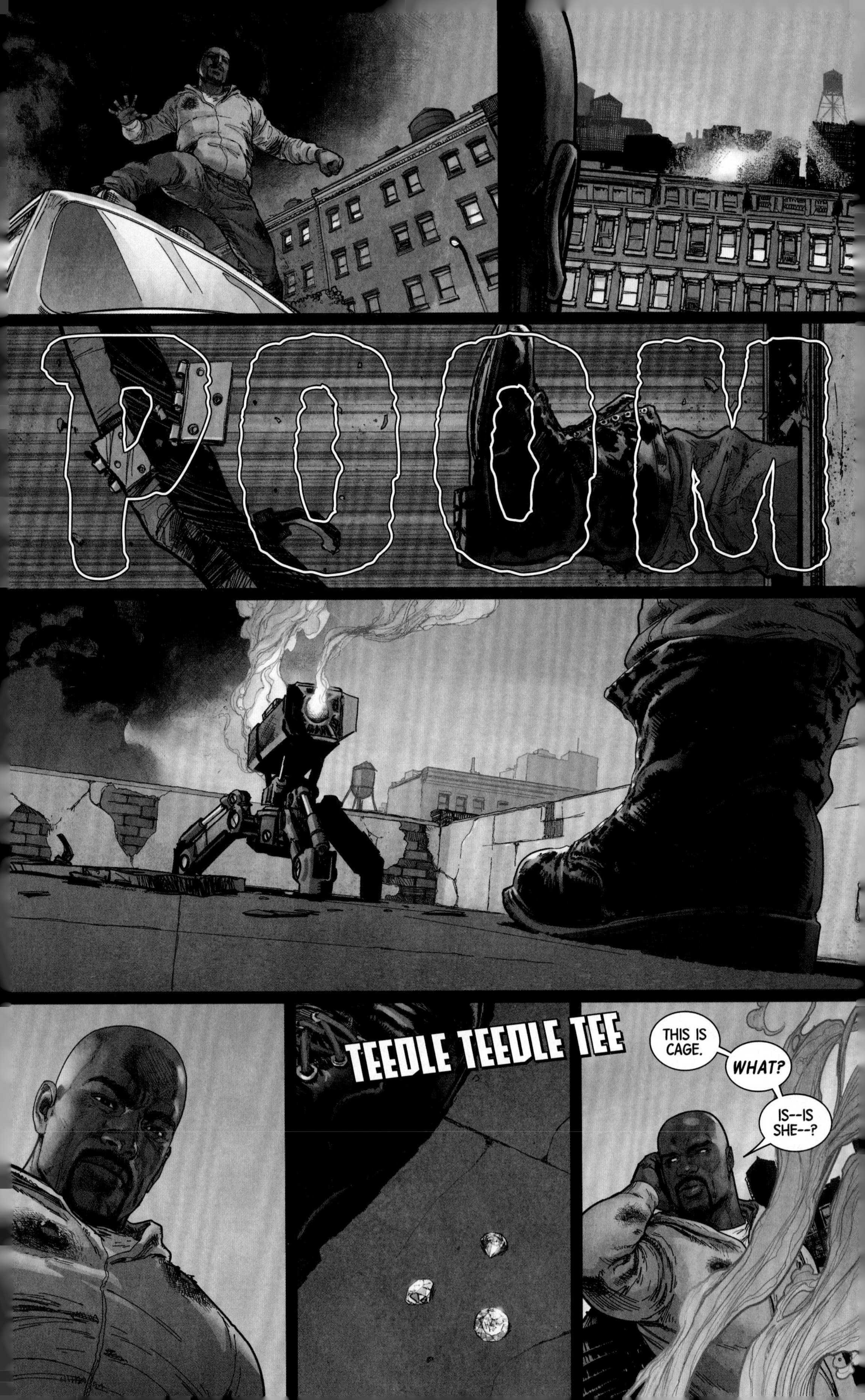
POOM
TEEDLE TEEDLE TEE
THIS IS CAGE.
WHAT?
IS--IS SHE--?

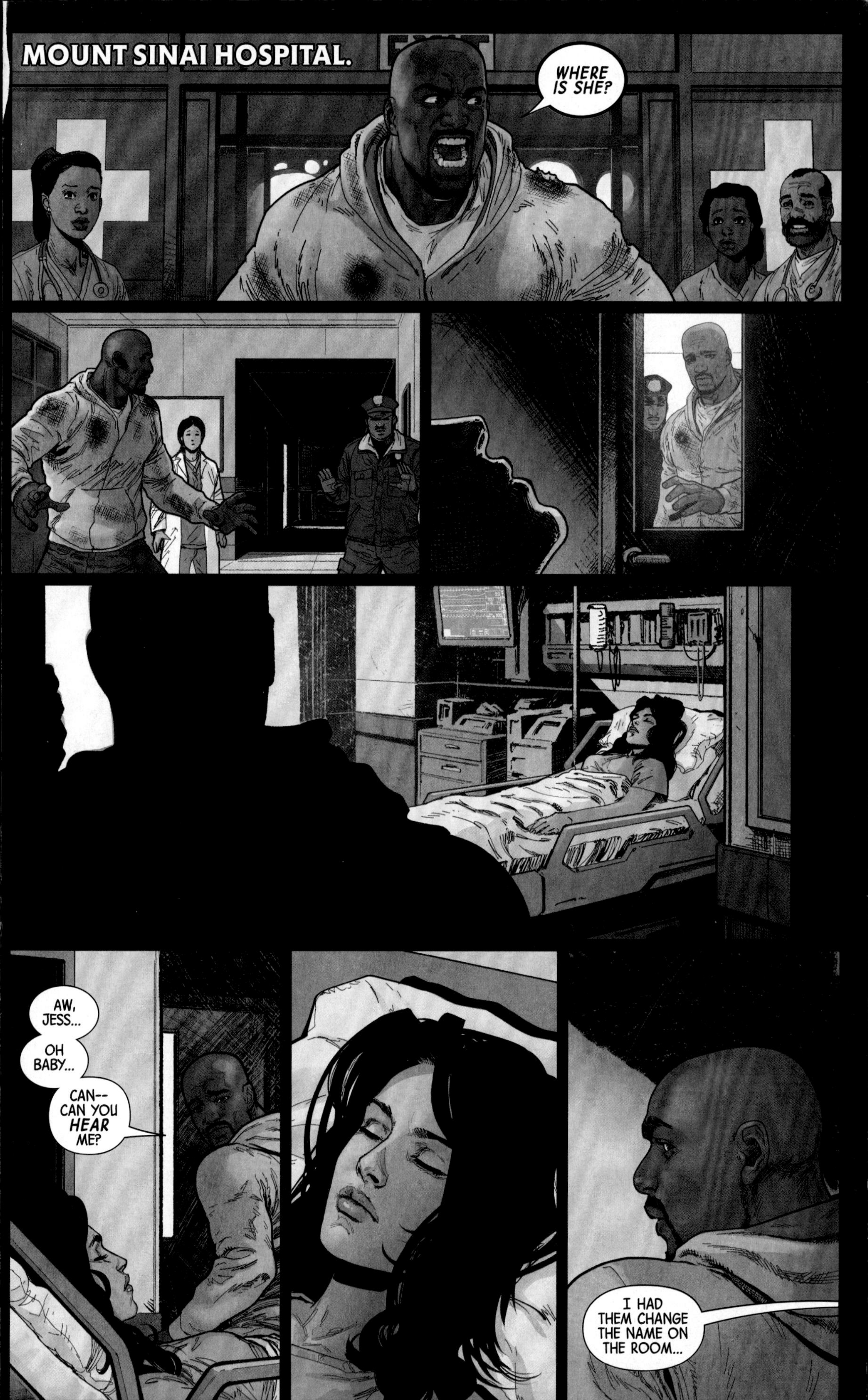
MOUNT SINAI HOSPITAL.
WHERE IS SHE?
AW, JESS...
OH BABY...
CAN-- CAN YOU *HEAR* ME?
I HAD THEM CHANGE THE NAME ON THE ROOM...

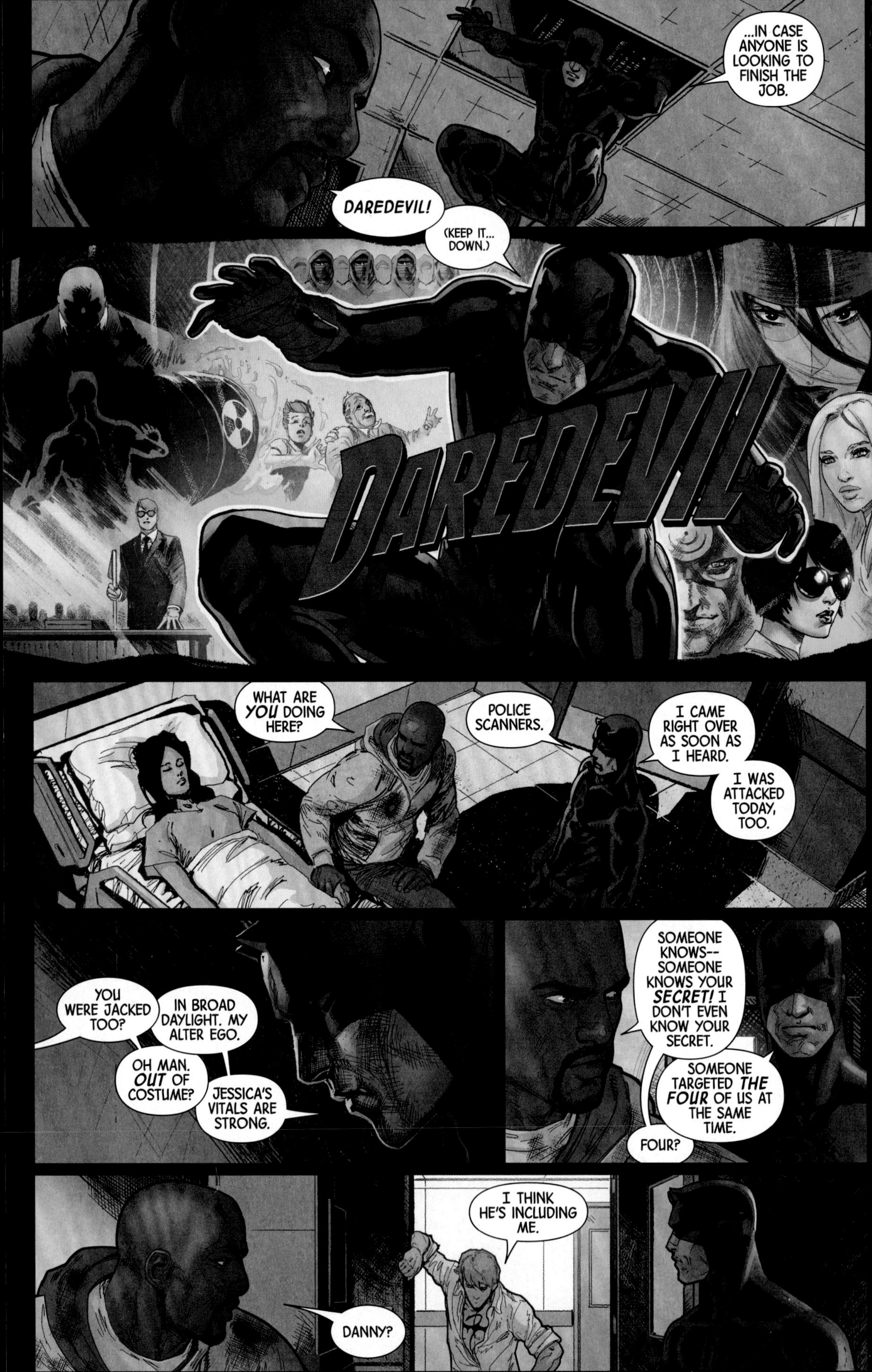

...IN CASE ANYONE IS LOOKING TO FINISH THE JOB.
DAREDEVIL!
(KEEP IT... DOWN.)
DAREDEVIL
WHAT ARE YOU DOING HERE?
POLICE SCANNERS.
I CAME RIGHT OVER AS SOON AS I HEARD.
I WAS ATTACKED TODAY, TOO.
YOU WERE JACKED TOO?
IN BROAD DAYLIGHT. MY ALTER EGO.
OH MAN. OUT OF COSTUME?
JESSICA'S VITALS ARE STRONG.
SOMEONE KNOWS-- SOMEONE KNOWS YOUR SECRET! I DON'T EVEN KNOW YOUR SECRET.
SOMEONE TARGETED THE FOUR OF US AT THE SAME TIME.
FOUR?
I THINK HE'S INCLUDING ME.
DANNY?

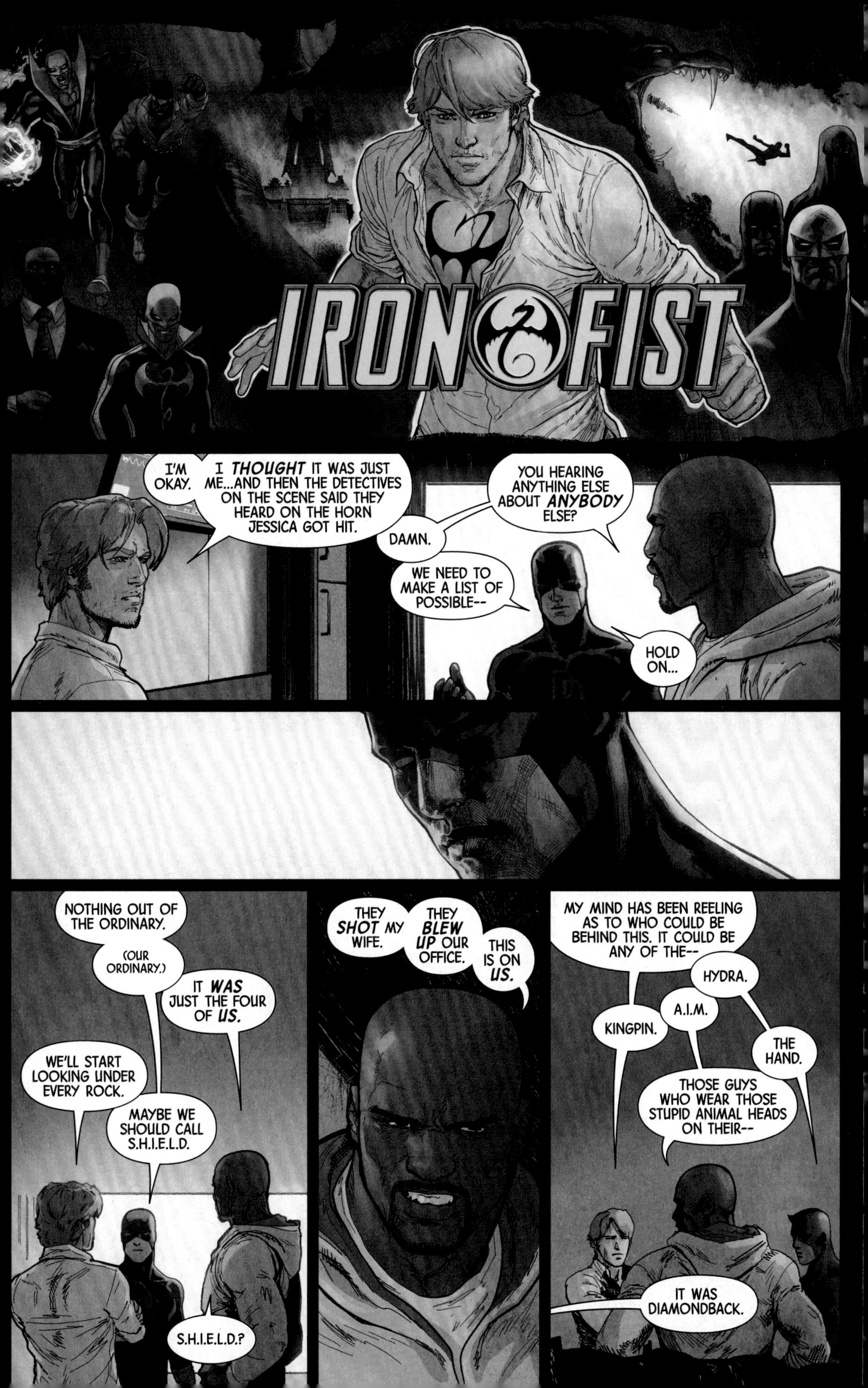
IRON FIST
I'M OKAY.
I THOUGHT IT WAS JUST ME...AND THEN THE DETECTIVES ON THE SCENE SAID THEY HEARD ON THE HORN JESSICA GOT HIT.
DAMN.
YOU HEARING ANYTHING ELSE ABOUT ANYBODY ELSE?
WE NEED TO MAKE A LIST OF POSSIBLE--
HOLD ON...
NOTHING OUT OF THE ORDINARY.
(OUR ORDINARY.)
IT WAS JUST THE FOUR OF US.
WE'LL START LOOKING UNDER EVERY ROCK.
MAYBE WE SHOULD CALL S.H.I.E.L.D.
S.H.I.E.L.D.?
THEY SHOT MY WIFE.
THEY BLEW UP OUR OFFICE.
THIS IS ON US.
MY MIND HAS BEEN REELING AS TO WHO COULD BE BEHIND THIS. IT COULD BE ANY OF THE--
HYDRA.
KINGPIN.
A.I.M.
THE HAND.
THOSE GUYS WHO WEAR THOSE STUPID ANIMAL HEADS ON THEIR--
IT WAS DIAMONDBACK.

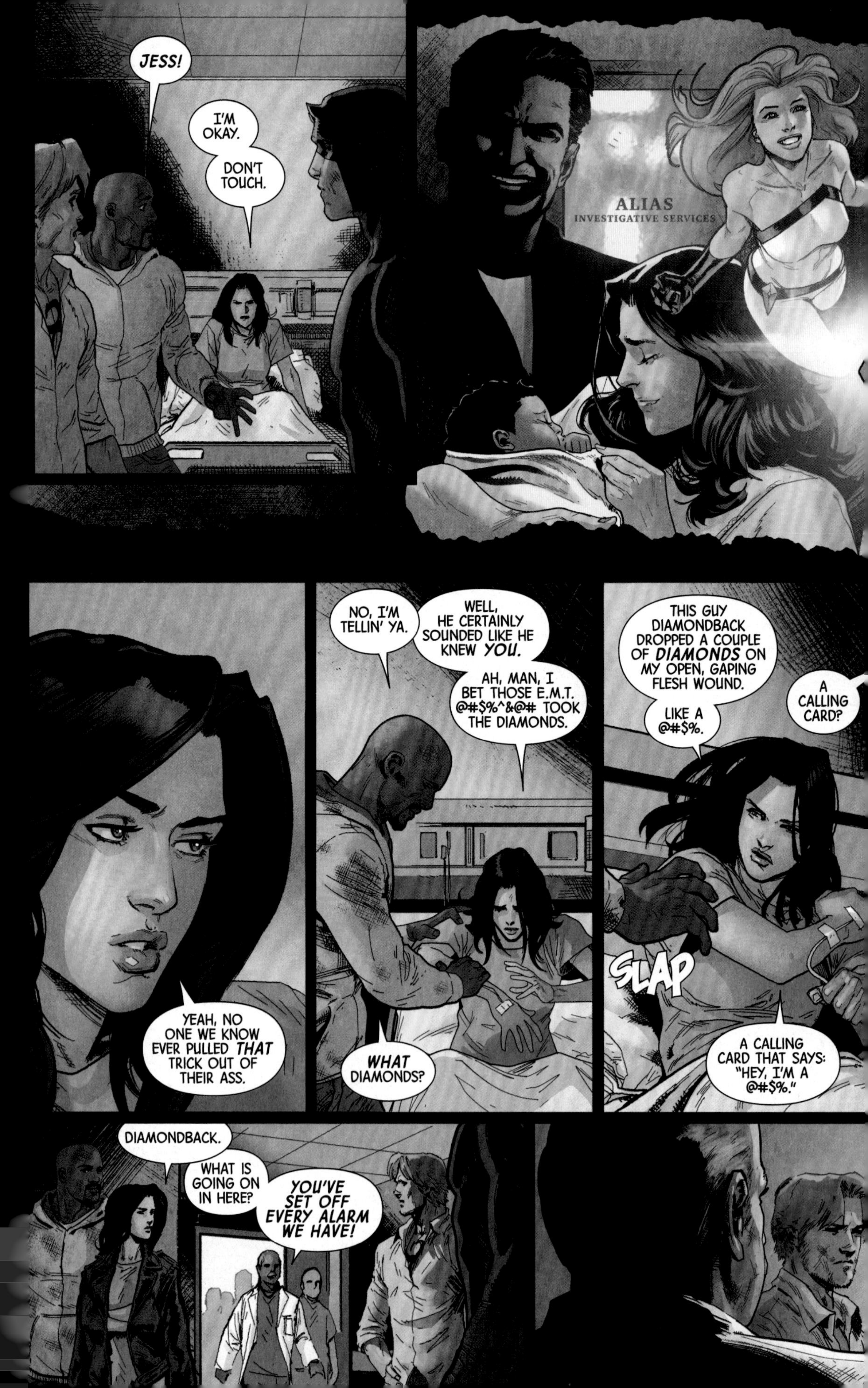
JESS!
I'M OKAY.
DON'T TOUCH.
ALIAS
INVESTIGATIVE SERVICES
YEAH, NO ONE WE KNOW EVER PULLED THAT TRICK OUT OF THEIR ASS.
NO, I'M TELLIN' YA.
WELL, HE CERTAINLY SOUNDED LIKE HE KNEW YOU.
AH, MAN, I BET THOSE E.M.T. @#$%^&@# TOOK THE DIAMONDS.
WHAT DIAMONDS?
THIS GUY DIAMONDBACK DROPPED A COUPLE OF DIAMONDS ON MY OPEN, GAPING FLESH WOUND.
LIKE A @#$%.
A CALLING CARD?
SLAP
A CALLING CARD THAT SAYS: "HEY, I'M A @#$%."
DIAMONDBACK.
WHAT IS GOING ON IN HERE?
YOU'VE SET OFF EVERY ALARM WE HAVE!

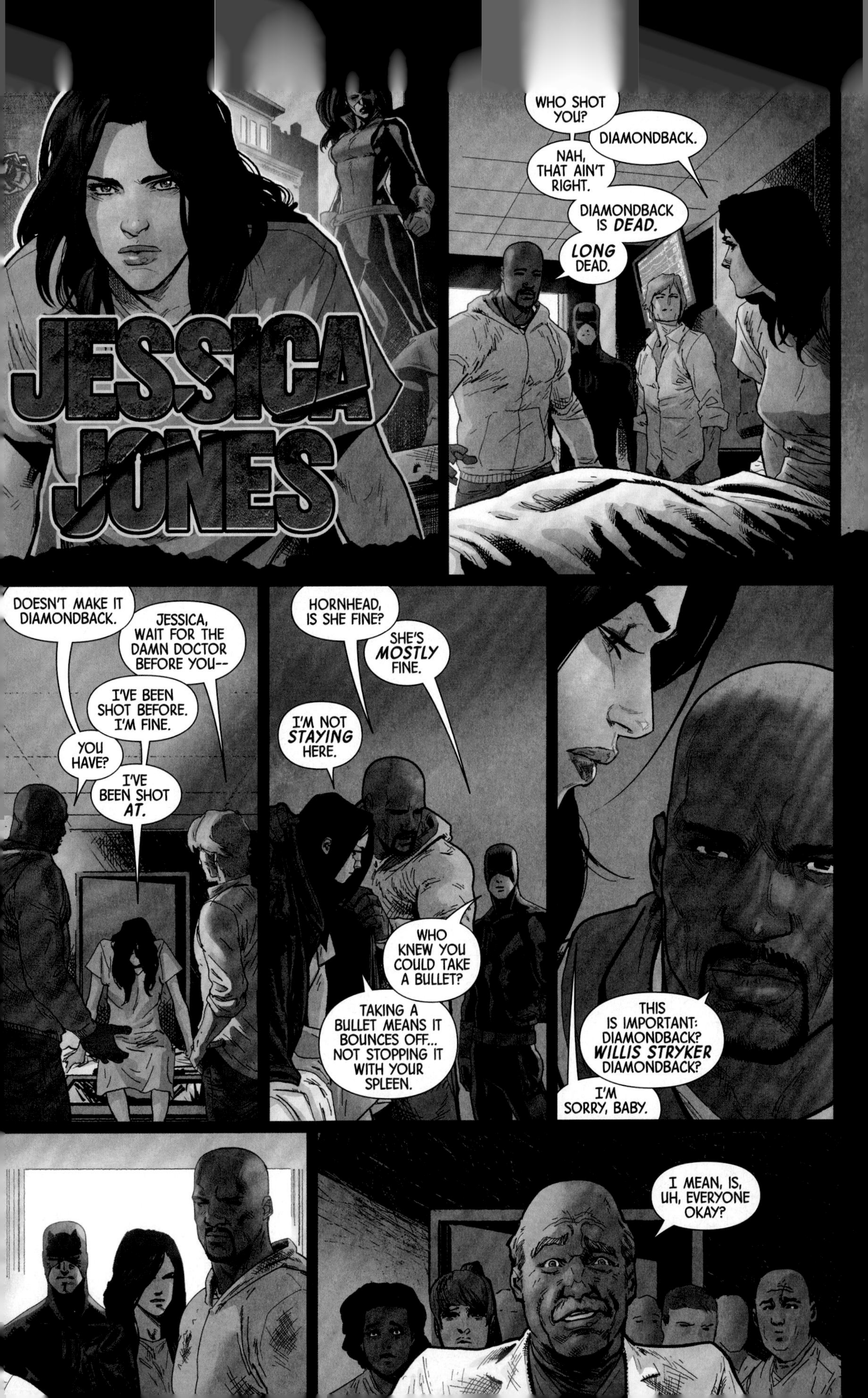
JESSICA JONES
WHO SHOT YOU?
DIAMONDBACK.
NAH, THAT AIN'T RIGHT.
DIAMONDBACK IS DEAD.
LONG DEAD.
DOESN'T MAKE IT DIAMONDBACK.
JESSICA, WAIT FOR THE DAMN DOCTOR BEFORE YOU--
I'VE BEEN SHOT BEFORE. I'M FINE.
YOU HAVE?
I'VE BEEN SHOT AT.
HORNHEAD, IS SHE FINE?
SHE'S MOSTLY FINE.
I'M NOT STAYING HERE.
WHO KNEW YOU COULD TAKE A BULLET?
TAKING A BULLET MEANS IT BOUNCES OFF... NOT STOPPING IT WITH YOUR SPLEEN.
THIS IS IMPORTANT: DIAMONDBACK? WILLIS STRYKER DIAMONDBACK?
I'M SORRY, BABY.
I MEAN, IS, UH, EVERYONE OKAY?

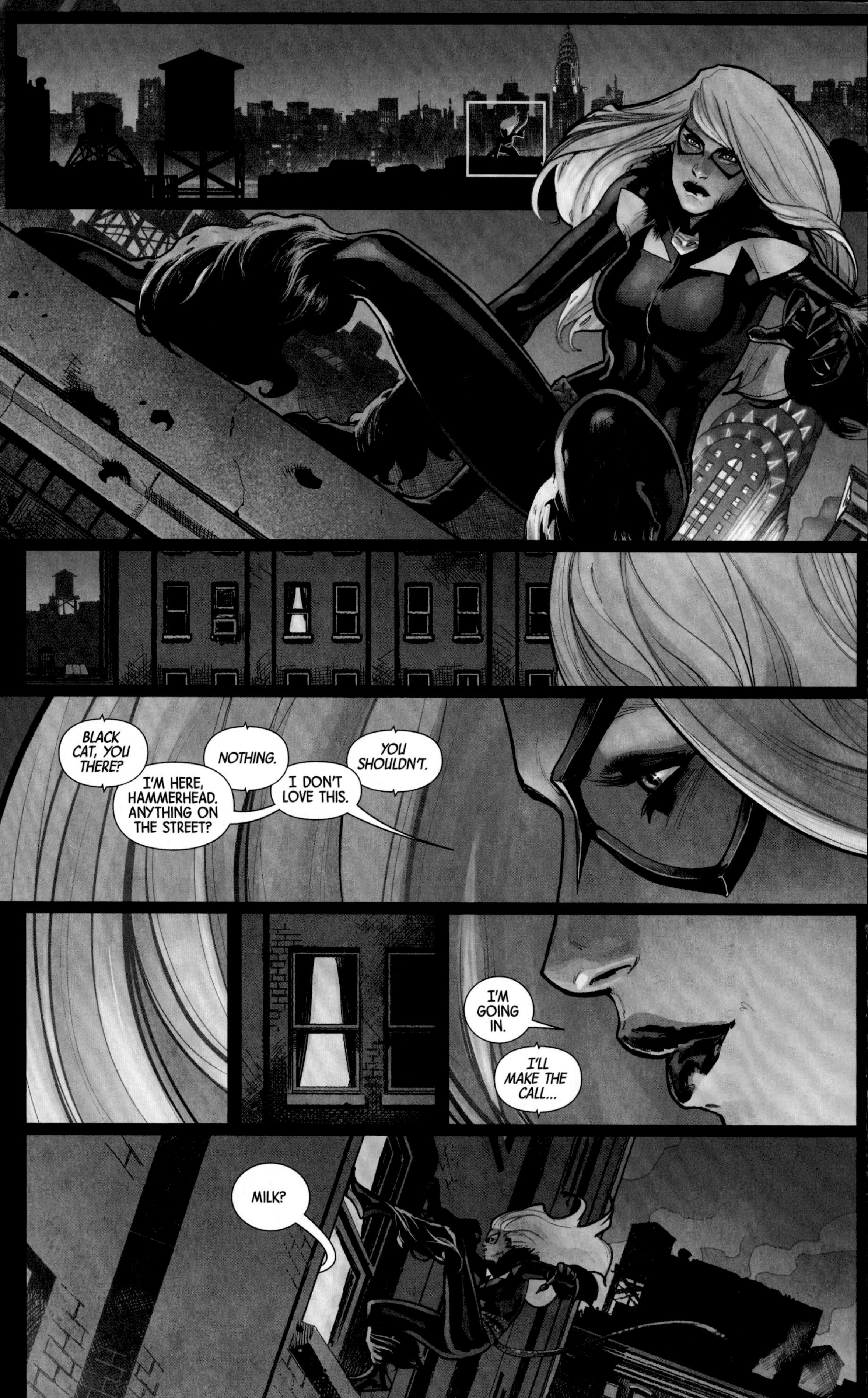
BLACK CAT, YOU THERE?
I'M HERE, HAMMERHEAD. ANYTHING ON THE STREET?
NOTHING.
I DON'T LOVE THIS.
YOU SHOULDN'T.
I'M GOING IN.
I'LL MAKE THE CALL...
MILK?

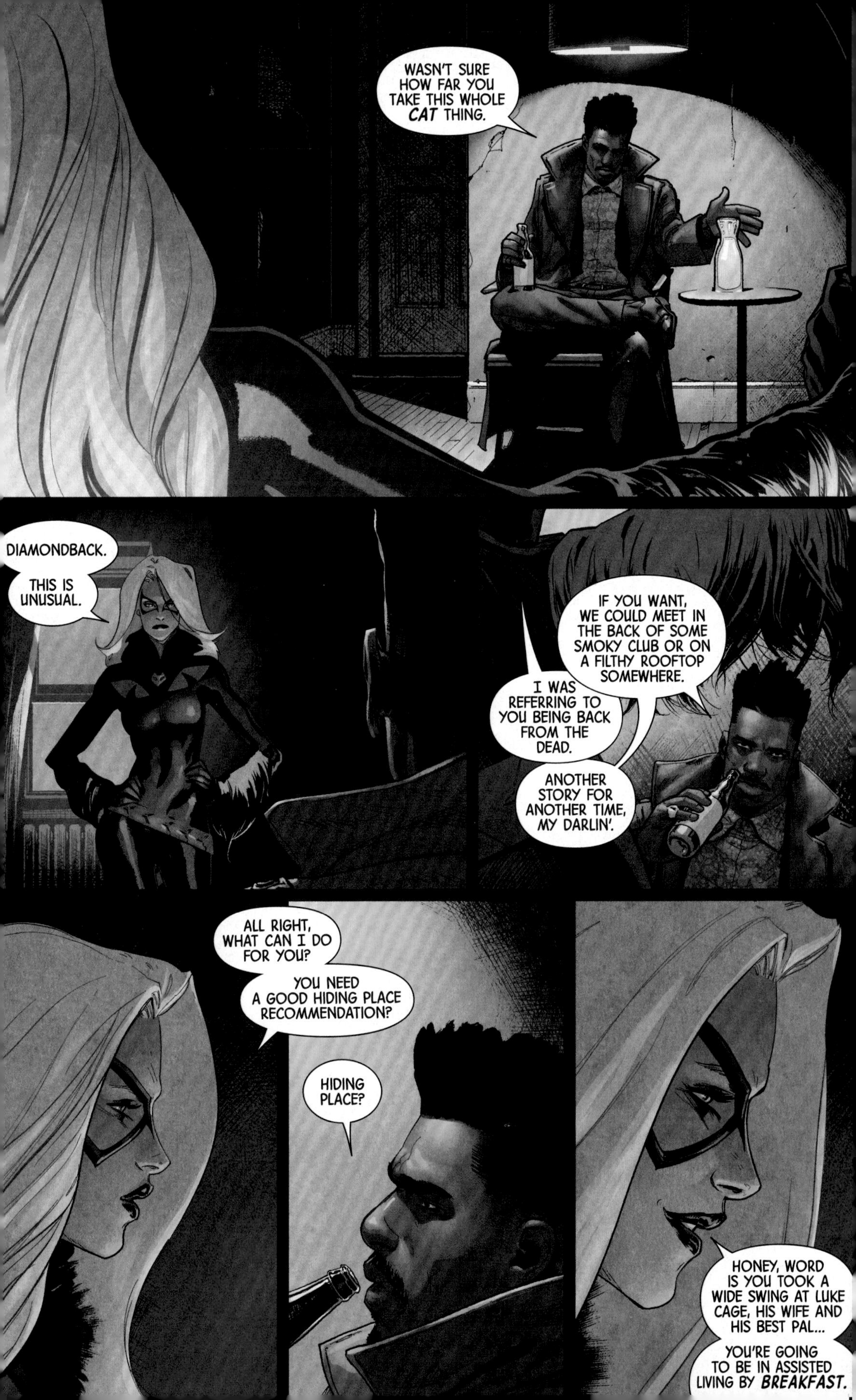
WASN'T SURE HOW FAR YOU TAKE THIS WHOLE CAT THING.
DIAMONDBACK.
THIS IS UNUSUAL.
IF YOU WANT, WE COULD MEET IN THE BACK OF SOME SMOKY CLUB OR ON A FILTHY ROOFTOP SOMEWHERE.
I WAS REFERRING TO YOU BEING BACK FROM THE DEAD.
ANOTHER STORY FOR ANOTHER TIME, MY DARLIN'.
ALL RIGHT, WHAT CAN I DO FOR YOU?
YOU NEED A GOOD HIDING PLACE RECOMMENDATION?
HIDING PLACE?
HONEY, WORD IS YOU TOOK A WIDE SWING AT LUKE CAGE, HIS WIFE AND HIS BEST PAL...
YOU'RE GOING TO BE IN ASSISTED LIVING BY BREAKFAST.

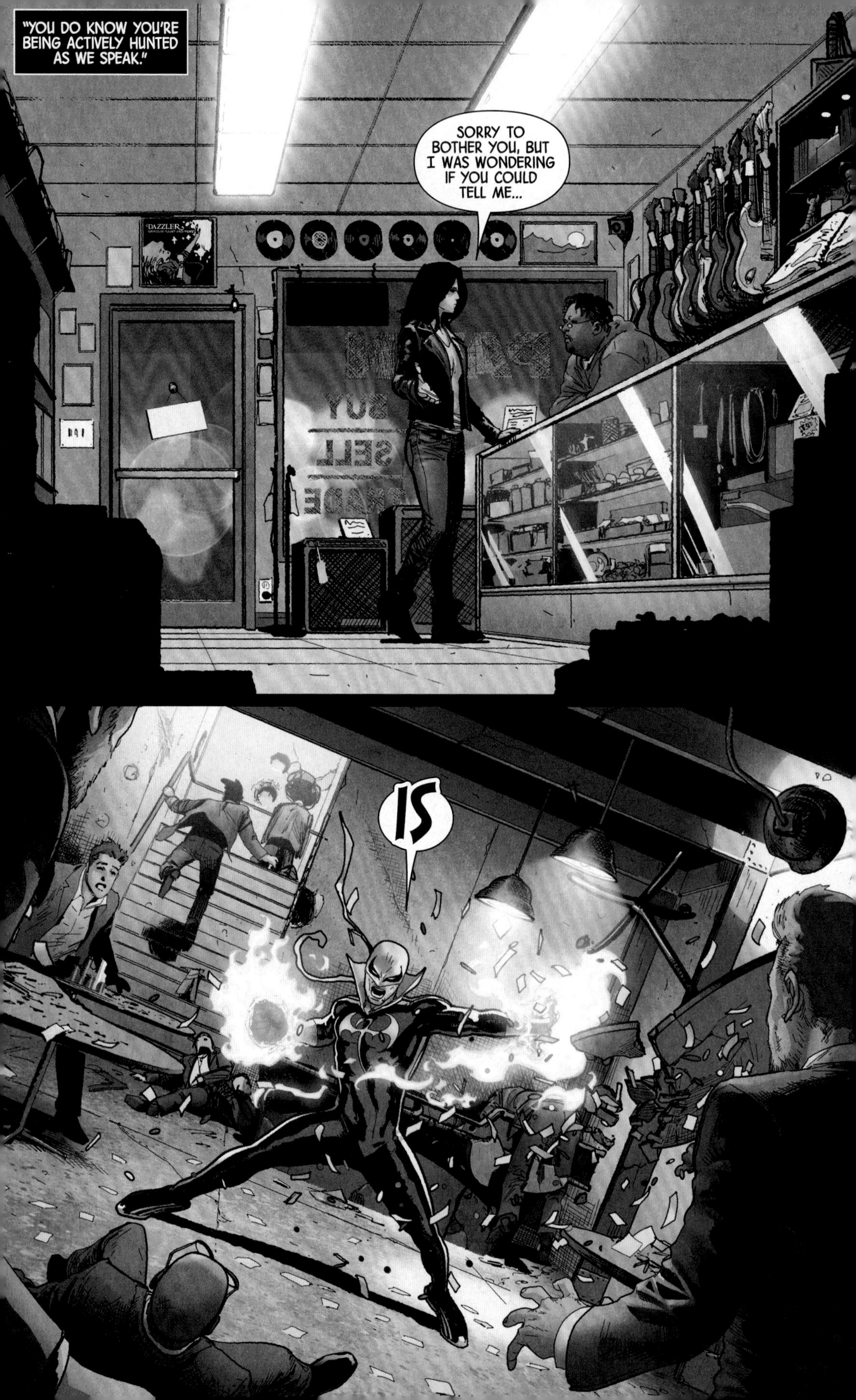
"YOU DO KNOW YOU'RE BEING ACTIVELY HUNTED AS WE SPEAK."
SORRY TO BOTHER YOU, BUT I WAS WONDERING IF YOU COULD TELL ME...
BUY
SELL
IS

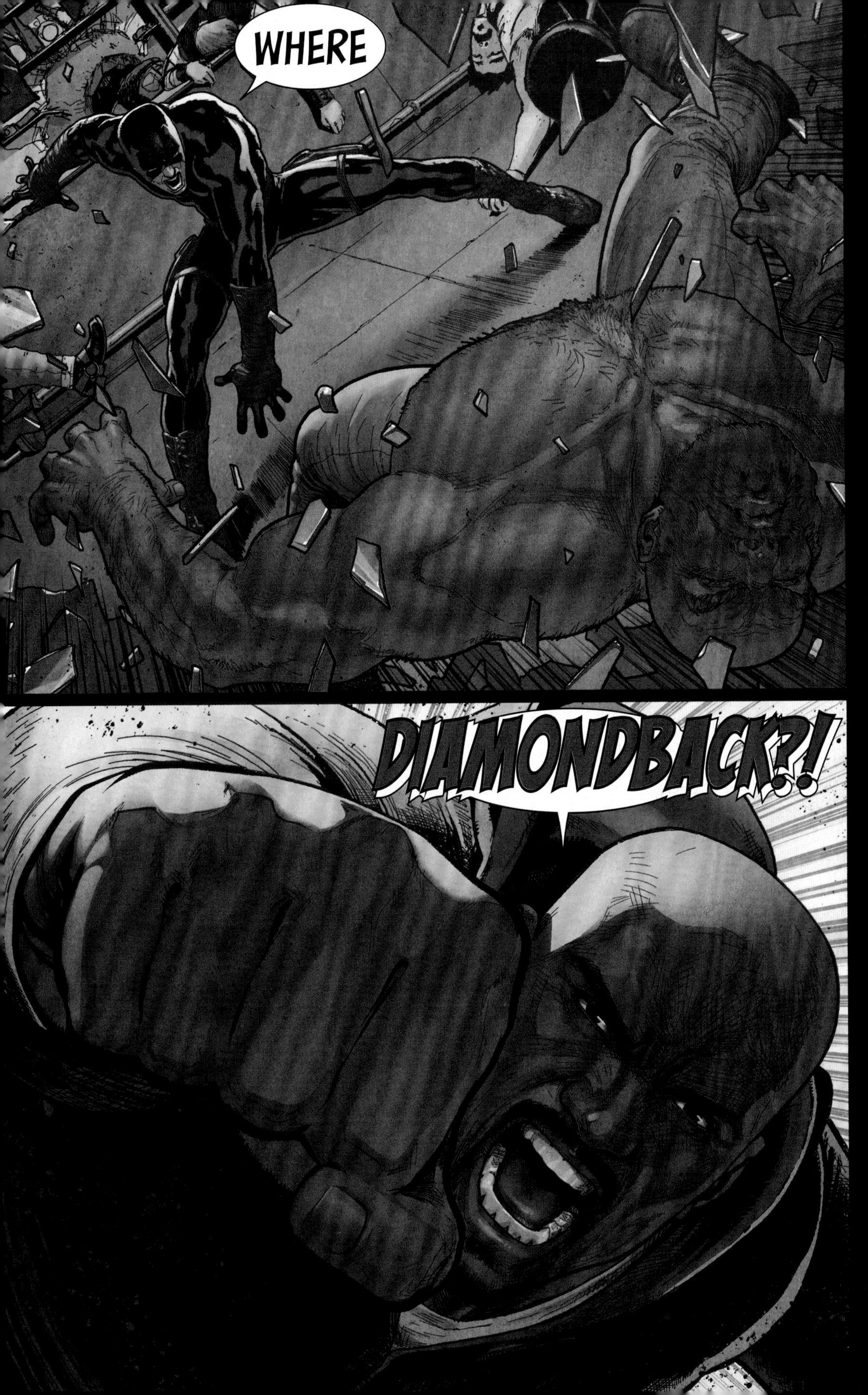
WHERE
DIAMONDBACK?!

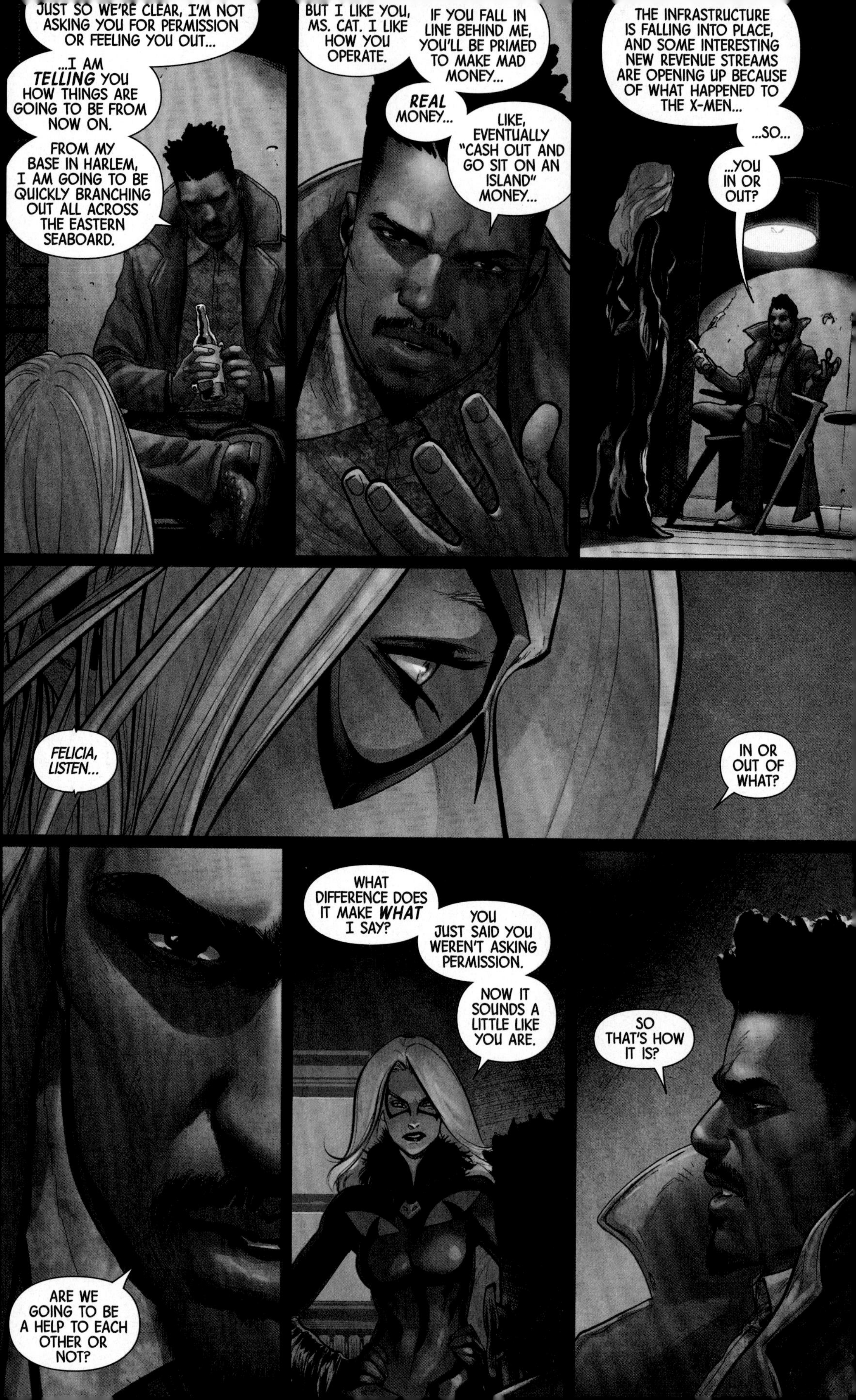
JUST SO WE'RE CLEAR, I'M NOT ASKING YOU FOR PERMISSION OR FEELING YOU OUT...
...I AM TELLING YOU HOW THINGS ARE GOING TO BE FROM NOW ON.
FROM MY BASE IN HARLEM, I AM GOING TO BE QUICKLY BRANCHING OUT ALL ACROSS THE EASTERN SEABOARD.
BUT I LIKE YOU, MS. CAT. I LIKE HOW YOU OPERATE.
IF YOU FALL IN LINE BEHIND ME, YOU'LL BE PRIMED TO MAKE MAD MONEY...
REAL MONEY...
LIKE, EVENTUALLY "CASH OUT AND GO SIT ON AN ISLAND" MONEY...
THE INFRASTRUCTURE IS FALLING INTO PLACE, AND SOME INTERESTING NEW REVENUE STREAMS ARE OPENING UP BECAUSE OF WHAT HAPPENED TO THE X-MEN...
...SO...
...YOU IN OR OUT?
FELICIA, LISTEN...
IN OR OUT OF WHAT?
ARE WE GOING TO BE A HELP TO EACH OTHER OR NOT?
WHAT DIFFERENCE DOES IT MAKE WHAT I SAY?
YOU JUST SAID YOU WEREN'T ASKING PERMISSION.
NOW IT SOUNDS A LITTLE LIKE YOU ARE.
SO THAT'S HOW IT IS?

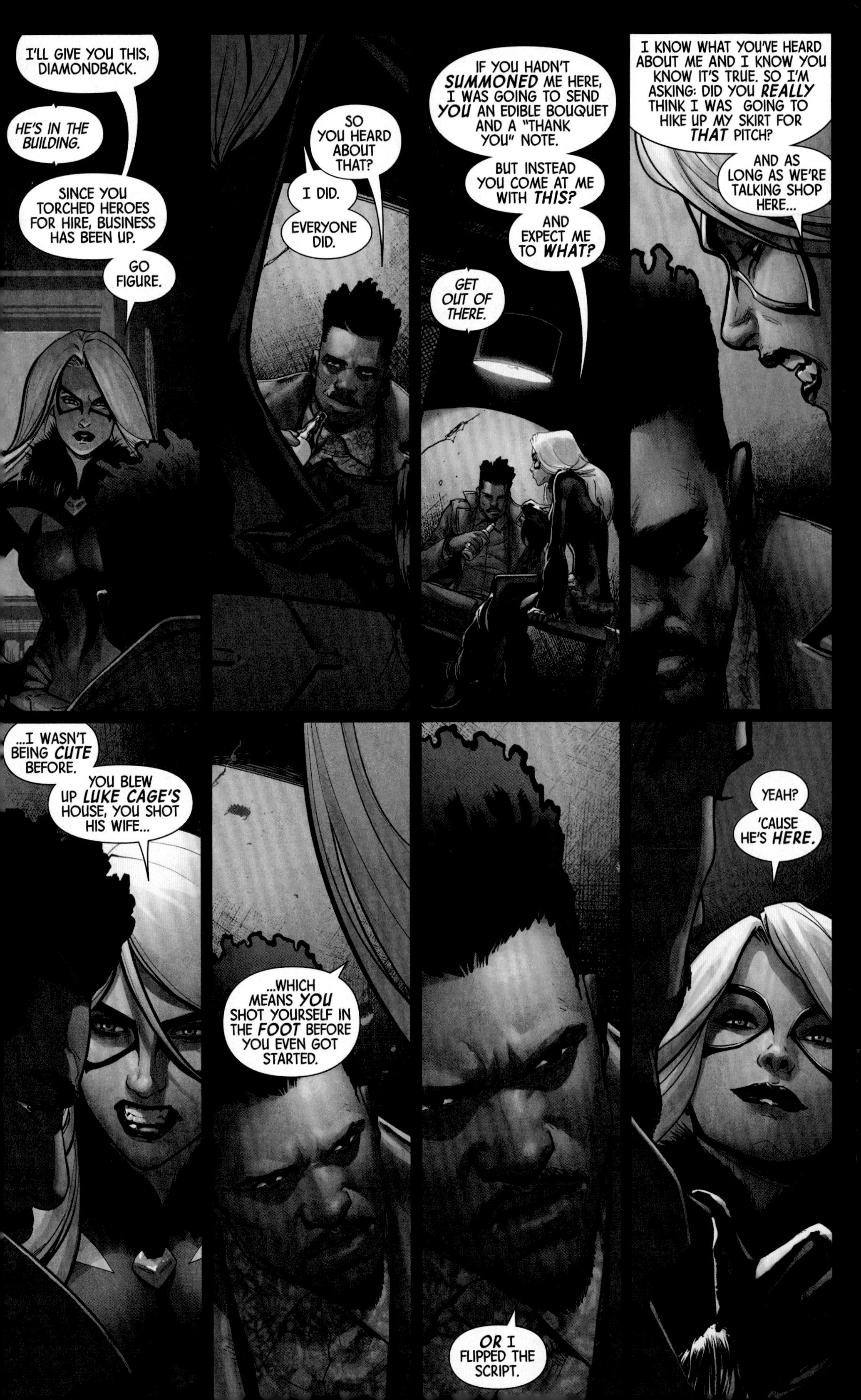
I'LL GIVE YOU THIS, DIAMONDBACK.
HE'S IN THE BUILDING.
SINCE YOU TORCHED HEROES FOR HIRE, BUSINESS HAS BEEN UP.
GO FIGURE.
SO YOU HEARD ABOUT THAT?
I DID.
EVERYONE DID.
IF YOU HADN'T SUMMONED ME HERE, I WAS GOING TO SEND YOU AN EDIBLE BOUQUET AND A "THANK YOU" NOTE.
BUT INSTEAD YOU COME AT ME WITH THIS?
AND EXPECT ME TO WHAT?
GET OUT OF THERE.
I KNOW WHAT YOU'VE HEARD ABOUT ME AND I KNOW YOU KNOW IT'S TRUE. SO I'M ASKING: DID YOU REALLY THINK I WAS GOING TO HIKE UP MY SKIRT FOR THAT PITCH?
AND AS LONG AS WE'RE TALKING SHOP HERE...
...I WASN'T BEING CUTE BEFORE.
YOU BLEW UP LUKE CAGE'S HOUSE, YOU SHOT HIS WIFE...
...WHICH MEANS YOU SHOT YOURSELF IN THE FOOT BEFORE YOU EVEN GOT STARTED.
OR I FLIPPED THE SCRIPT.
YEAH?
'CAUSE HE'S HERE.

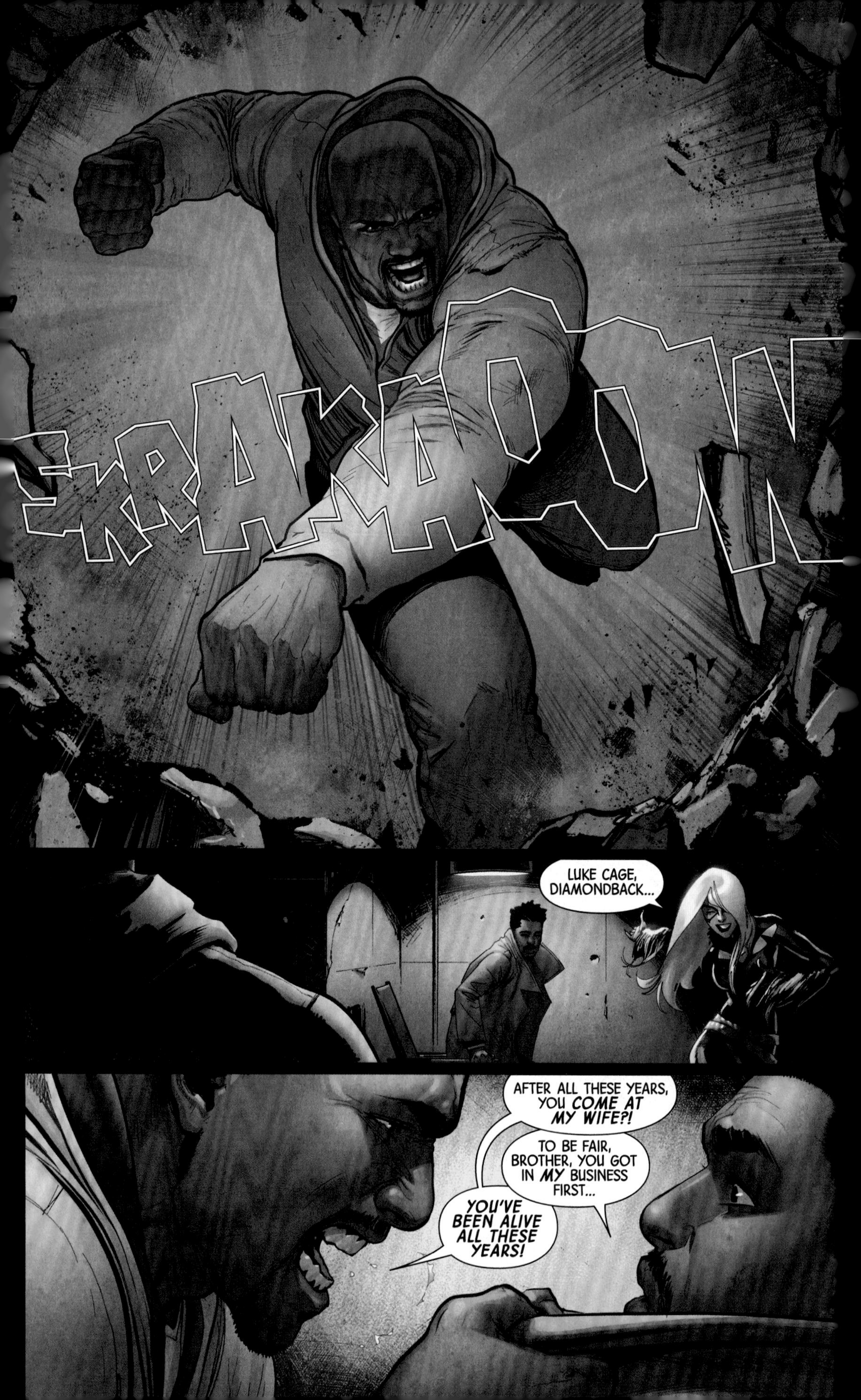
LUKE CAGE, DIAMONDBACK...
AFTER ALL THESE YEARS, YOU *COME AT MY WIFE?!*
TO BE FAIR, BROTHER, YOU GOT IN *MY* BUSINESS FIRST...
YOU'VE BEEN ALIVE ALL THESE YEARS!

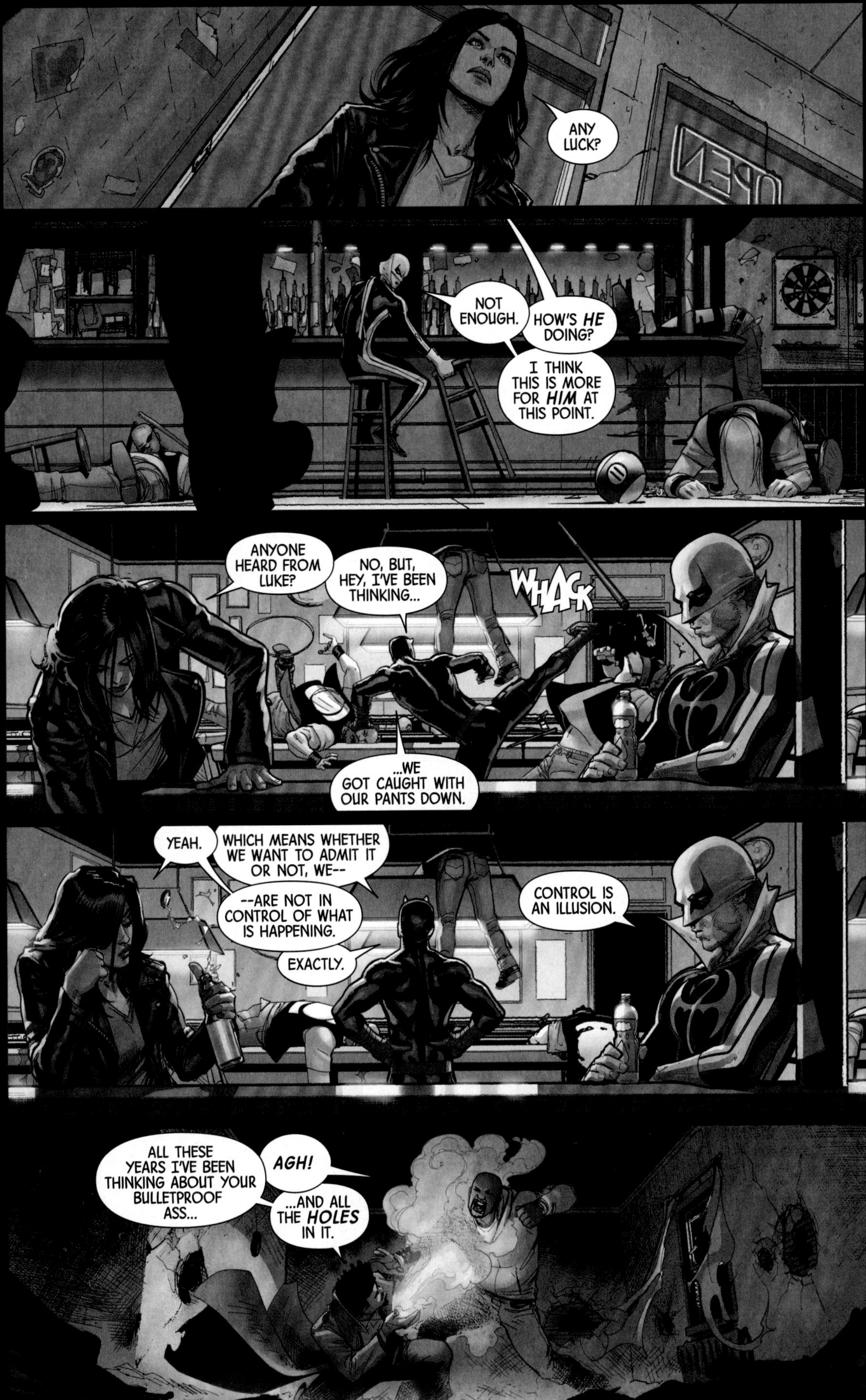
ANY LUCK?
NOT ENOUGH.
HOW'S HE DOING?
I THINK THIS IS MORE FOR HIM AT THIS POINT.
ANYONE HEARD FROM LUKE?
NO, BUT, HEY, I'VE BEEN THINKING...
WHACK
...WE GOT CAUGHT WITH OUR PANTS DOWN.
YEAH.
WHICH MEANS WHETHER WE WANT TO ADMIT IT OR NOT, WE--
--ARE NOT IN CONTROL OF WHAT IS HAPPENING.
EXACTLY.
CONTROL IS AN ILLUSION.
ALL THESE YEARS I'VE BEEN THINKING ABOUT YOUR BULLETPROOF ASS...
AGH!
...AND ALL THE HOLES IN IT.

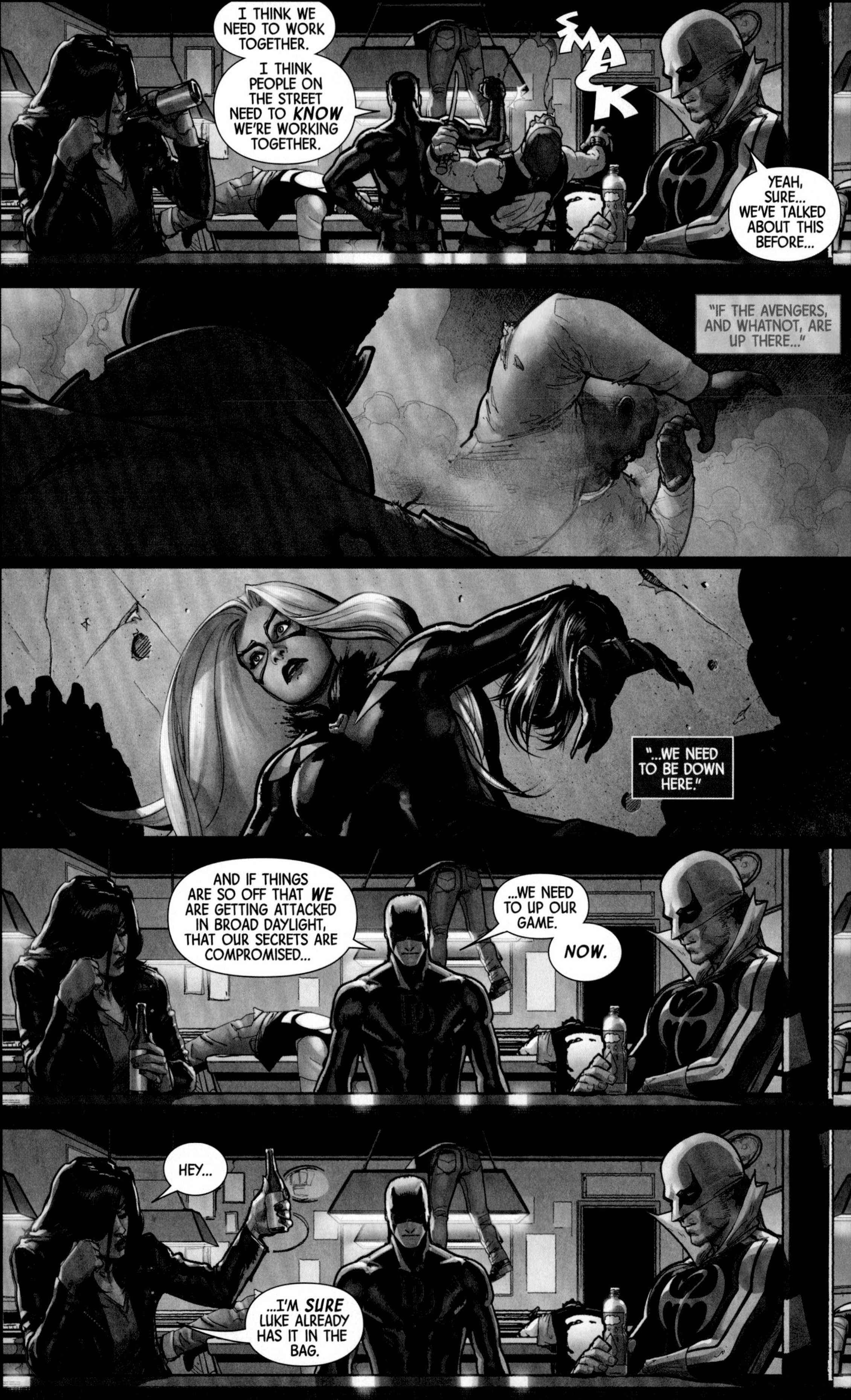
I THINK WE NEED TO WORK TOGETHER.
I THINK PEOPLE ON THE STREET NEED TO KNOW WE'RE WORKING TOGETHER.
SMACK
YEAH, SURE... WE'VE TALKED ABOUT THIS BEFORE...
"IF THE AVENGERS, AND WHATNOT, ARE UP THERE..."
"...WE NEED TO BE DOWN HERE."
AND IF THINGS ARE SO OFF THAT WE ARE GETTING ATTACKED IN BROAD DAYLIGHT, THAT OUR SECRETS ARE COMPROMISED...
...WE NEED TO UP OUR GAME.
NOW.
HEY...
...I'M SURE LUKE ALREADY HAS IT IN THE BAG.

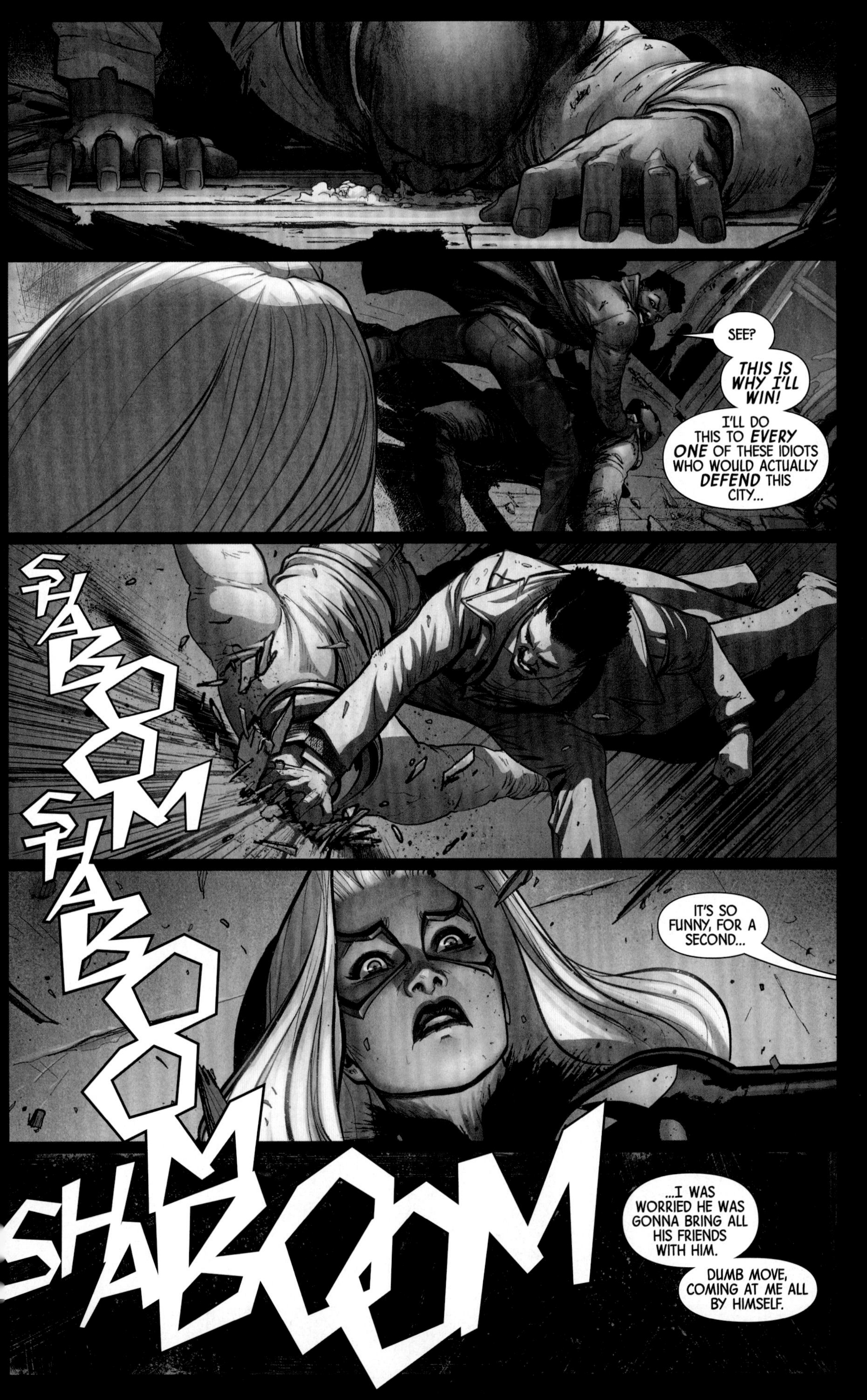
SEE?
THIS IS WHY I'LL WIN!
I'LL DO THIS TO EVERY ONE OF THESE IDIOTS WHO WOULD ACTUALLY DEFEND THIS CITY...
SHABOOM
SHABOOM
IT'S SO FUNNY, FOR A SECOND...
SHABOOM
...I WAS WORRIED HE WAS GONNA BRING ALL HIS FRIENDS WITH HIM.
DUMB MOVE, COMING AT ME ALL BY HIMSELF.

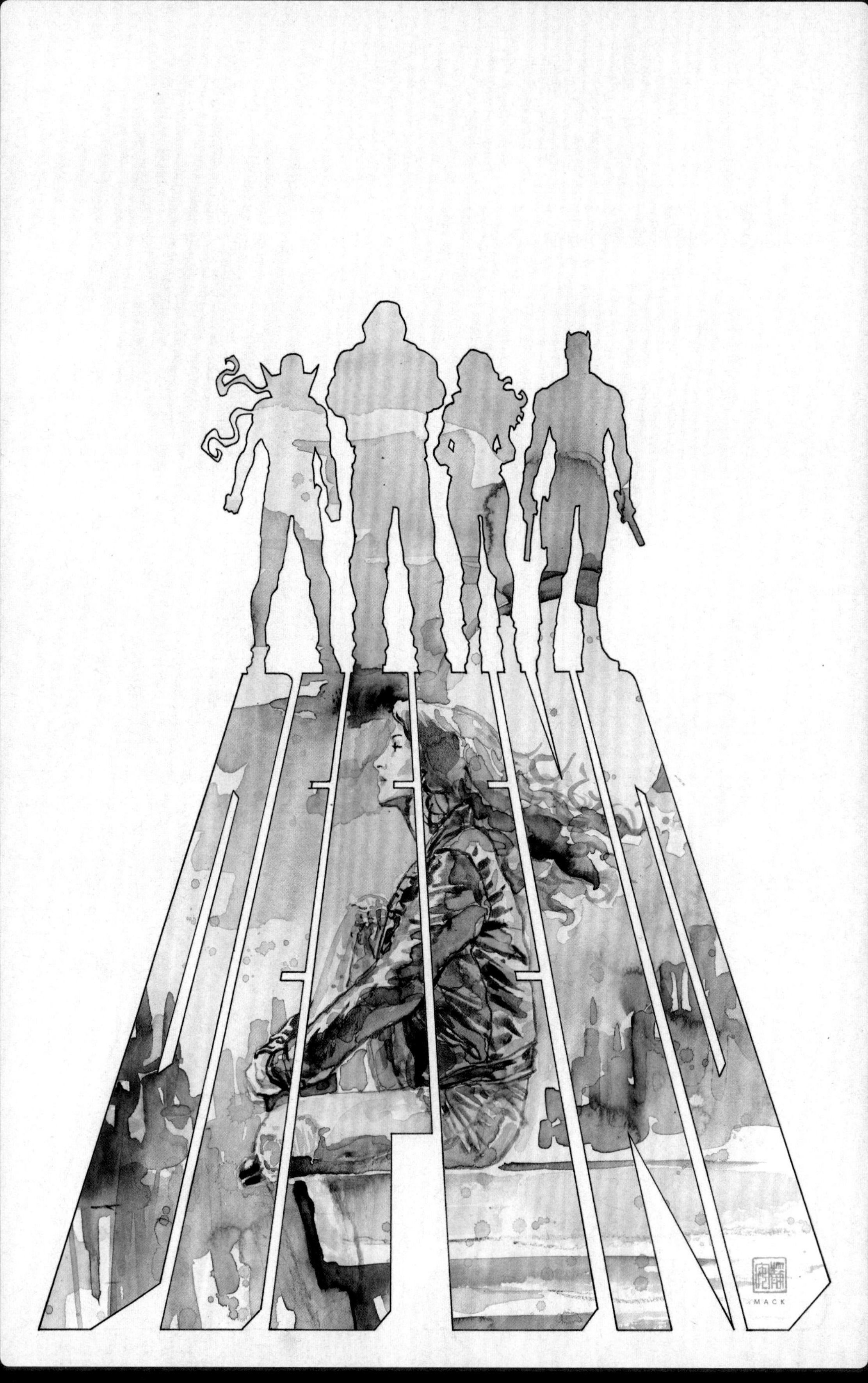
MACK

NO. 1 VARIANT BY **DAVID MACK**

2

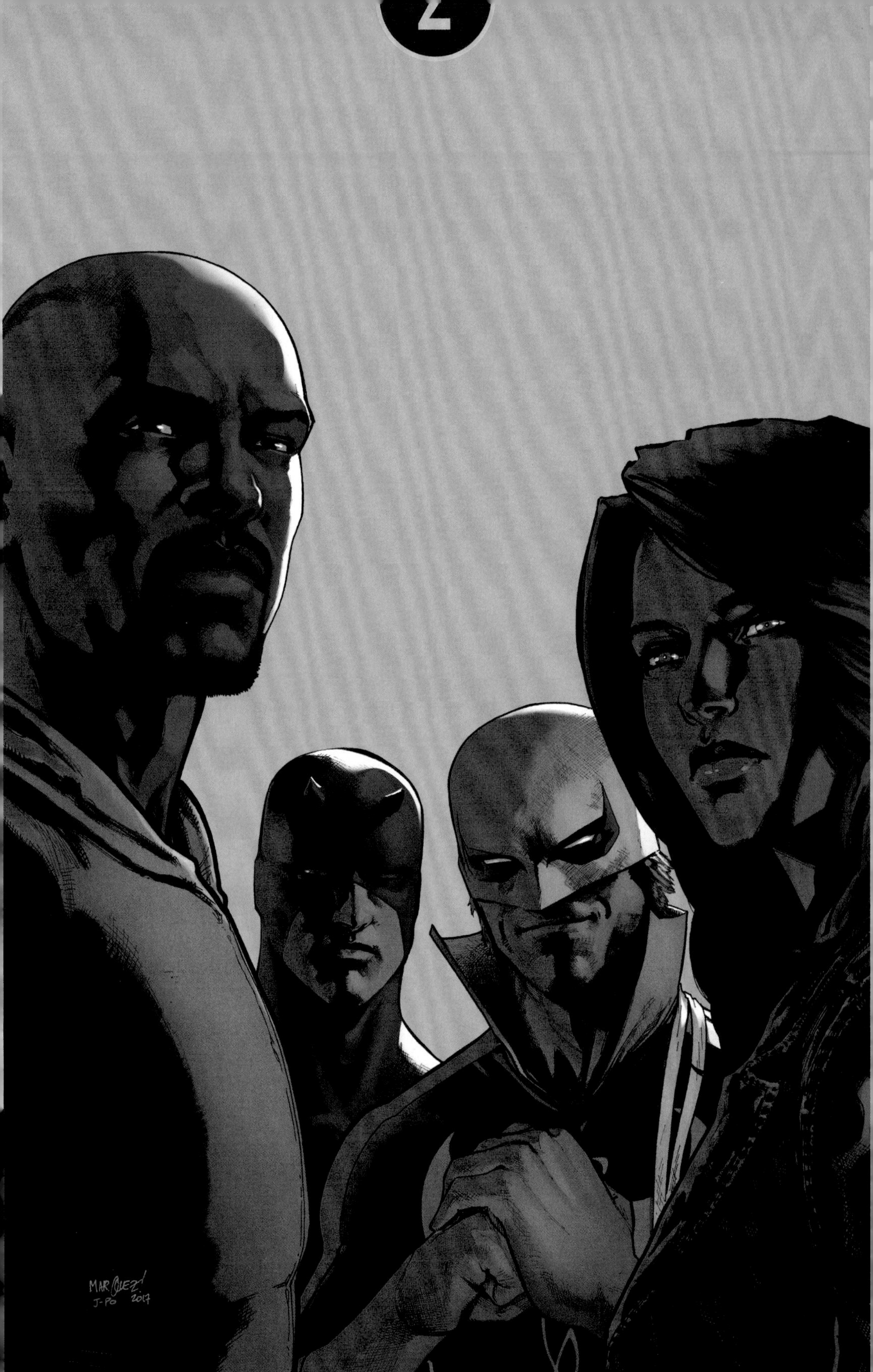
MARQUEZ!
J-PO 2017

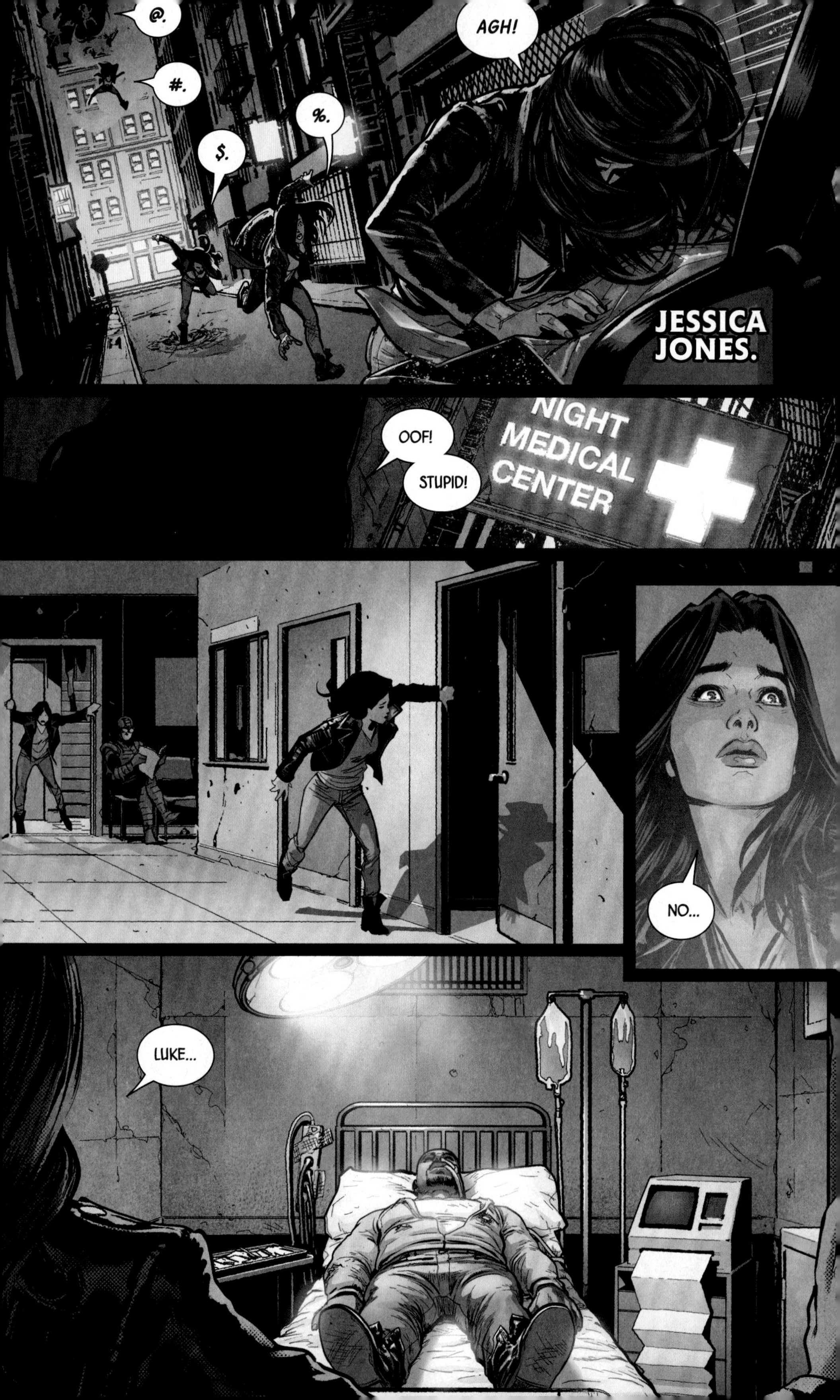
@.
#.
$.
%.
AGH!
JESSICA JONES.
NIGHT MEDICAL CENTER
OOF!
STUPID!
NO...
LUKE...

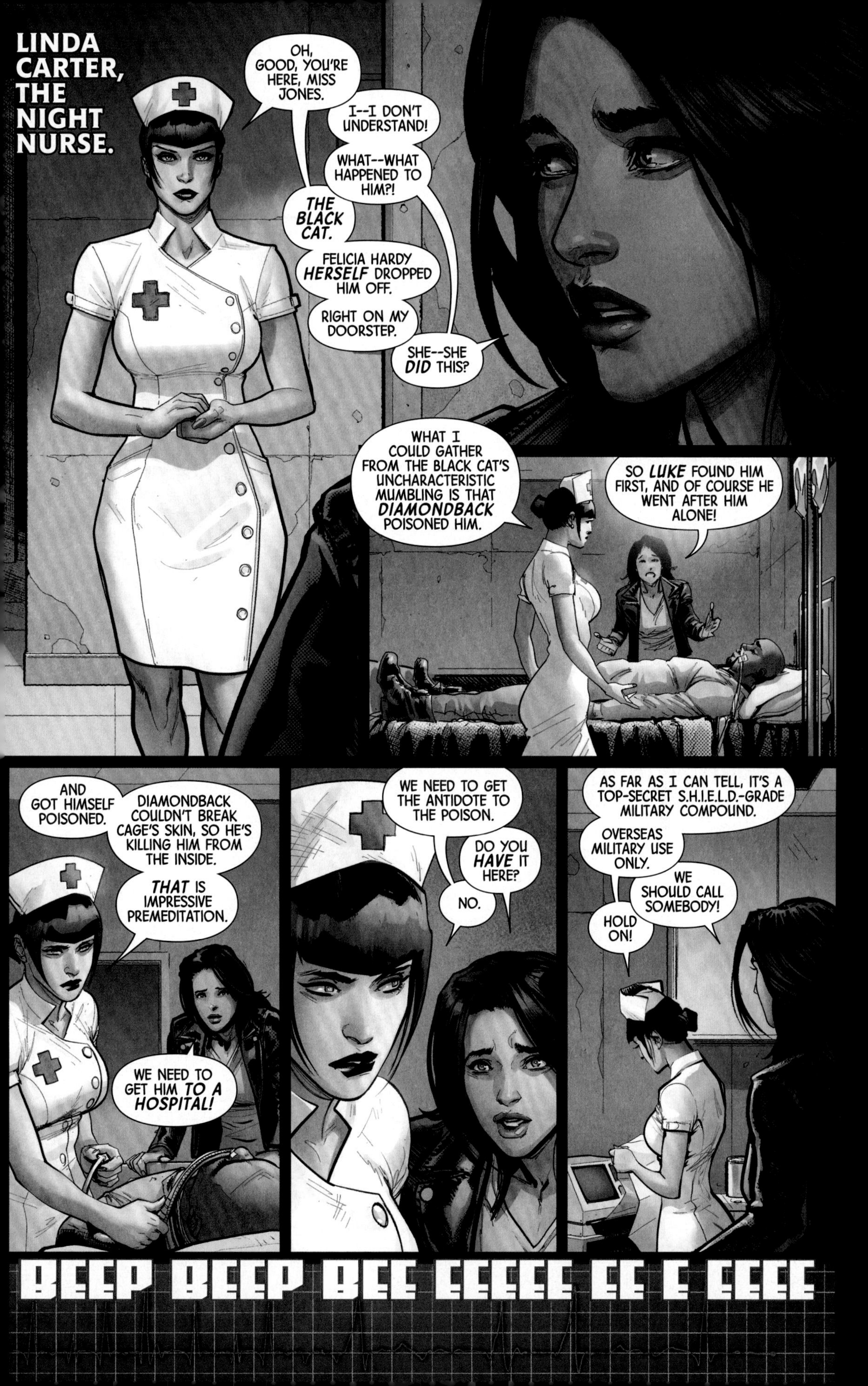
LINDA CARTER, THE NIGHT NURSE.
OH, GOOD, YOU'RE HERE, MISS JONES.
I--I DON'T UNDERSTAND!
WHAT--WHAT HAPPENED TO HIM?!
THE BLACK CAT.
FELICIA HARDY HERSELF DROPPED HIM OFF.
RIGHT ON MY DOORSTEP.
SHE--SHE DID THIS?
WHAT I COULD GATHER FROM THE BLACK CAT'S UNCHARACTERISTIC MUMBLING IS THAT DIAMONDBACK POISONED HIM.
SO LUKE FOUND HIM FIRST, AND OF COURSE HE WENT AFTER HIM ALONE!
AND GOT HIMSELF POISONED.
DIAMONDBACK COULDN'T BREAK CAGE'S SKIN, SO HE'S KILLING HIM FROM THE INSIDE.
THAT IS IMPRESSIVE PREMEDITATION.
WE NEED TO GET HIM TO A HOSPITAL!
WE NEED TO GET THE ANTIDOTE TO THE POISON.
DO YOU HAVE IT HERE?
NO.
AS FAR AS I CAN TELL, IT'S A TOP-SECRET S.H.I.E.L.D.-GRADE MILITARY COMPOUND.
OVERSEAS MILITARY USE ONLY.
WE SHOULD CALL SOMEBODY!
HOLD ON!
BEEP BEEP BEE EEEEE EE E EEEE

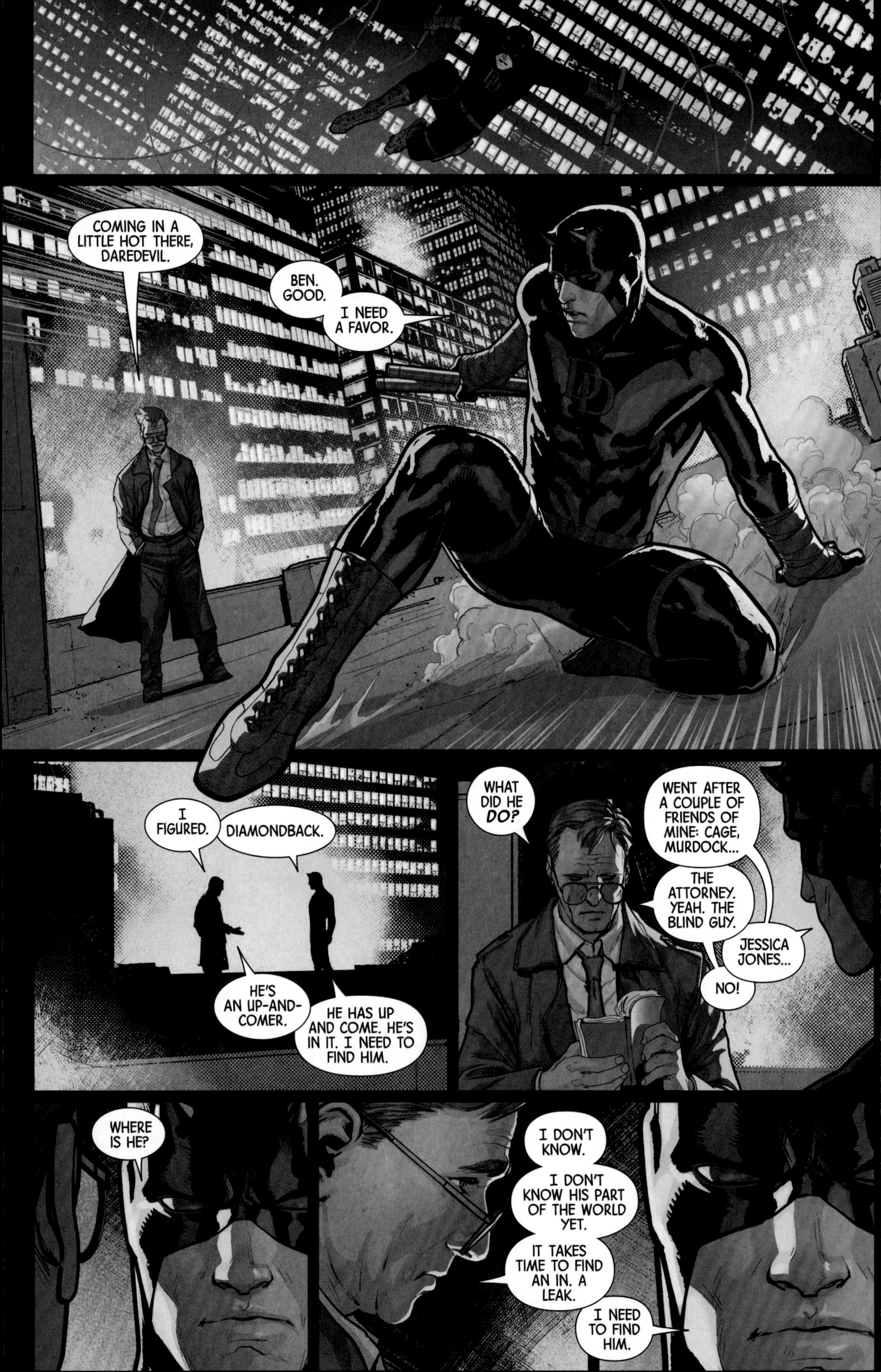
COMING IN A LITTLE HOT THERE, DAREDEVIL.
BEN. GOOD.
I NEED A FAVOR.
I FIGURED.
DIAMONDBACK.
HE'S AN UP-AND-COMER.
HE HAS UP AND COME. HE'S IN IT. I NEED TO FIND HIM.
WHAT DID HE DO?
WENT AFTER A COUPLE OF FRIENDS OF MINE: CAGE, MURDOCK...
THE ATTORNEY. YEAH. THE BLIND GUY.
JESSICA JONES...
NO!
WHERE IS HE?
I DON'T KNOW.
I DON'T KNOW HIS PART OF THE WORLD YET.
IT TAKES TIME TO FIND AN IN. A LEAK.
I NEED TO FIND HIM.

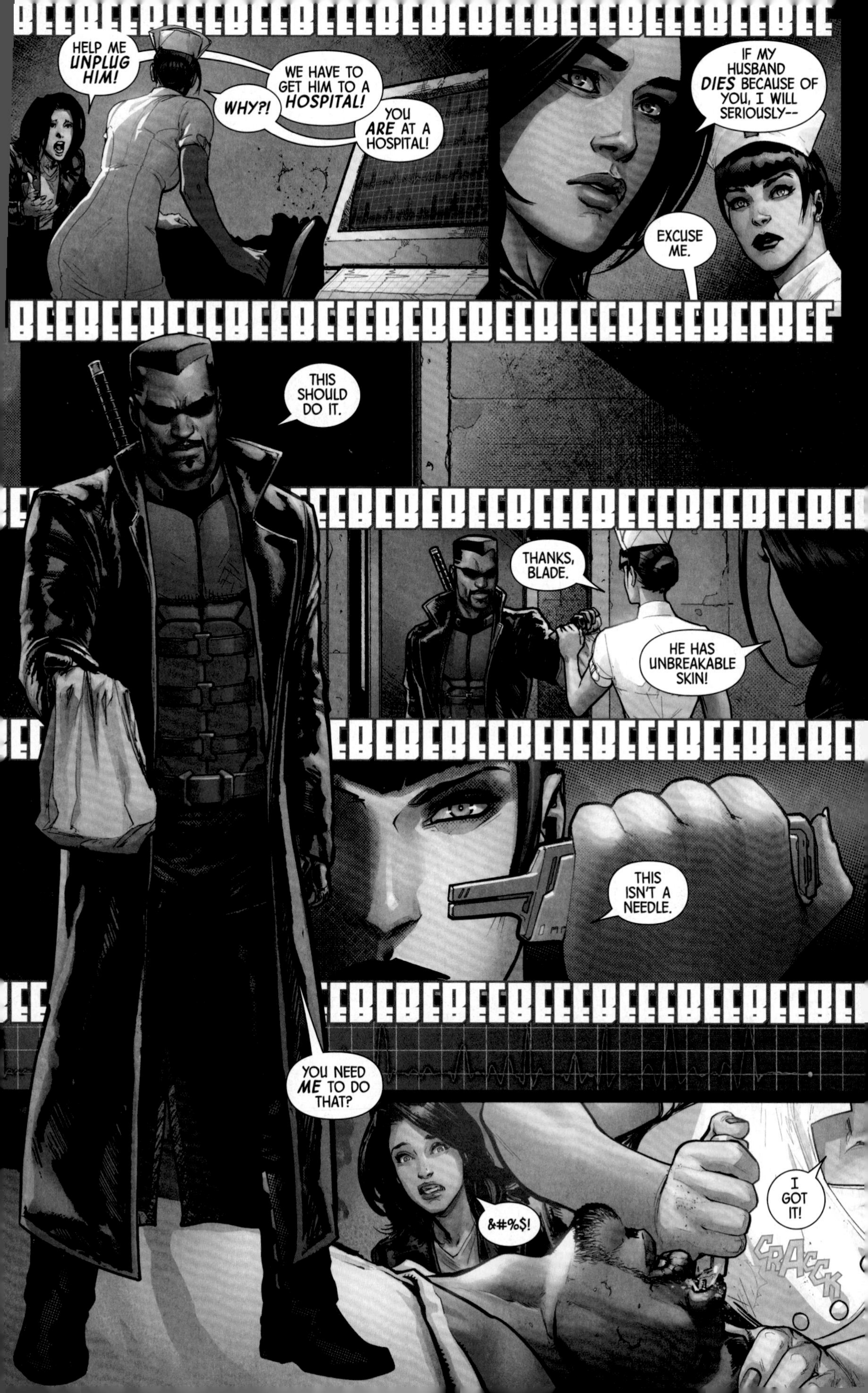
BEEBEEBEEBEEBEEBEEBEEBEEBEEBEEBEE
HELP ME UNPLUG HIM!
WE HAVE TO GET HIM TO A HOSPITAL!
WHY?!
YOU ARE AT A HOSPITAL!
IF MY HUSBAND DIES BECAUSE OF YOU, I WILL SERIOUSLY--
EXCUSE ME.
THIS SHOULD DO IT.
THANKS, BLADE.
HE HAS UNBREAKABLE SKIN!
THIS ISN'T A NEEDLE.
YOU NEED ME TO DO THAT?
&#%$!
I GOT IT!
CRACCK

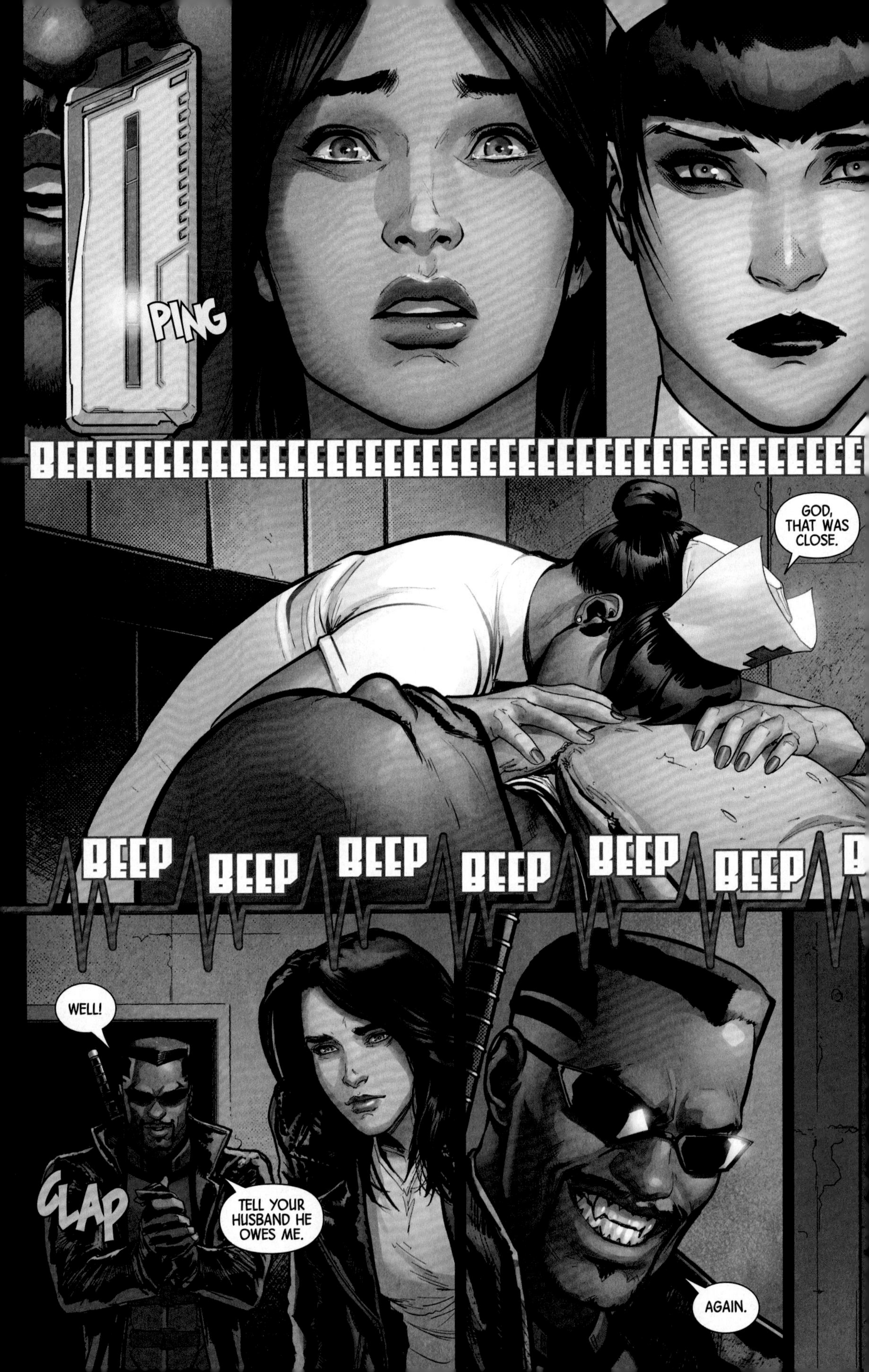
PING
BEEEEEEEEEEEEEEEEEEEEEEEEEEEEEEEEEEEEEEE
GOD, THAT WAS CLOSE.
BEEP BEEP BEEP BEEP BEEP BEEP
WELL!
CLAP
TELL YOUR HUSBAND HE OWES ME.
AGAIN.

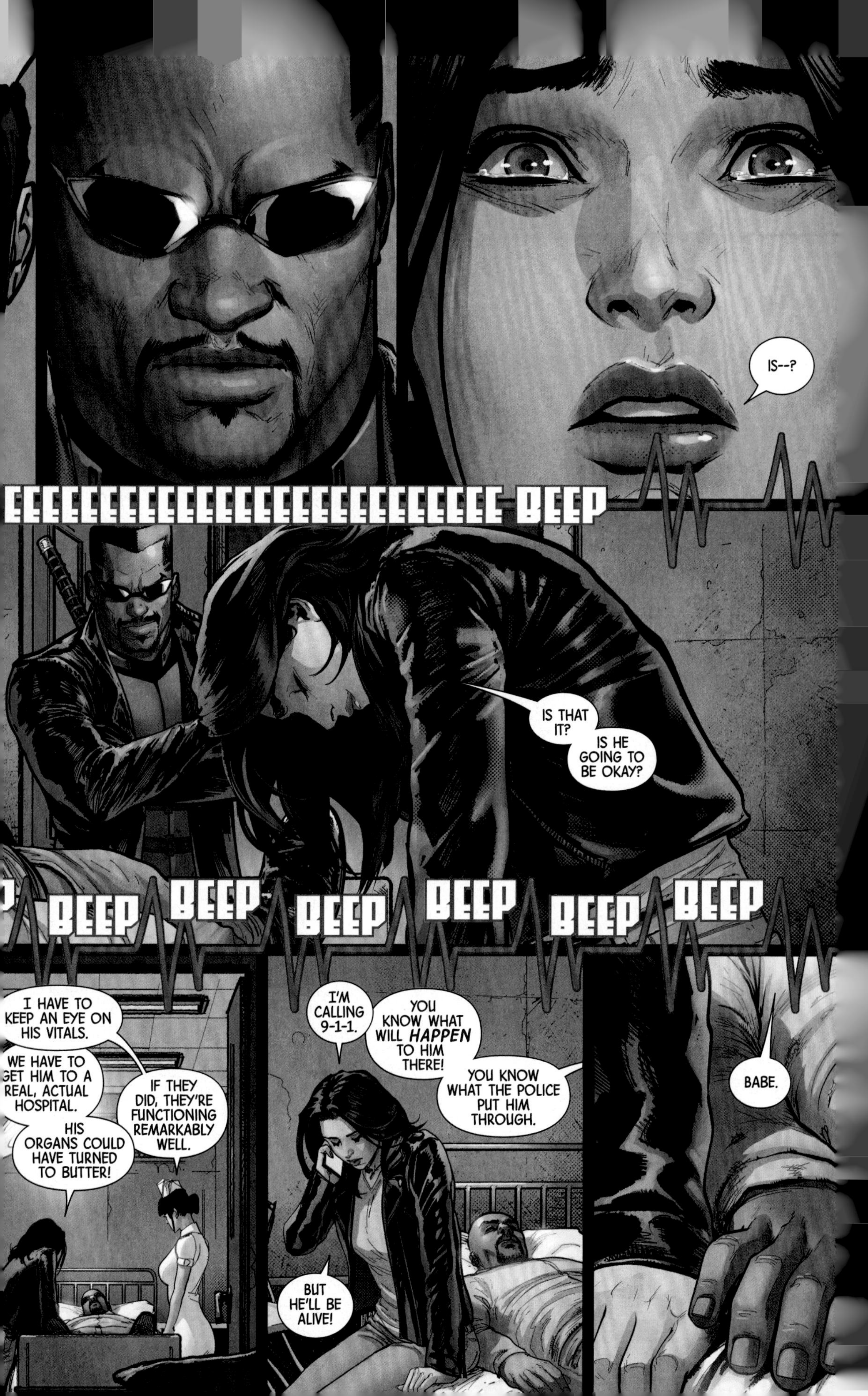
IS--?
EEEEEEEEEEEEEEEEEEEEEEEEEEEEE BEEP
IS THAT IT?
IS HE GOING TO BE OKAY?
BEEP
BEEP
BEEP
BEEP
BEEP
BEEP
I HAVE TO KEEP AN EYE ON HIS VITALS.
WE HAVE TO GET HIM TO A REAL, ACTUAL HOSPITAL.
HIS ORGANS COULD HAVE TURNED TO BUTTER!
IF THEY DID, THEY'RE FUNCTIONING REMARKABLY WELL.
I'M CALLING 9-1-1.
YOU KNOW WHAT WILL *HAPPEN* TO HIM THERE!
YOU KNOW WHAT THE POLICE PUT HIM THROUGH.
BUT HE'LL BE ALIVE!
BABE.

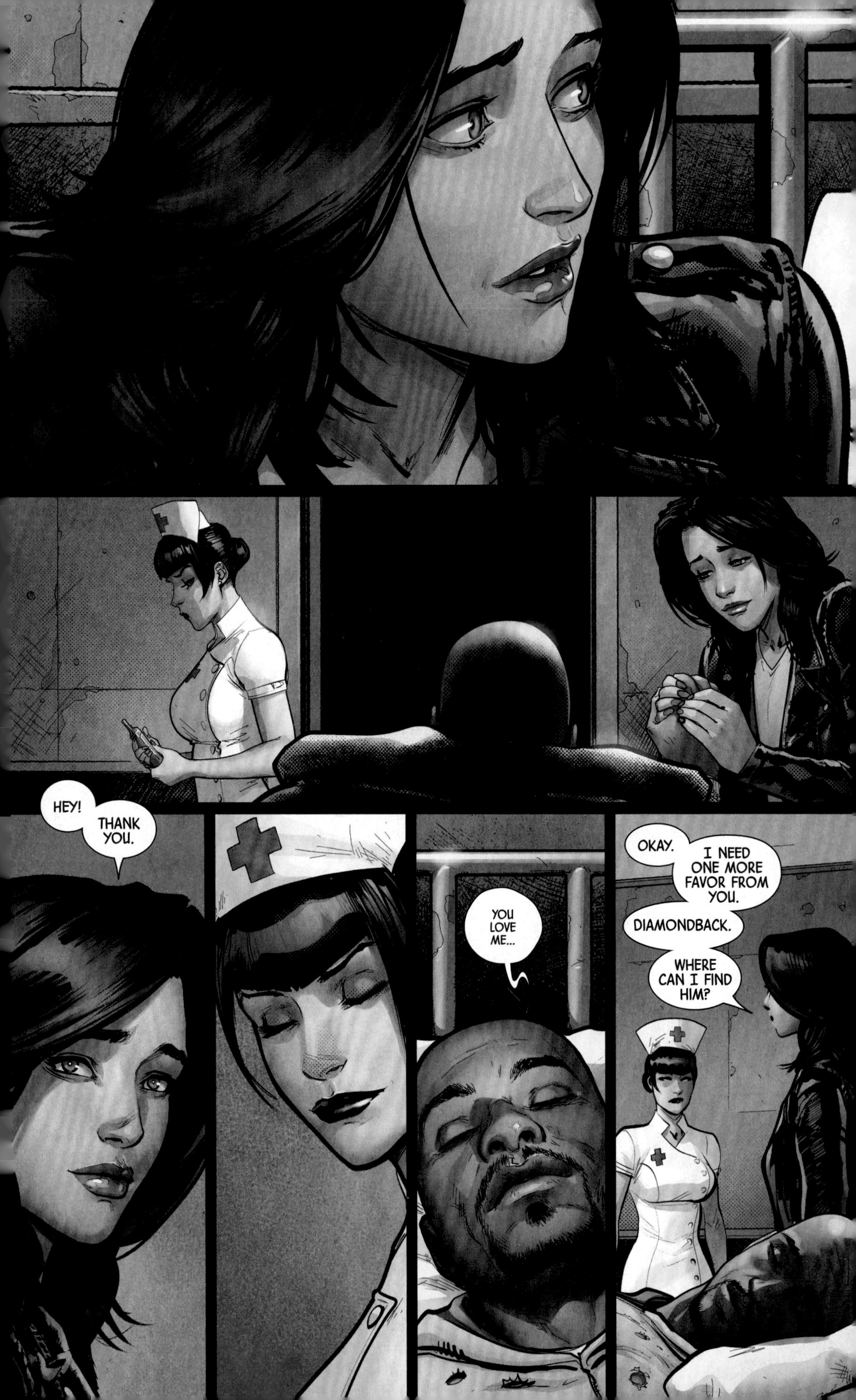
HEY!
THANK YOU.
YOU LOVE ME...
OKAY.
I NEED ONE MORE FAVOR FROM YOU.
DIAMONDBACK.
WHERE CAN I FIND HIM?

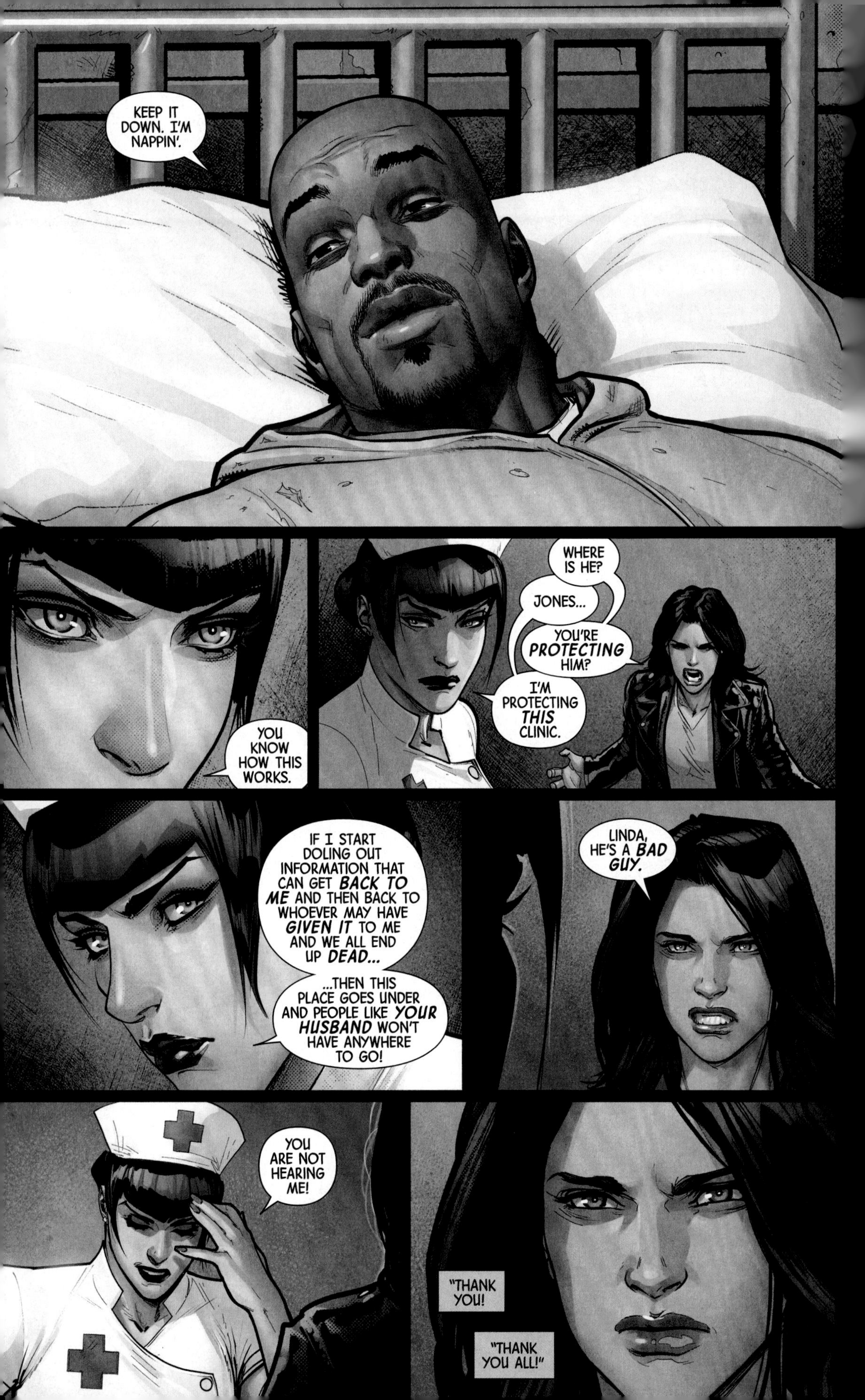
KEEP IT DOWN. I'M NAPPIN'.
YOU KNOW HOW THIS WORKS.
WHERE IS HE?
JONES...
YOU'RE *PROTECTING* HIM?
I'M PROTECTING *THIS* CLINIC.
IF I START DOLING OUT INFORMATION THAT CAN GET *BACK TO ME* AND THEN BACK TO WHOEVER MAY HAVE *GIVEN IT* TO ME AND WE ALL END UP *DEAD...*
...THEN THIS PLACE GOES UNDER AND PEOPLE LIKE *YOUR HUSBAND* WON'T HAVE ANYWHERE TO GO!
LINDA, HE'S A *BAD GUY.*
YOU ARE NOT HEARING ME!
"THANK YOU!
"THANK YOU ALL!"

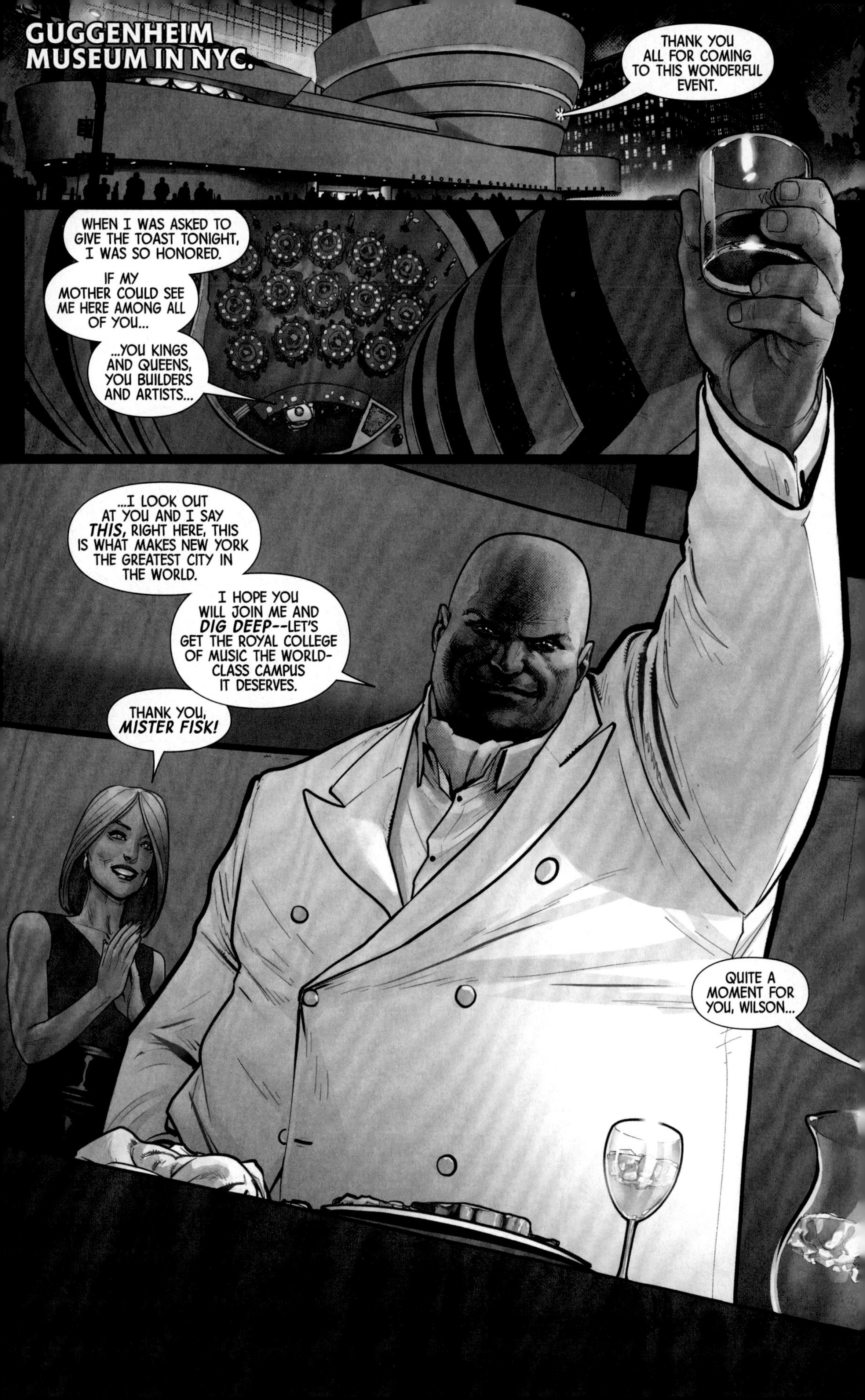
GUGGENHEIM MUSEUM IN NYC.
THANK YOU ALL FOR COMING TO THIS WONDERFUL EVENT.
WHEN I WAS ASKED TO GIVE THE TOAST TONIGHT, I WAS SO HONORED.
IF MY MOTHER COULD SEE ME HERE AMONG ALL OF YOU...
...YOU KINGS AND QUEENS, YOU BUILDERS AND ARTISTS...
...I LOOK OUT AT YOU AND I SAY *THIS,* RIGHT HERE, THIS IS WHAT MAKES NEW YORK THE GREATEST CITY IN THE WORLD.
I HOPE YOU WILL JOIN ME AND *DIG DEEP*--LET'S GET THE ROYAL COLLEGE OF MUSIC THE WORLD-CLASS CAMPUS IT DESERVES.
THANK YOU, *MISTER FISK!*
QUITE A MOMENT FOR YOU, WILSON...

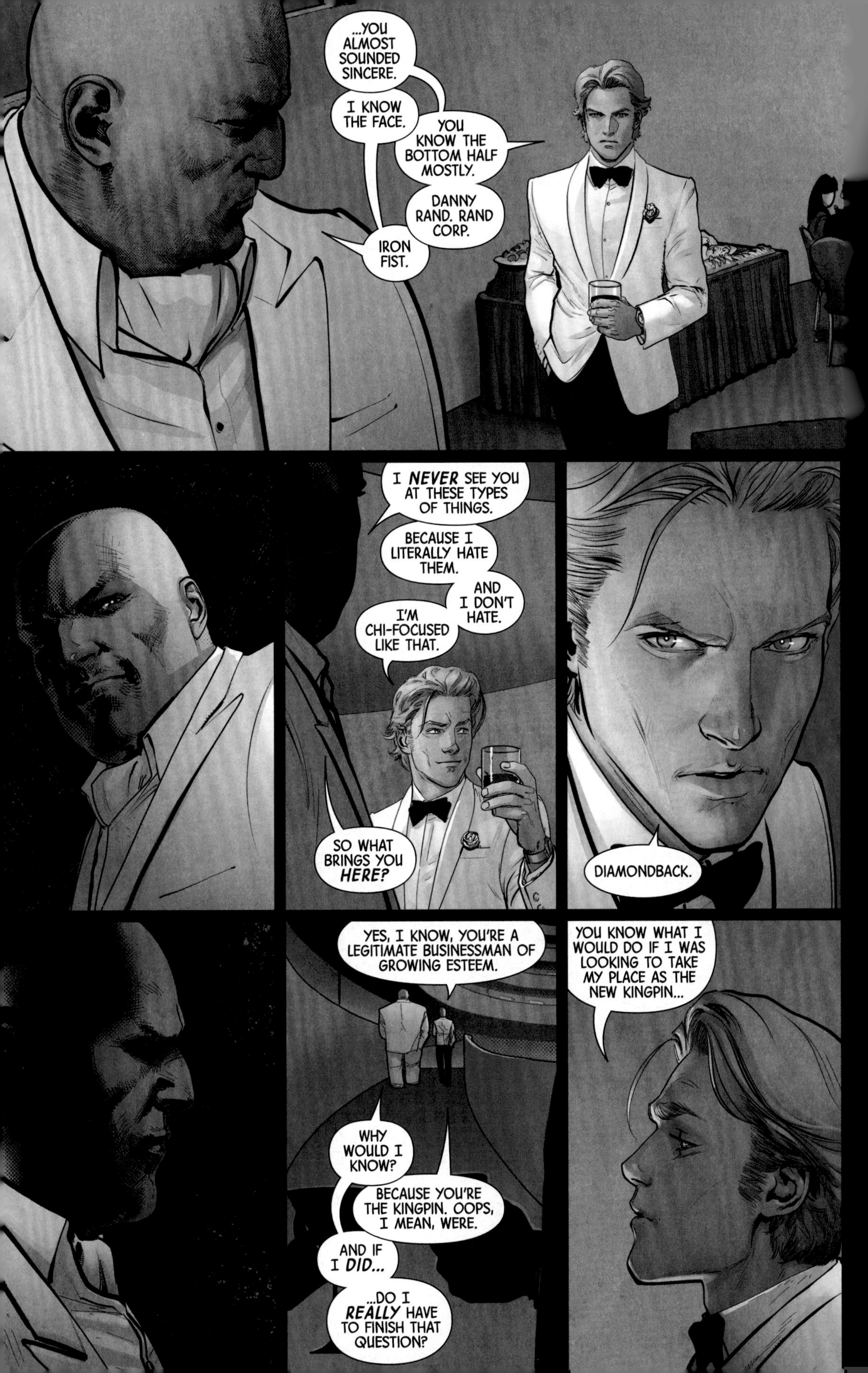
...YOU ALMOST SOUNDED SINCERE.
I KNOW THE FACE.
YOU KNOW THE BOTTOM HALF MOSTLY.
DANNY RAND. RAND CORP.
IRON FIST.
I *NEVER* SEE YOU AT THESE TYPES OF THINGS.
BECAUSE I LITERALLY HATE THEM.
AND I DON'T HATE.
I'M CHI-FOCUSED LIKE THAT.
SO WHAT BRINGS YOU *HERE?*
DIAMONDBACK.
YES, I KNOW, YOU'RE A LEGITIMATE BUSINESSMAN OF GROWING ESTEEM.
YOU KNOW WHAT I WOULD DO IF I WAS LOOKING TO TAKE MY PLACE AS THE NEW KINGPIN...
WHY WOULD I KNOW?
BECAUSE YOU'RE THE KINGPIN. OOPS, I MEAN, WERE.
AND IF I *DID...*
...DO I *REALLY* HAVE TO FINISH THAT QUESTION?

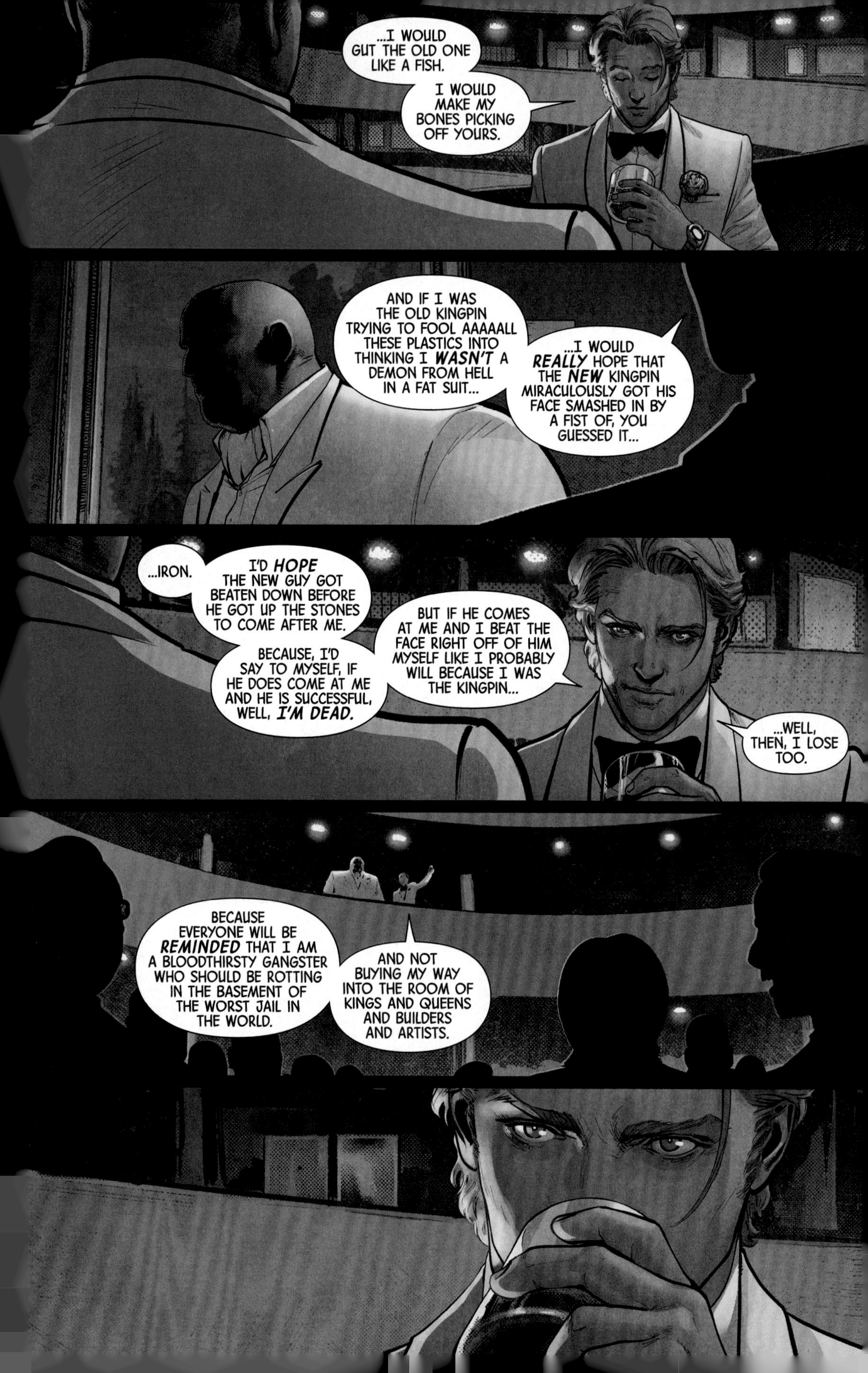
...I WOULD GUT THE OLD ONE LIKE A FISH.
I WOULD MAKE MY BONES PICKING OFF YOURS.
AND IF I WAS THE OLD KINGPIN TRYING TO FOOL AAAAALL THESE PLASTICS INTO THINKING I WASN'T A DEMON FROM HELL IN A FAT SUIT...
...I WOULD REALLY HOPE THAT THE NEW KINGPIN MIRACULOUSLY GOT HIS FACE SMASHED IN BY A FIST OF, YOU GUESSED IT...
...IRON.
I'D HOPE THE NEW GUY GOT BEATEN DOWN BEFORE HE GOT UP THE STONES TO COME AFTER ME.
BECAUSE, I'D SAY TO MYSELF, IF HE DOES COME AT ME AND HE IS SUCCESSFUL, WELL, I'M DEAD.
BUT IF HE COMES AT ME AND I BEAT THE FACE RIGHT OFF OF HIM MYSELF LIKE I PROBABLY WILL BECAUSE I WAS THE KINGPIN...
...WELL, THEN, I LOSE TOO.
BECAUSE EVERYONE WILL BE REMINDED THAT I AM A BLOODTHIRSTY GANGSTER WHO SHOULD BE ROTTING IN THE BASEMENT OF THE WORST JAIL IN THE WORLD.
AND NOT BUYING MY WAY INTO THE ROOM OF KINGS AND QUEENS AND BUILDERS AND ARTISTS.

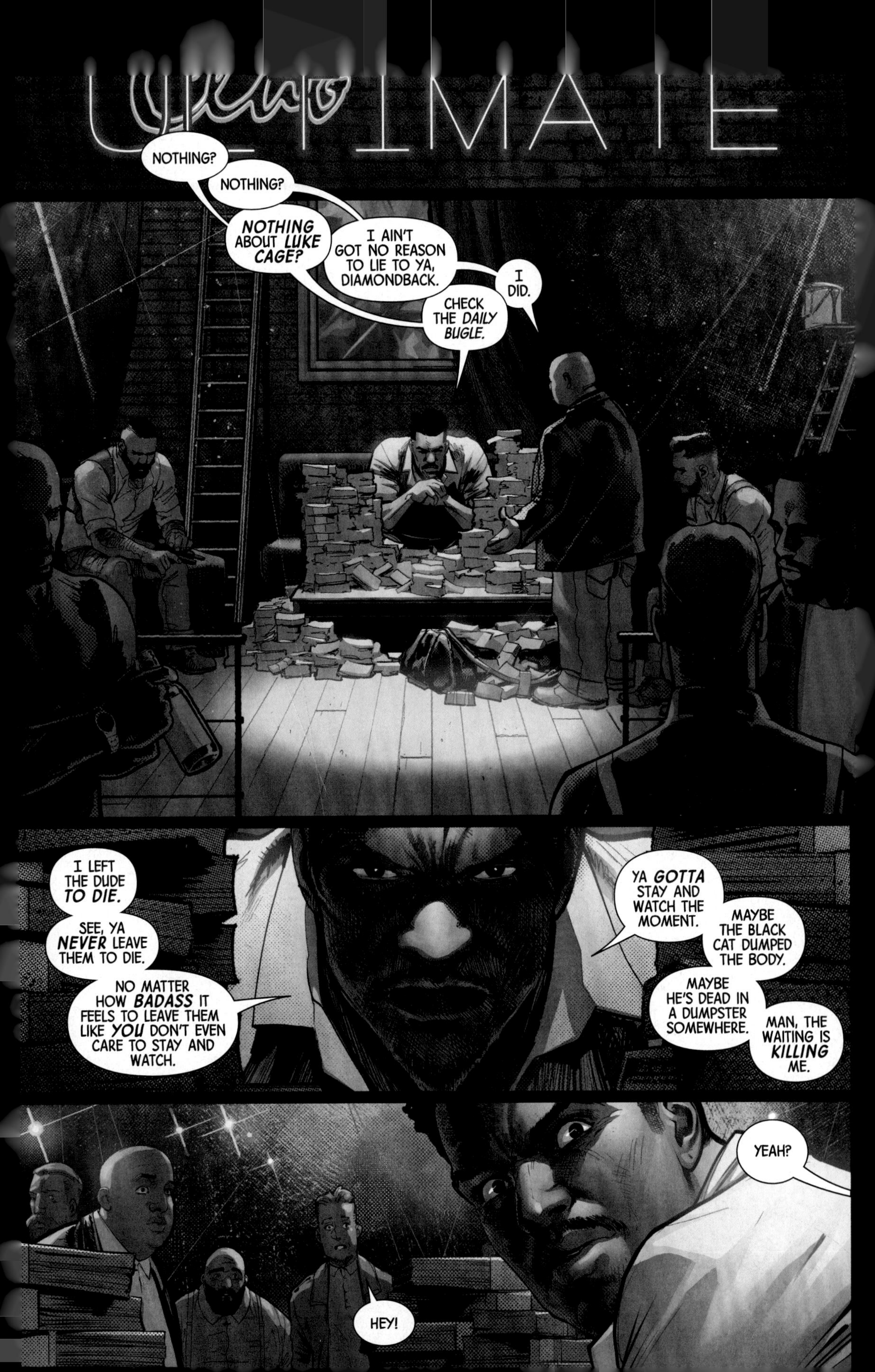
NOTHING?
NOTHING?
NOTHING ABOUT LUKE CAGE?
I AIN'T GOT NO REASON TO LIE TO YA, DIAMONDBACK.
I DID.
CHECK THE DAILY BUGLE.
I LEFT THE DUDE TO DIE.
SEE, YA NEVER LEAVE THEM TO DIE.
NO MATTER HOW BADASS IT FEELS TO LEAVE THEM LIKE YOU DON'T EVEN CARE TO STAY AND WATCH.
YA GOTTA STAY AND WATCH THE MOMENT.
MAYBE THE BLACK CAT DUMPED THE BODY.
MAYBE HE'S DEAD IN A DUMPSTER SOMEWHERE.
MAN, THE WAITING IS KILLING ME.
HEY!
YEAH?

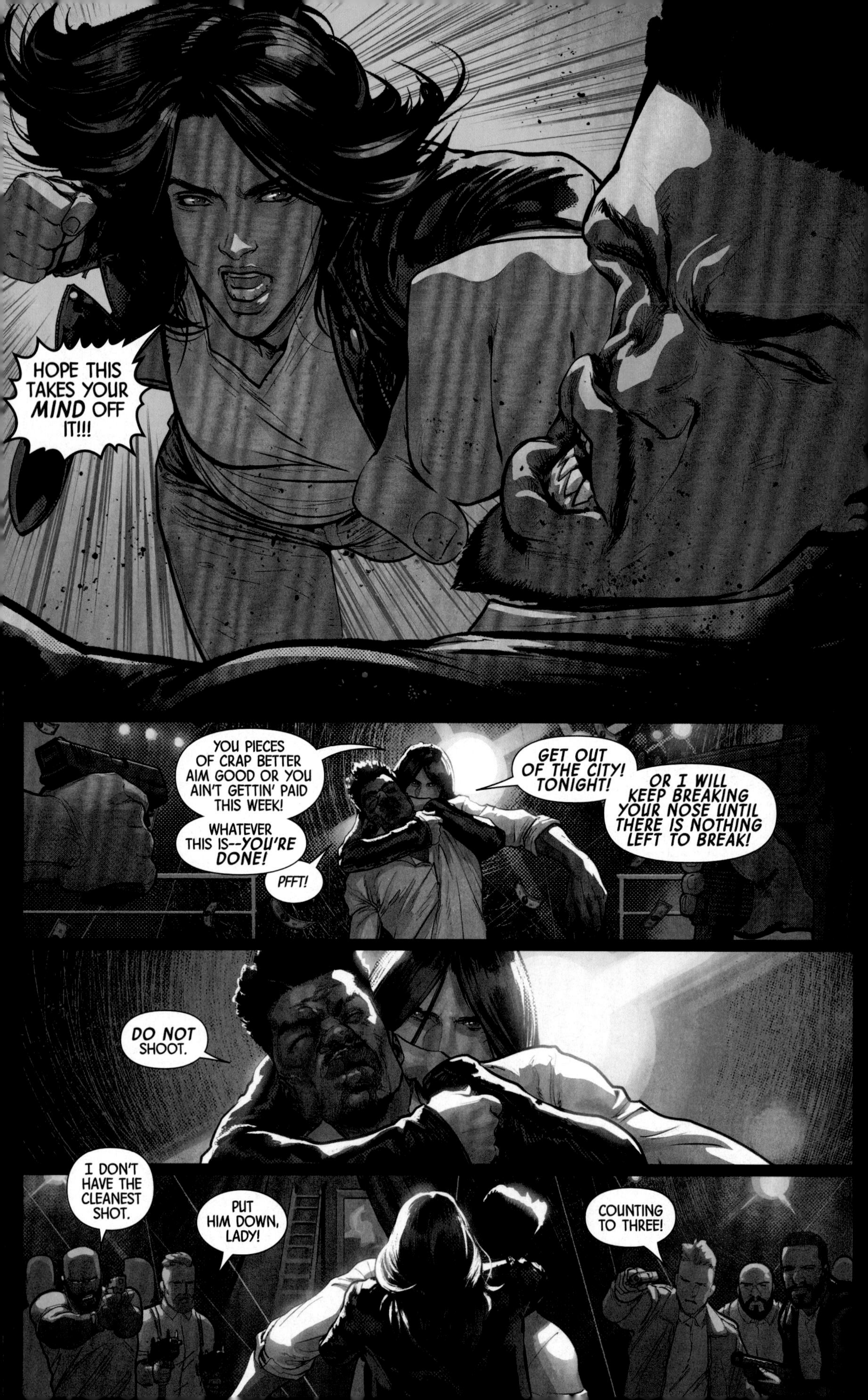
HOPE THIS TAKES YOUR MIND OFF IT!!!
YOU PIECES OF CRAP BETTER AIM GOOD OR YOU AIN'T GETTIN' PAID THIS WEEK!
WHATEVER THIS IS--YOU'RE DONE!
PFFT!
GET OUT OF THE CITY! TONIGHT!
OR I WILL KEEP BREAKING YOUR NOSE UNTIL THERE IS NOTHING LEFT TO BREAK!
DO NOT SHOOT.
I DON'T HAVE THE CLEANEST SHOT.
PUT HIM DOWN, LADY!
COUNTING TO THREE!

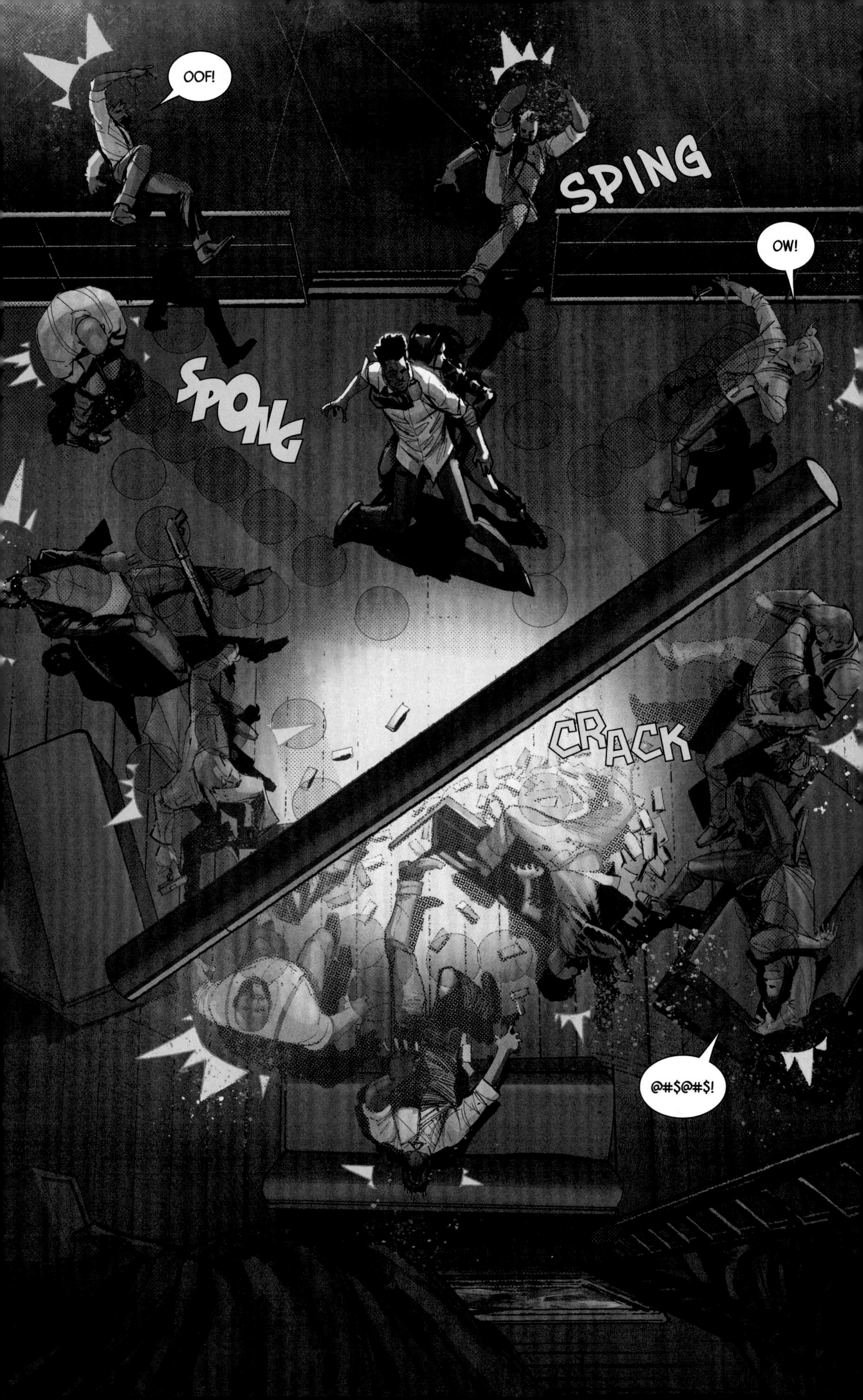
OOF!
SPING
OW!
SPONG
CRACK
@#$@#$!

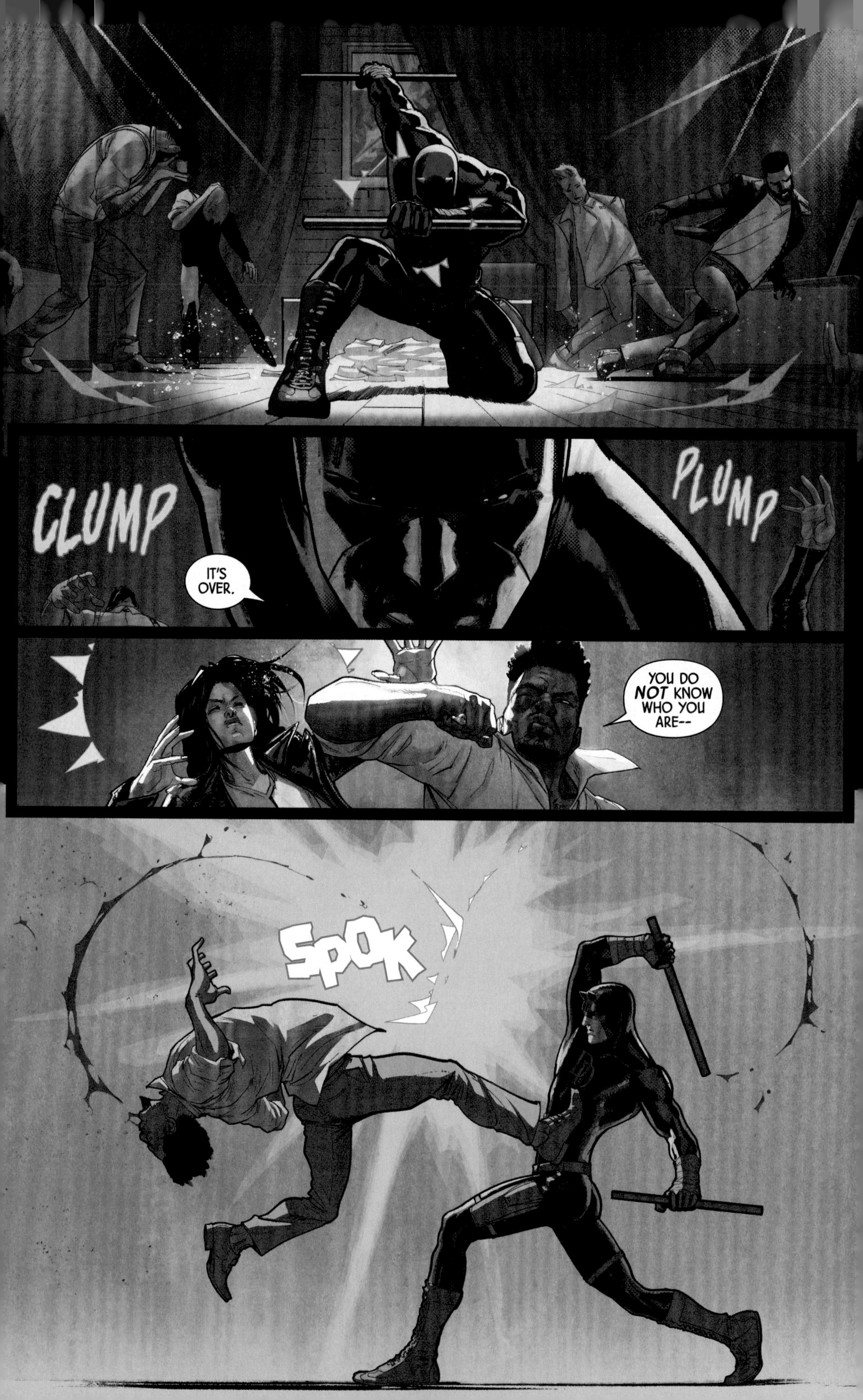
CLUMP
PLUMP
IT'S OVER.
YOU DO NOT KNOW WHO YOU ARE--
SPOK

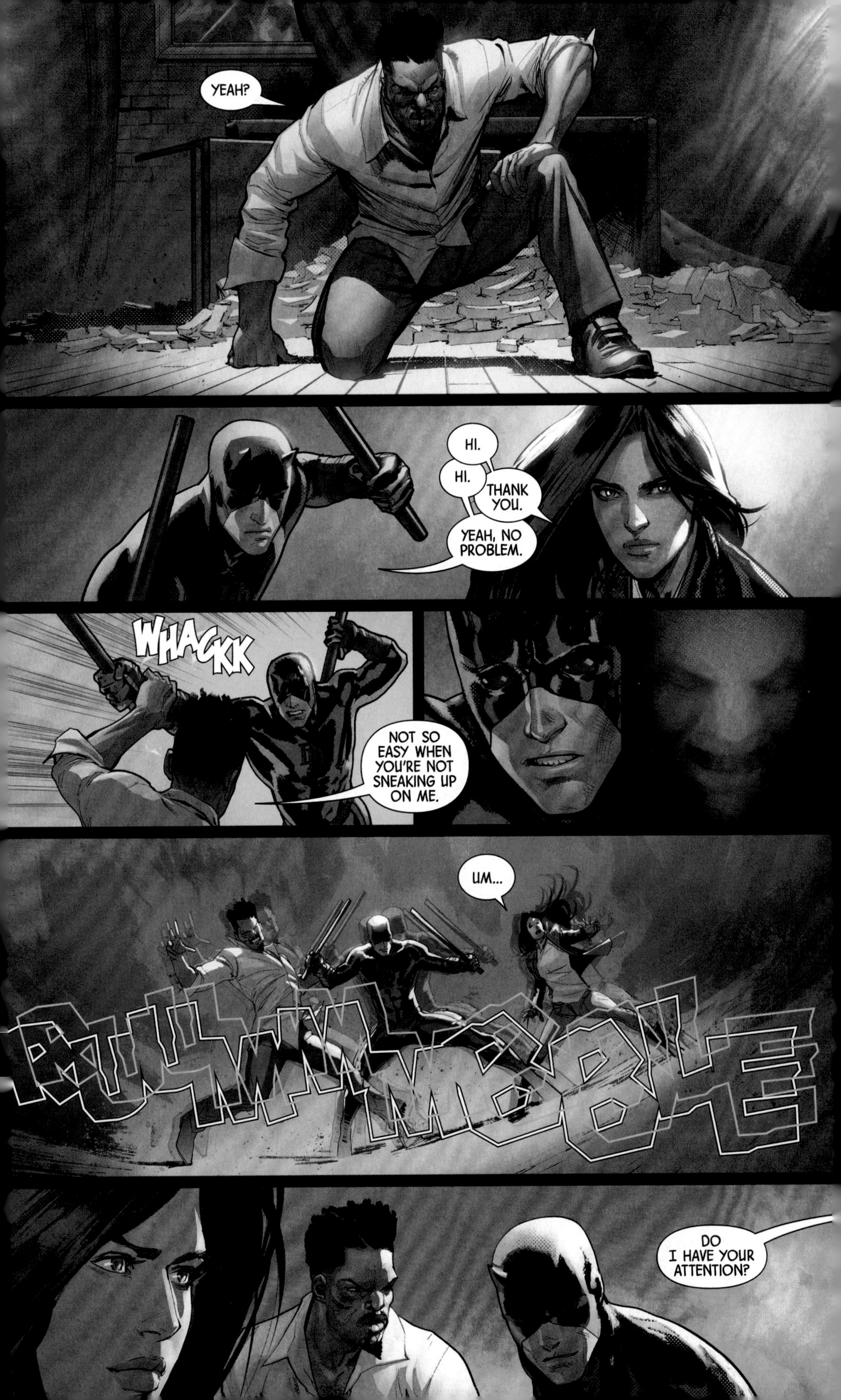
YEAH?
HI.
HI.
THANK YOU.
YEAH, NO PROBLEM.
WHACKK
NOT SO EASY WHEN YOU'RE NOT SNEAKING UP ON ME.
UM...
DO I HAVE YOUR ATTENTION?

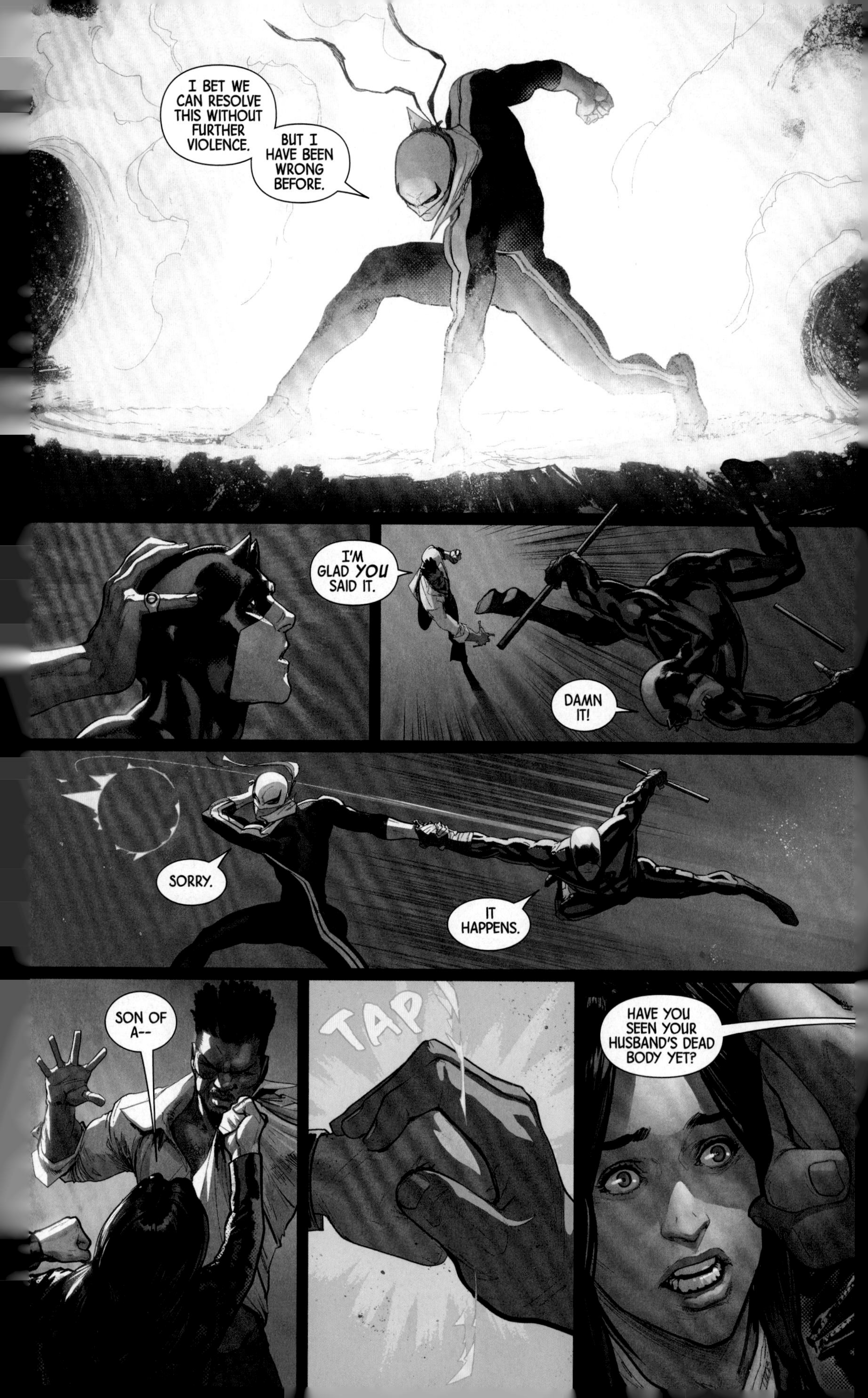
I BET WE CAN RESOLVE THIS WITHOUT FURTHER VIOLENCE.
BUT I HAVE BEEN WRONG BEFORE.
I'M GLAD YOU SAID IT.
DAMN IT!
SORRY.
IT HAPPENS.
SON OF A--
TAP
HAVE YOU SEEN YOUR HUSBAND'S DEAD BODY YET?

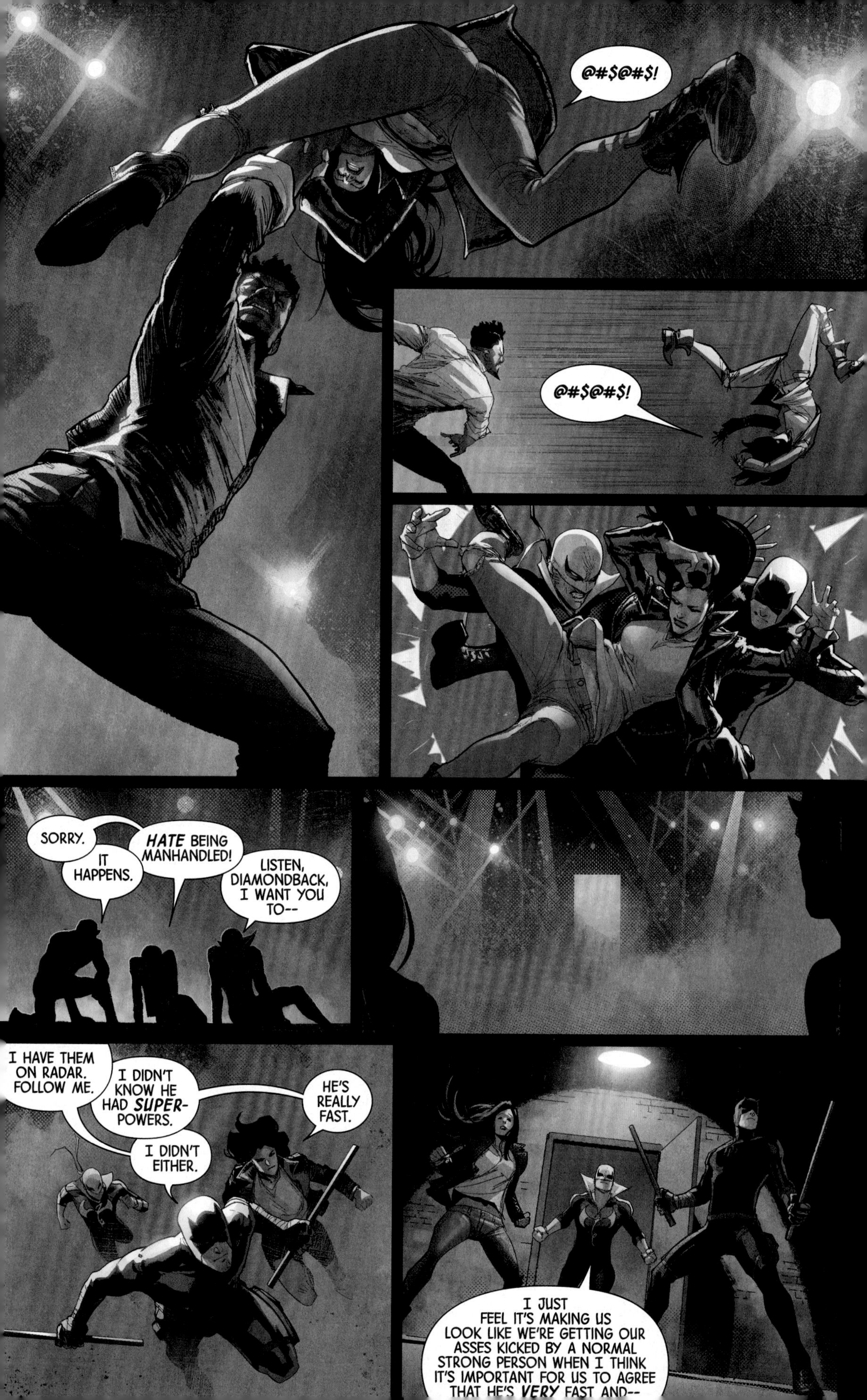
@#$@#$!
@#$@#$!
SORRY.
IT HAPPENS.
HATE BEING MANHANDLED!
LISTEN, DIAMONDBACK, I WANT YOU TO--
I HAVE THEM ON RADAR. FOLLOW ME.
I DIDN'T KNOW HE HAD SUPER-POWERS.
HE'S REALLY FAST.
I DIDN'T EITHER.
I JUST FEEL IT'S MAKING US LOOK LIKE WE'RE GETTING OUR ASSES KICKED BY A NORMAL STRONG PERSON WHEN I THINK IT'S IMPORTANT FOR US TO AGREE THAT HE'S VERY FAST AND--

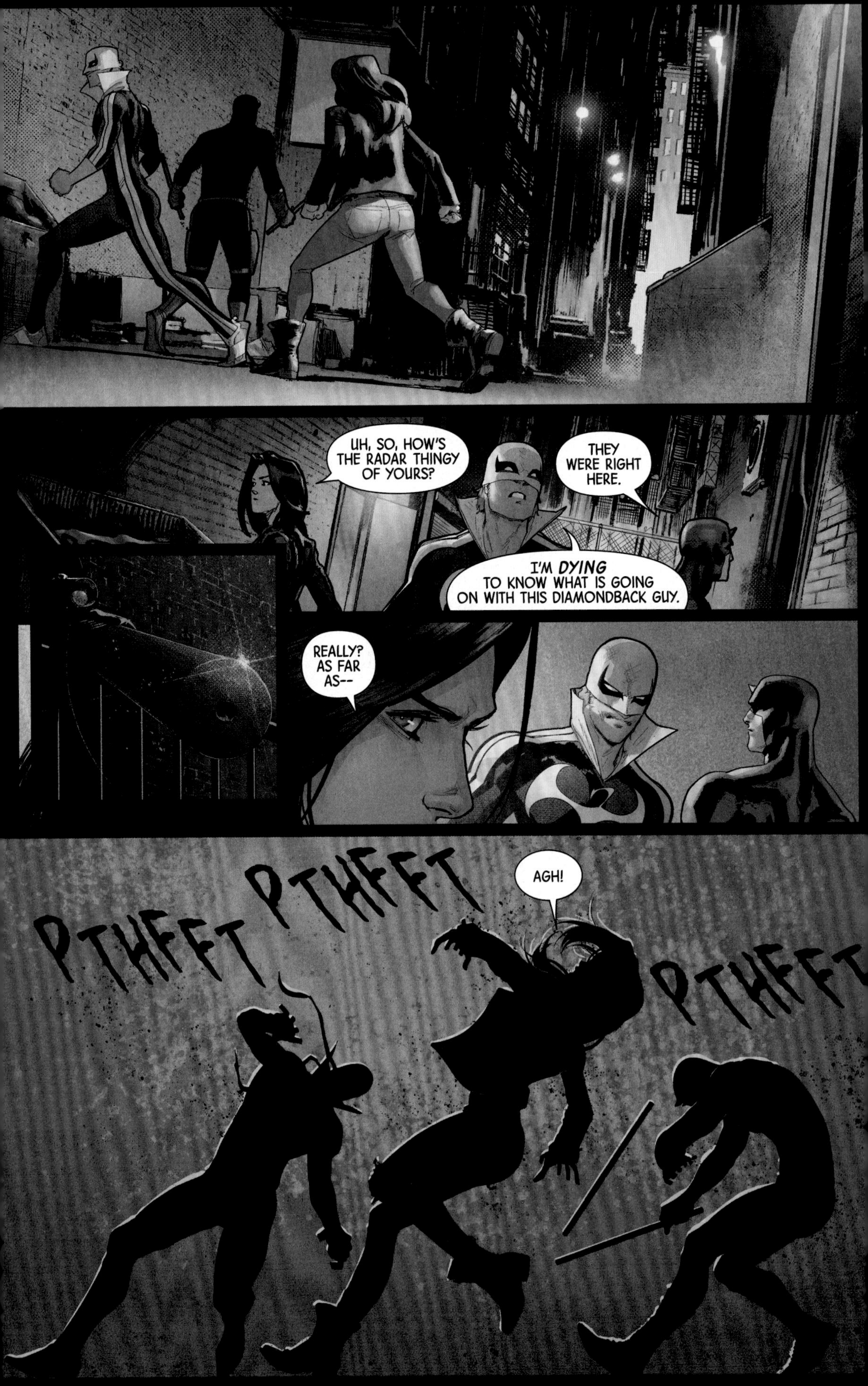
UH, SO, HOW'S THE RADAR THINGY OF YOURS?
THEY WERE RIGHT HERE.
I'M DYING TO KNOW WHAT IS GOING ON WITH THIS DIAMONDBACK GUY.
REALLY? AS FAR AS--
PTHFFT PTHFFT
AGH!
PTHFFT

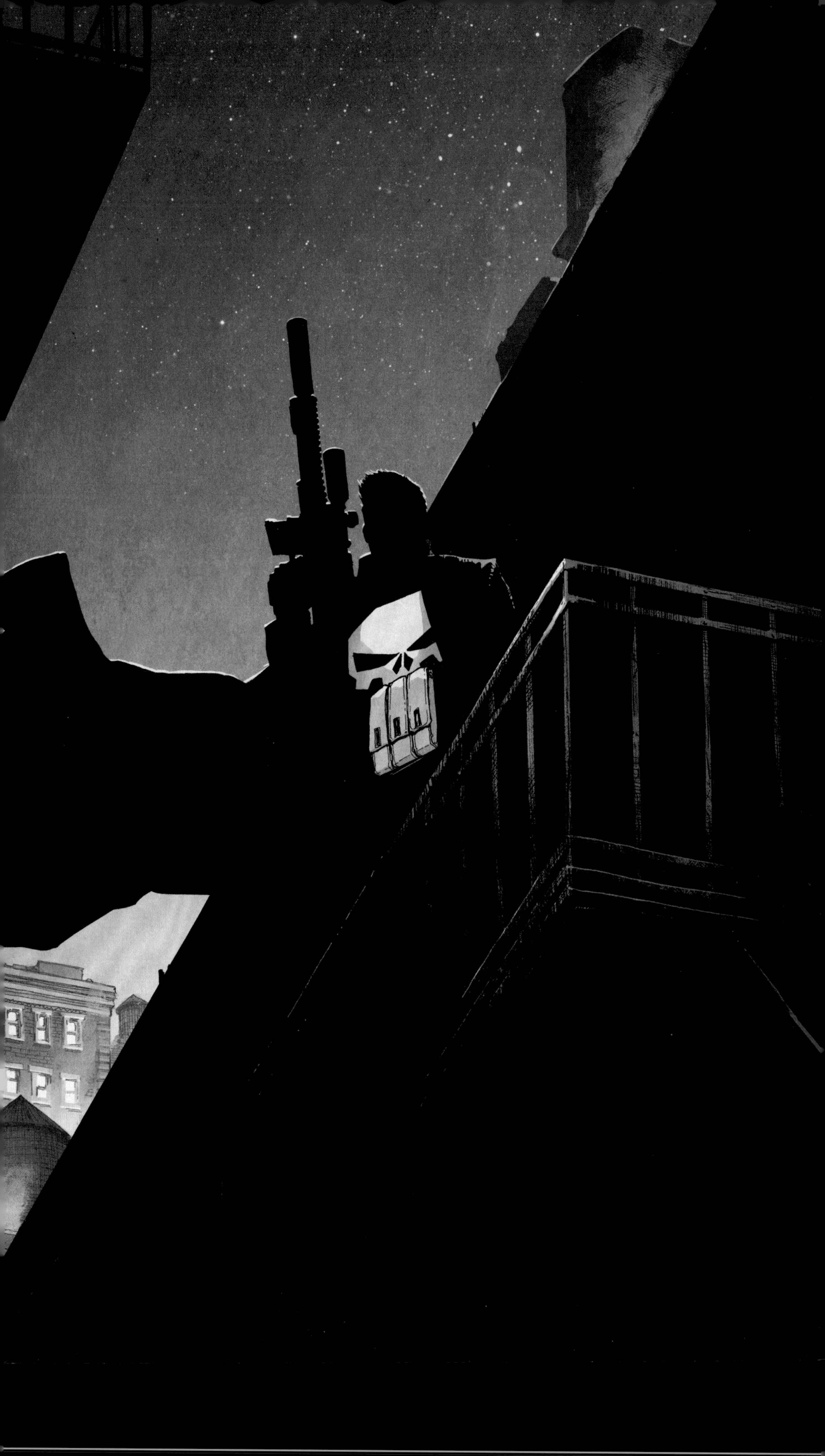

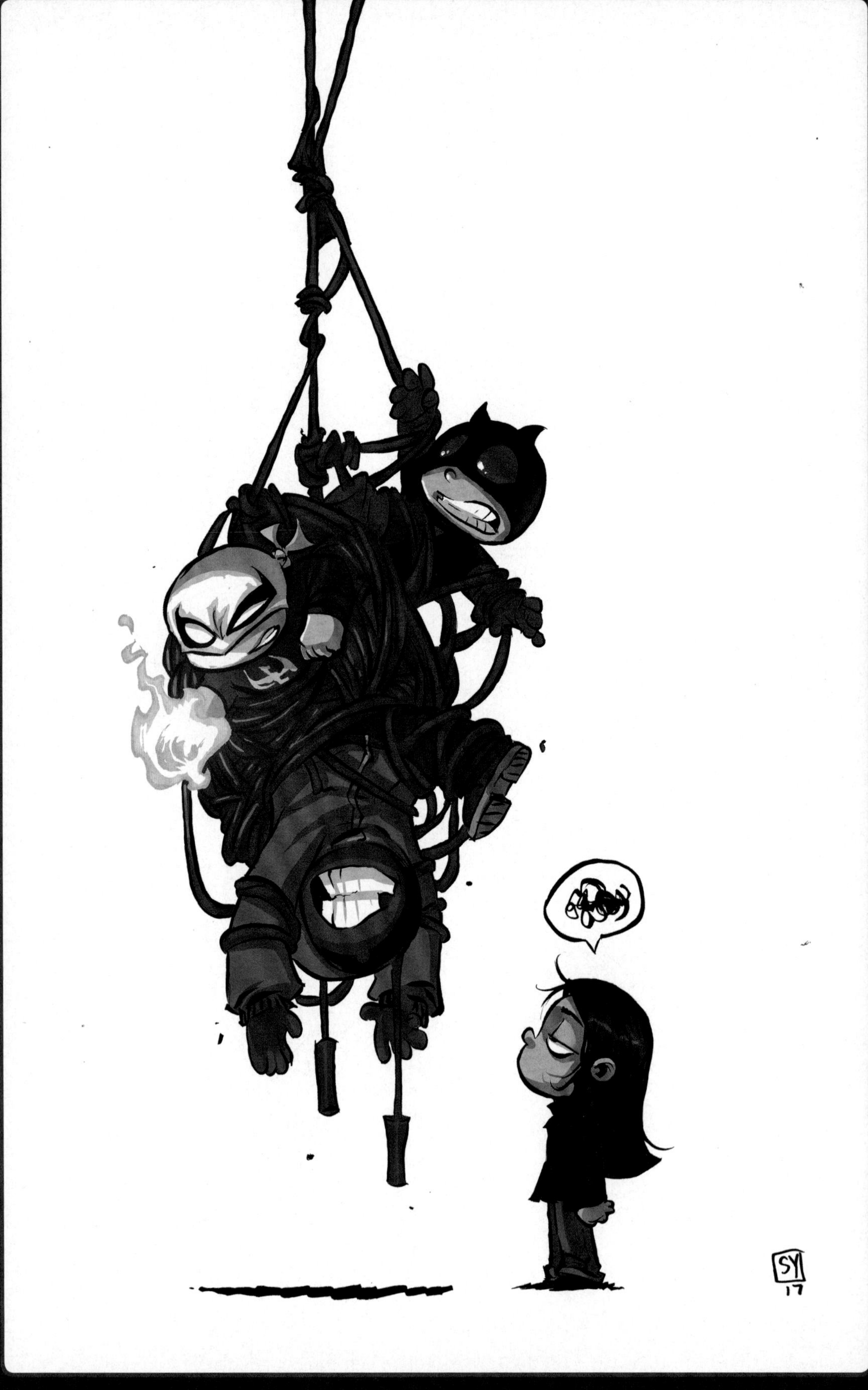
SY
17

NO. 1 VARIANT BY **SKOTTIE YOUNG**

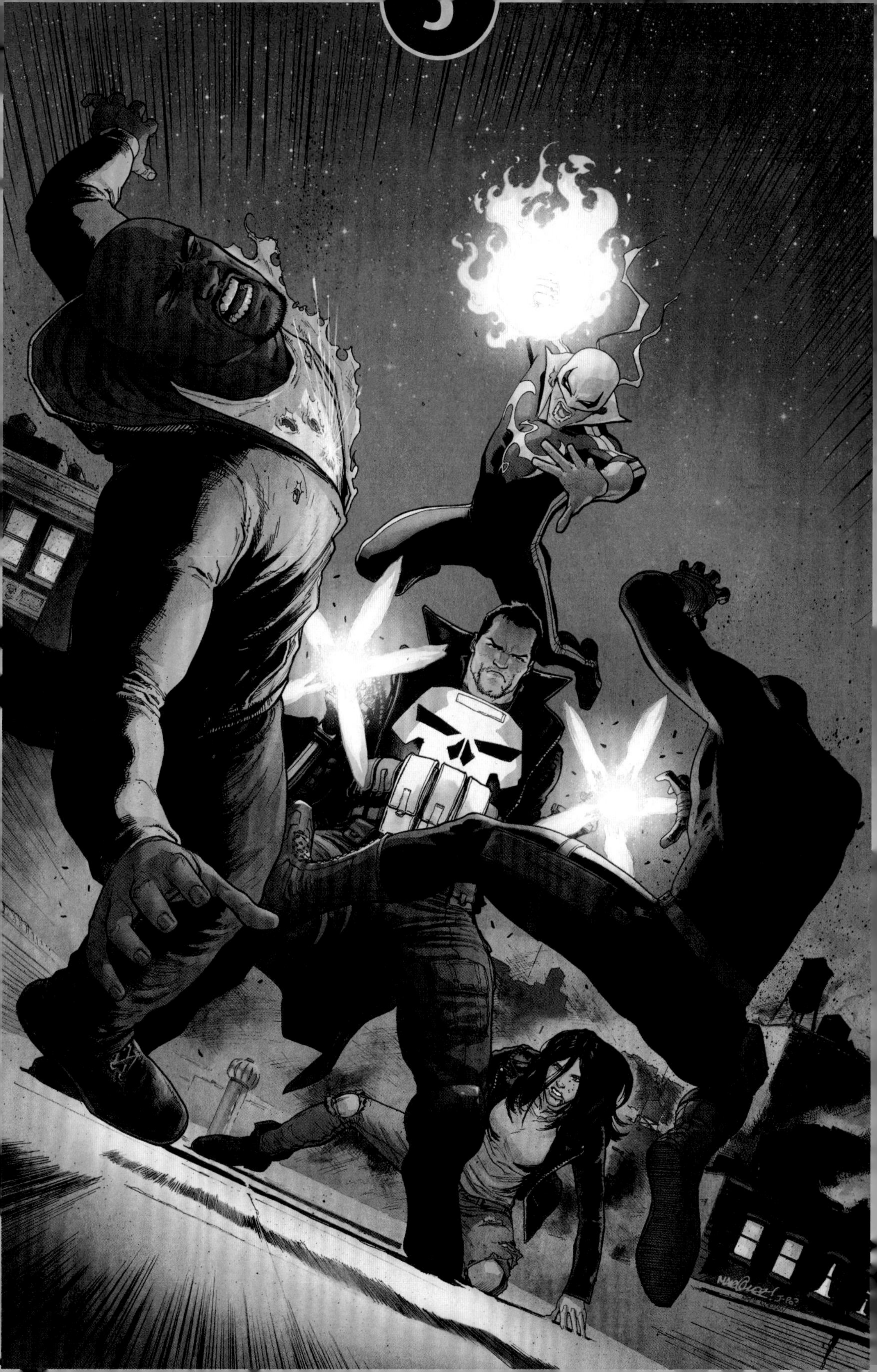

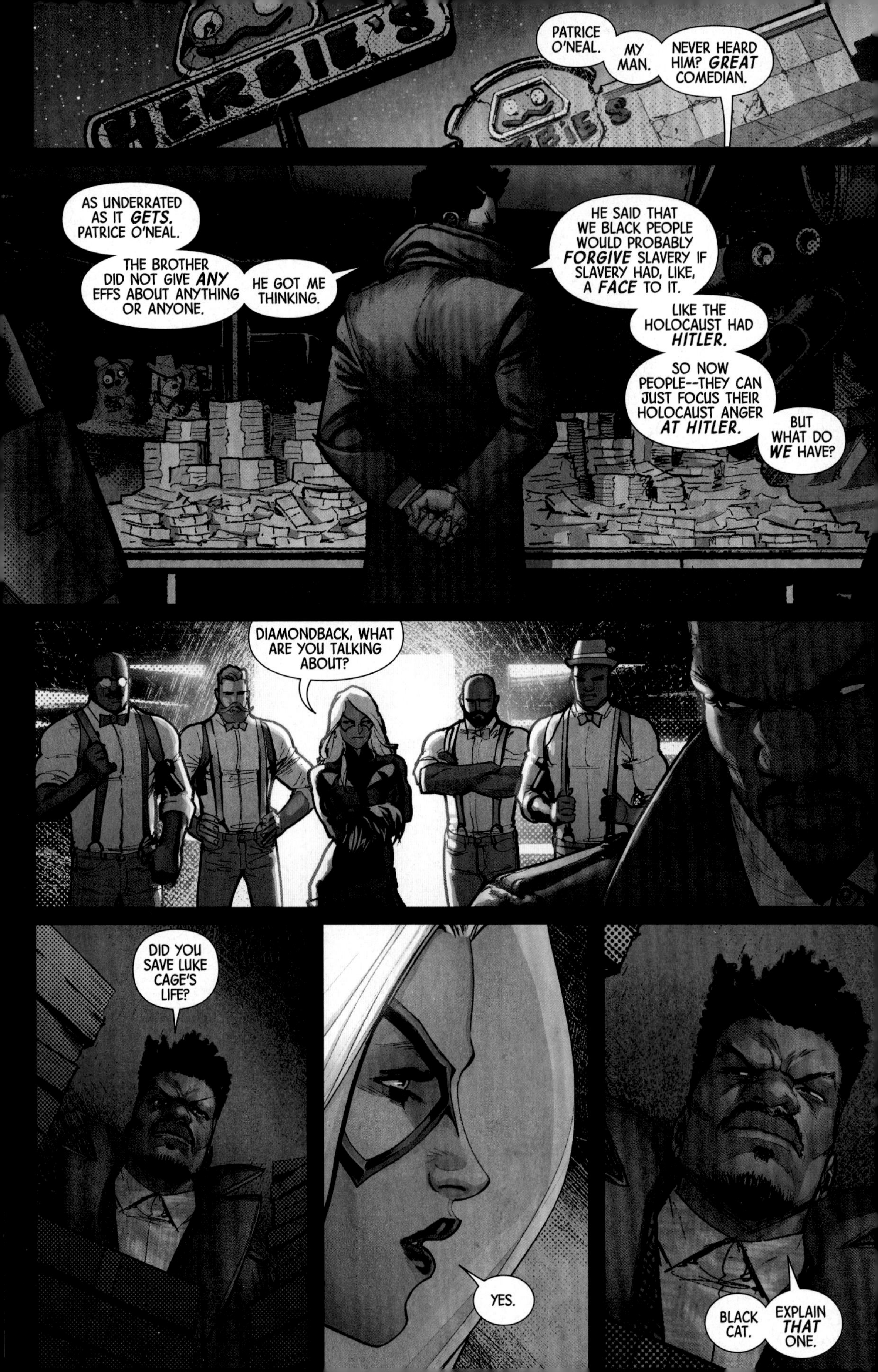

HERBIE'S
PATRICE O'NEAL.
MY MAN.
NEVER HEARD HIM? GREAT COMEDIAN.
AS UNDERRATED AS IT GETS. PATRICE O'NEAL.
THE BROTHER DID NOT GIVE ANY EFFS ABOUT ANYTHING OR ANYONE.
HE GOT ME THINKING.
HE SAID THAT WE BLACK PEOPLE WOULD PROBABLY FORGIVE SLAVERY IF SLAVERY HAD, LIKE, A FACE TO IT.
LIKE THE HOLOCAUST HAD HITLER.
SO NOW PEOPLE--THEY CAN JUST FOCUS THEIR HOLOCAUST ANGER AT HITLER.
BUT WHAT DO WE HAVE?
DIAMONDBACK, WHAT ARE YOU TALKING ABOUT?
DID YOU SAVE LUKE CAGE'S LIFE?
YES.
BLACK CAT.
EXPLAIN THAT ONE.

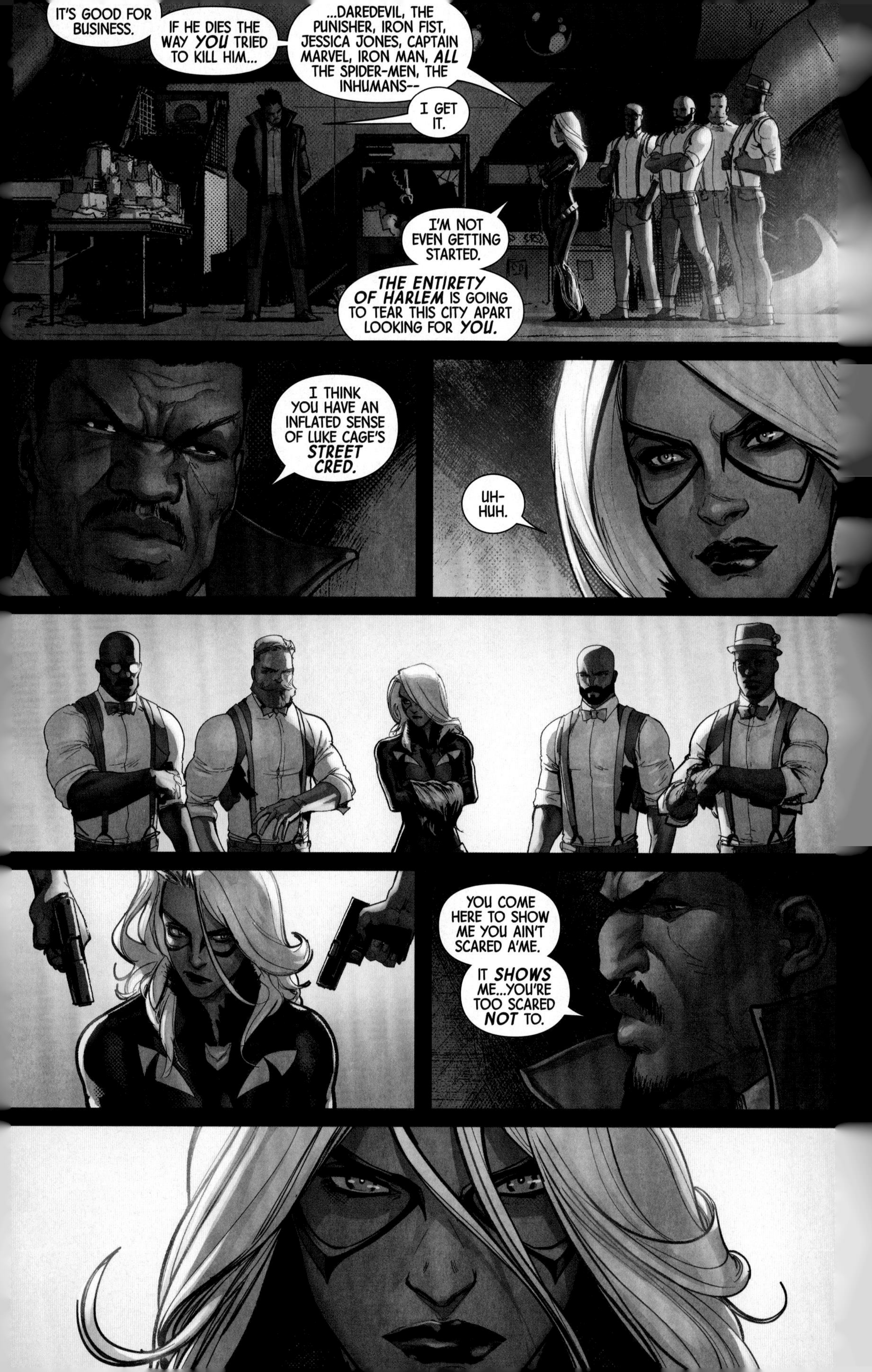
IT'S GOOD FOR BUSINESS.
IF HE DIES THE WAY YOU TRIED TO KILL HIM...
...DAREDEVIL, THE PUNISHER, IRON FIST, JESSICA JONES, CAPTAIN MARVEL, IRON MAN, ALL THE SPIDER-MEN, THE INHUMANS--
I GET IT.
I'M NOT EVEN GETTING STARTED.
THE ENTIRETY OF HARLEM IS GOING TO TEAR THIS CITY APART LOOKING FOR YOU.
I THINK YOU HAVE AN INFLATED SENSE OF LUKE CAGE'S STREET CRED.
UH-HUH.
YOU COME HERE TO SHOW ME YOU AIN'T SCARED A'ME.
IT SHOWS ME...YOU'RE TOO SCARED NOT TO.

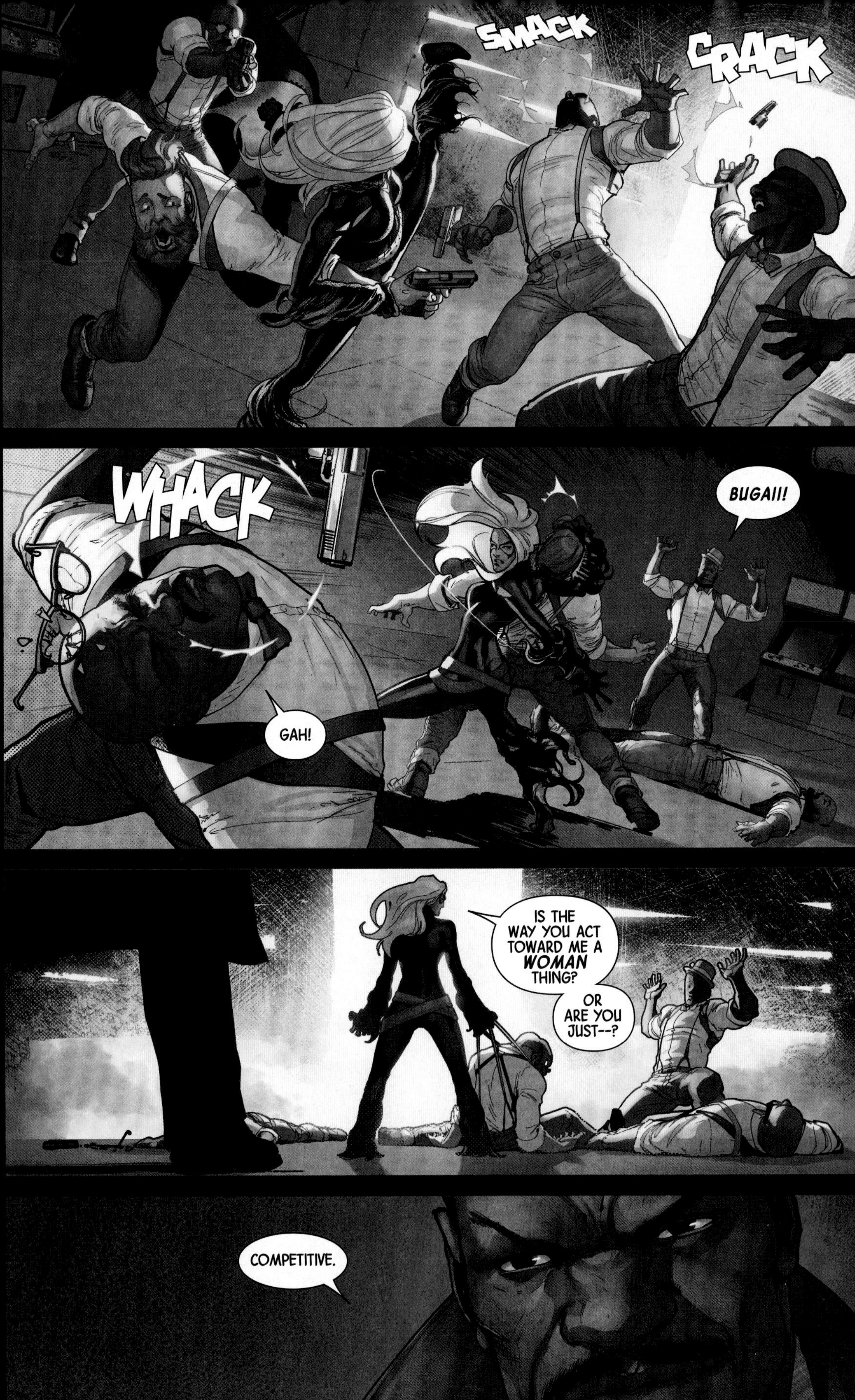
SMACK
CRACK
WHACK
BUGAII!
GAH!
IS THE WAY YOU ACT TOWARD ME A WOMAN THING?
OR ARE YOU JUST--?
COMPETITIVE.

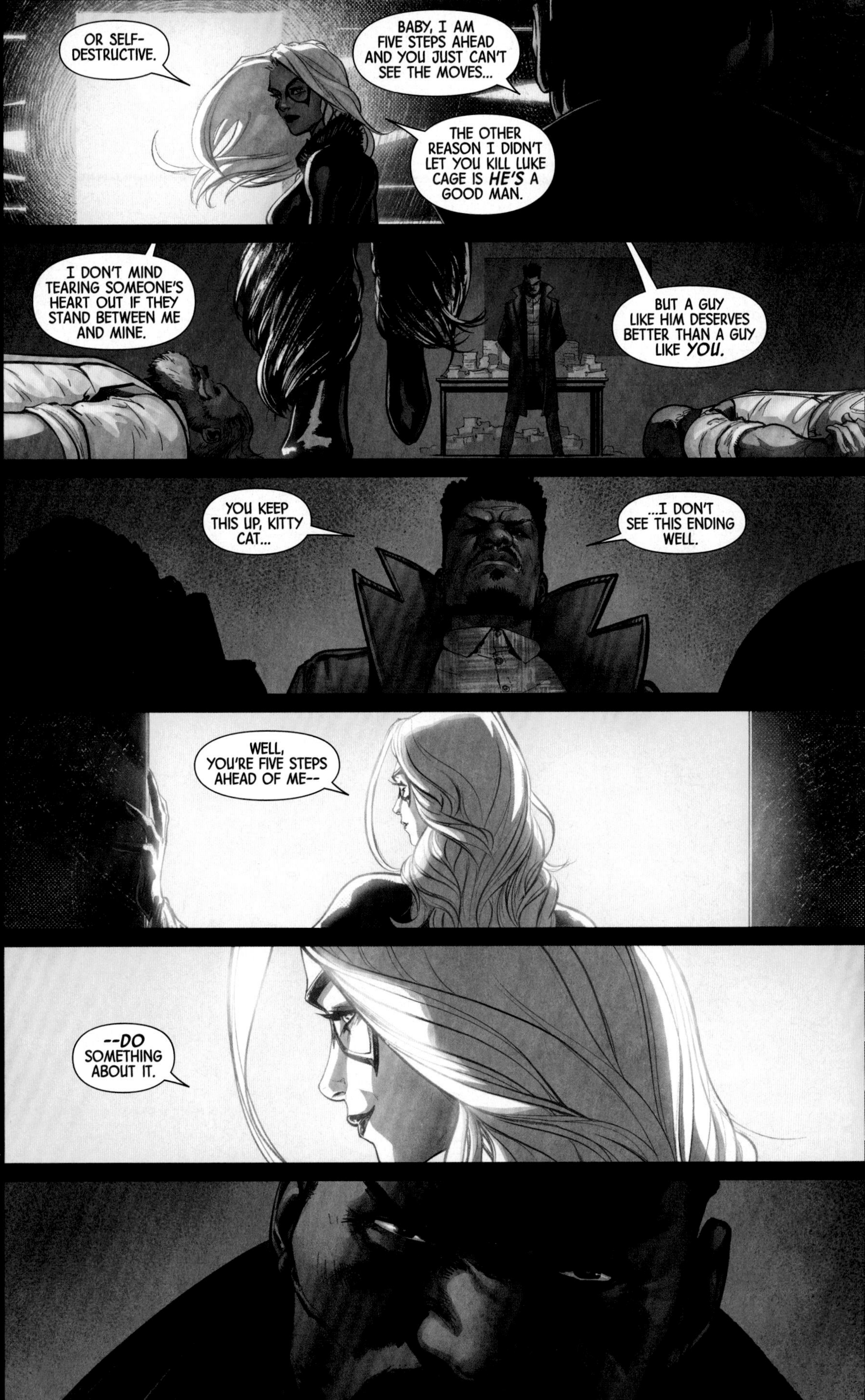
OR SELF-DESTRUCTIVE.
BABY, I AM FIVE STEPS AHEAD AND YOU JUST CAN'T SEE THE MOVES...
THE OTHER REASON I DIDN'T LET YOU KILL LUKE CAGE IS HE'S A GOOD MAN.
I DON'T MIND TEARING SOMEONE'S HEART OUT IF THEY STAND BETWEEN ME AND MINE.
BUT A GUY LIKE HIM DESERVES BETTER THAN A GUY LIKE YOU.
YOU KEEP THIS UP, KITTY CAT...
...I DON'T SEE THIS ENDING WELL.
WELL, YOU'RE FIVE STEPS AHEAD OF ME--
--DO SOMETHING ABOUT IT.

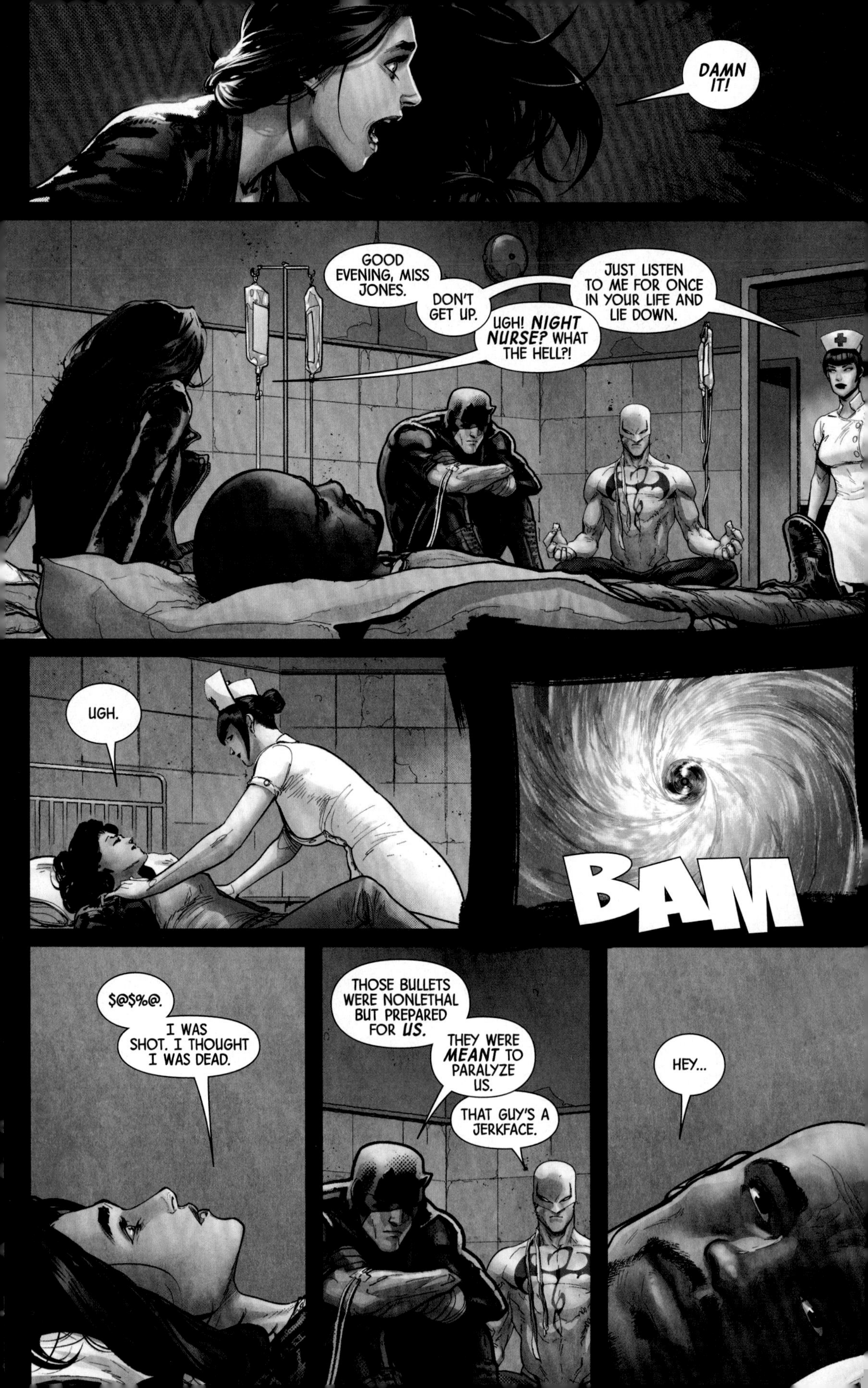
DAMN IT!
GOOD EVENING, MISS JONES.
DON'T GET UP.
UGH! NIGHT NURSE? WHAT THE HELL?!
JUST LISTEN TO ME FOR ONCE IN YOUR LIFE AND LIE DOWN.
UGH.
BAM
$@$%@.
I WAS SHOT. I THOUGHT I WAS DEAD.
THOSE BULLETS WERE NONLETHAL BUT PREPARED FOR US.
THEY WERE MEANT TO PARALYZE US.
THAT GUY'S A JERKFACE.
HEY...

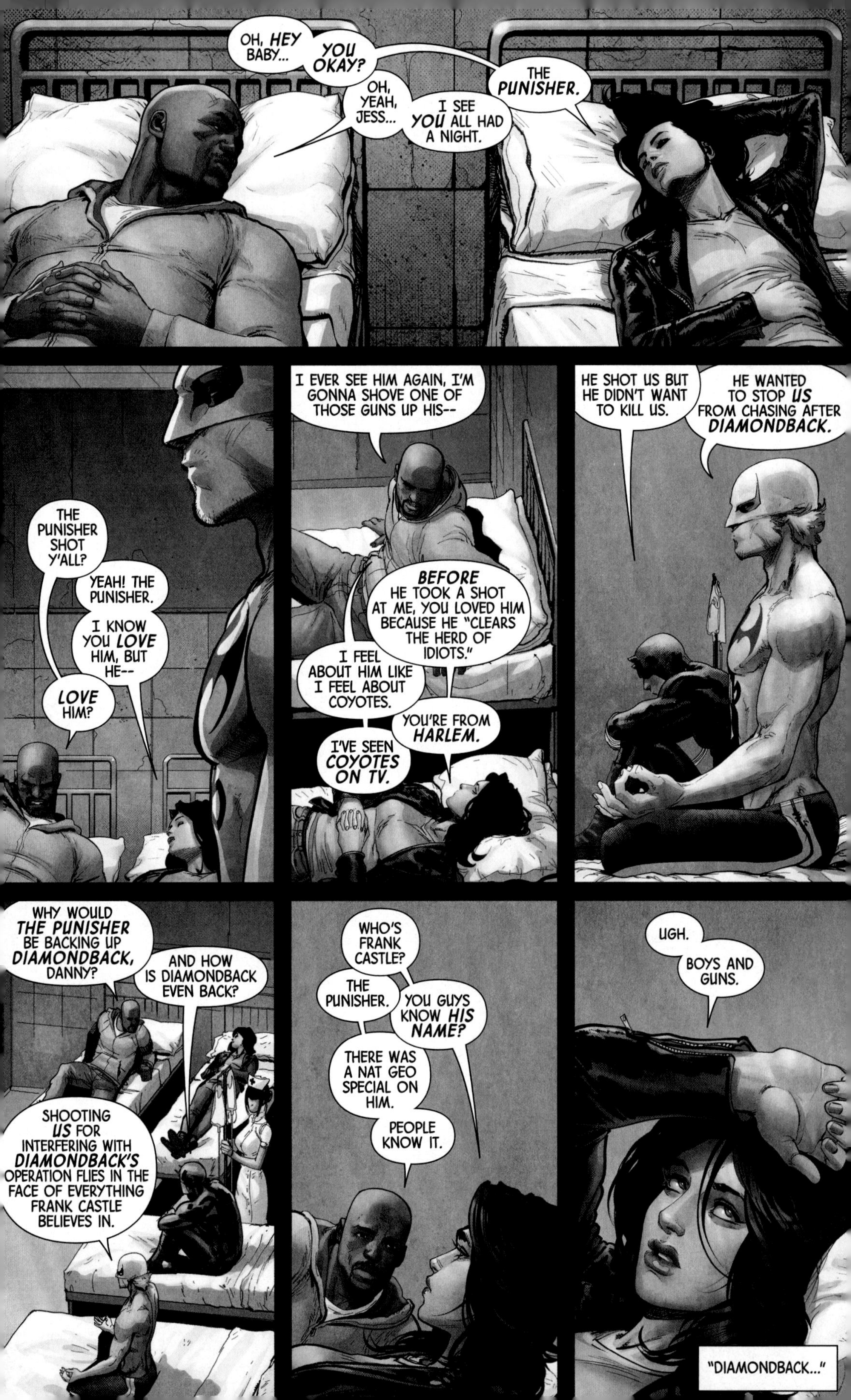
OH, HEY BABY... YOU OKAY?
OH, YEAH, JESS...
I SEE YOU ALL HAD A NIGHT.
THE PUNISHER.
THE PUNISHER SHOT Y'ALL?
YEAH! THE PUNISHER.
I KNOW YOU LOVE HIM, BUT HE--
LOVE HIM?
I EVER SEE HIM AGAIN, I'M GONNA SHOVE ONE OF THOSE GUNS UP HIS--
BEFORE HE TOOK A SHOT AT ME, YOU LOVED HIM BECAUSE HE "CLEARS THE HERD OF IDIOTS."
I FEEL ABOUT HIM LIKE I FEEL ABOUT COYOTES.
YOU'RE FROM HARLEM.
I'VE SEEN COYOTES ON TV.
HE SHOT US BUT HE DIDN'T WANT TO KILL US.
HE WANTED TO STOP US FROM CHASING AFTER DIAMONDBACK.
WHY WOULD THE PUNISHER BE BACKING UP DIAMONDBACK, DANNY?
AND HOW IS DIAMONDBACK EVEN BACK?
SHOOTING US FOR INTERFERING WITH DIAMONDBACK'S OPERATION FLIES IN THE FACE OF EVERYTHING FRANK CASTLE BELIEVES IN.
WHO'S FRANK CASTLE?
THE PUNISHER.
YOU GUYS KNOW HIS NAME?
THERE WAS A NAT GEO SPECIAL ON HIM.
PEOPLE KNOW IT.
UGH.
BOYS AND GUNS.
"DIAMONDBACK..."

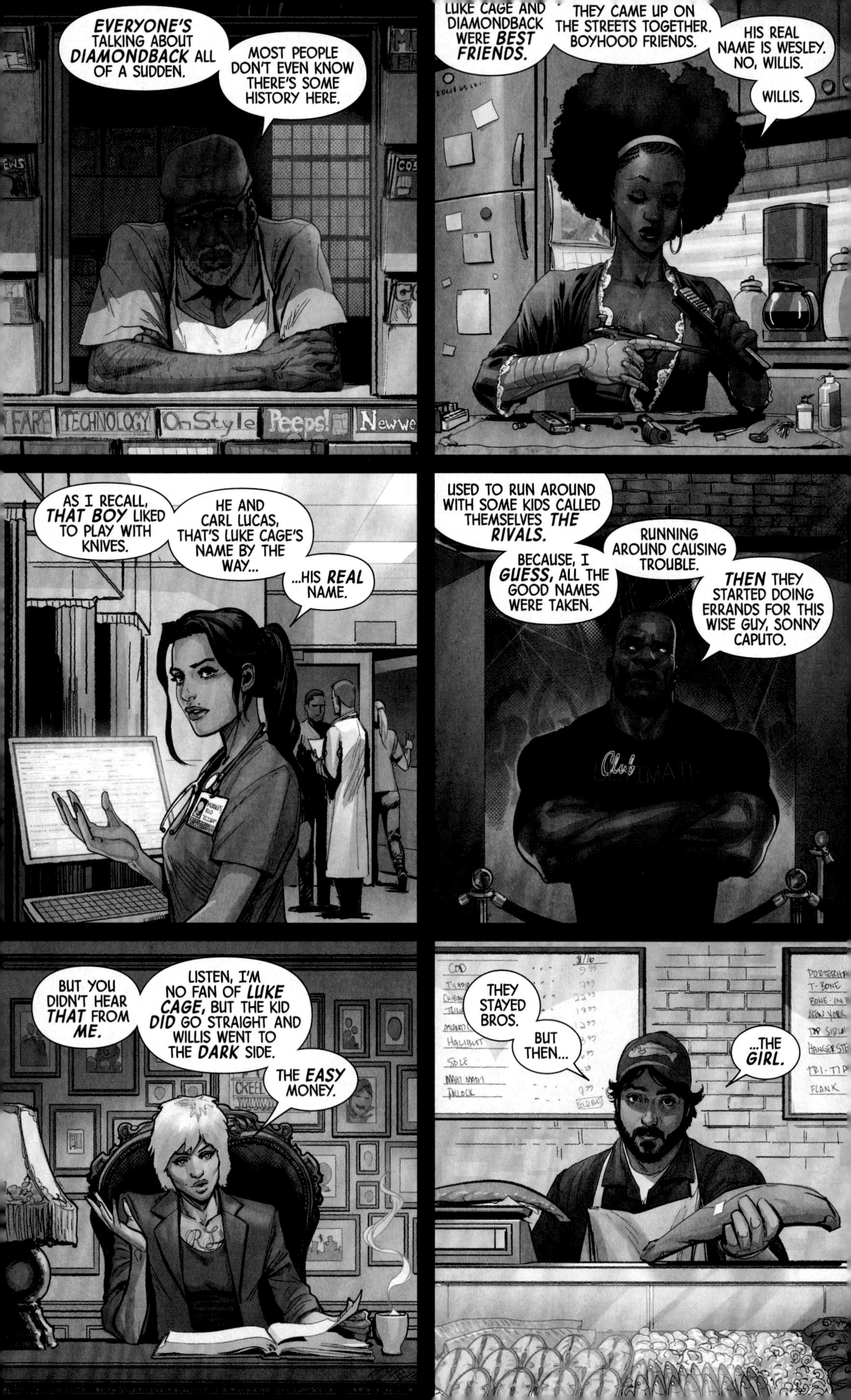
EVERYONE'S TALKING ABOUT DIAMONDBACK ALL OF A SUDDEN.
MOST PEOPLE DON'T EVEN KNOW THERE'S SOME HISTORY HERE.
FARE TECHNOLOGY OnStyle Peeps! Newwe
LUKE CAGE AND DIAMONDBACK WERE BEST FRIENDS.
THEY CAME UP ON THE STREETS TOGETHER. BOYHOOD FRIENDS.
HIS REAL NAME IS WESLEY. NO, WILLIS.
WILLIS.
AS I RECALL, THAT BOY LIKED TO PLAY WITH KNIVES.
HE AND CARL LUCAS, THAT'S LUKE CAGE'S NAME BY THE WAY...
...HIS REAL NAME.
USED TO RUN AROUND WITH SOME KIDS CALLED THEMSELVES THE RIVALS.
BECAUSE, I GUESS, ALL THE GOOD NAMES WERE TAKEN.
RUNNING AROUND CAUSING TROUBLE.
THEN THEY STARTED DOING ERRANDS FOR THIS WISE GUY, SONNY CAPUTO.
BUT YOU DIDN'T HEAR THAT FROM ME.
LISTEN, I'M NO FAN OF LUKE CAGE, BUT THE KID DID GO STRAIGHT AND WILLIS WENT TO THE DARK SIDE.
THE EASY MONEY.
THEY STAYED BROS.
BUT THEN...
...THE GIRL.

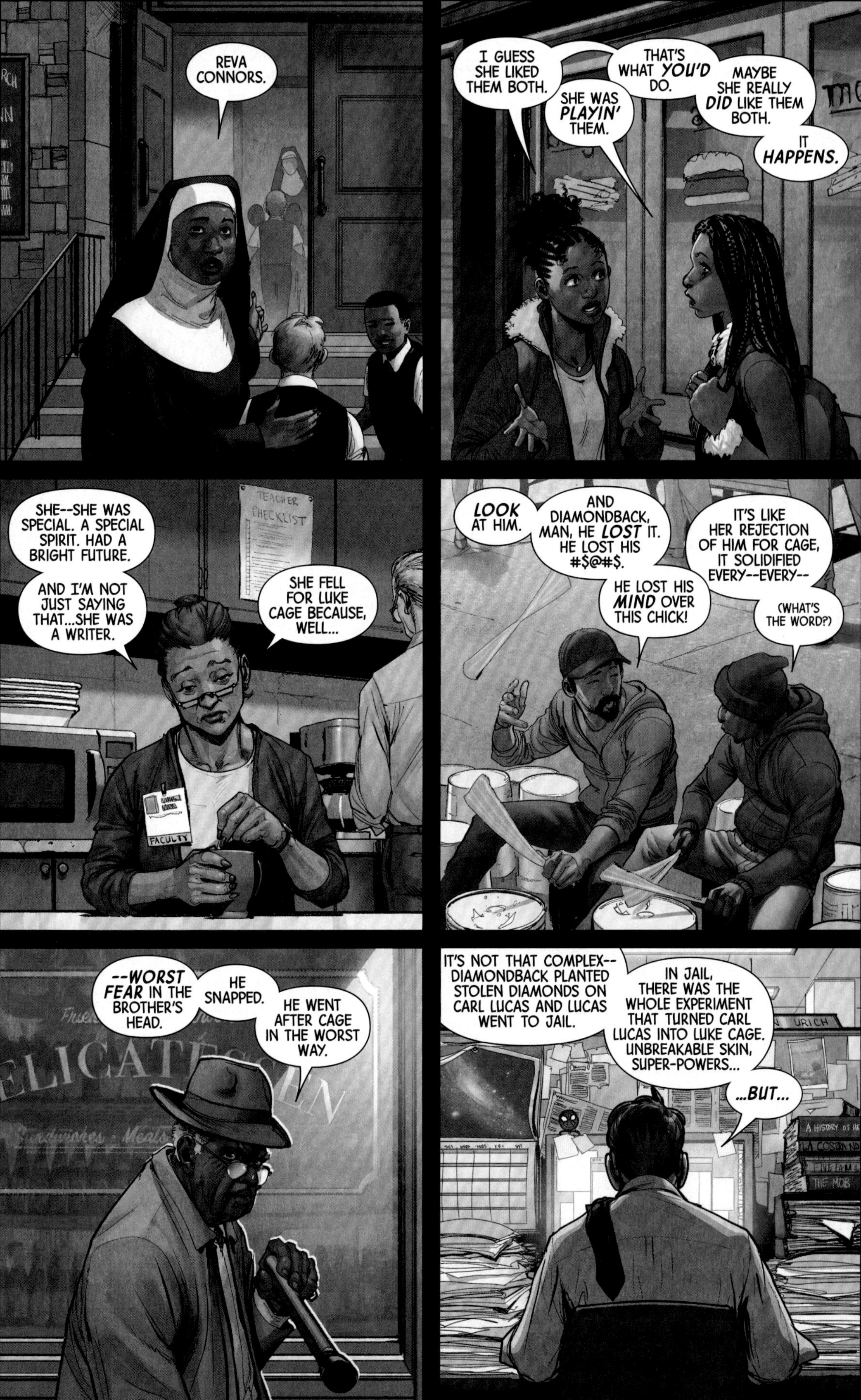

REVA CONNORS.
I GUESS SHE LIKED THEM BOTH.
THAT'S WHAT *YOU'D* DO.
SHE WAS *PLAYIN'* THEM.
MAYBE SHE REALLY *DID* LIKE THEM BOTH.
IT *HAPPENS.*
SHE--SHE WAS SPECIAL. A SPECIAL SPIRIT. HAD A BRIGHT FUTURE.
AND I'M NOT JUST SAYING THAT...SHE WAS A WRITER.
SHE FELL FOR LUKE CAGE BECAUSE, WELL...
TEACHER CHECKLIST
FACULTY
LOOK AT HIM.
AND DIAMONDBACK, MAN, HE *LOST* IT. HE LOST HIS #$@#$.
HE LOST HIS *MIND* OVER THIS CHICK!
IT'S LIKE HER REJECTION OF HIM FOR CAGE, IT SOLIDIFIED EVERY--EVERY--
(WHAT'S THE WORD?)
--*WORST FEAR* IN THE BROTHER'S HEAD.
HE SNAPPED.
HE WENT AFTER CAGE IN THE WORST WAY.
IT'S NOT THAT COMPLEX--DIAMONDBACK PLANTED STOLEN DIAMONDS ON CARL LUCAS AND LUCAS WENT TO JAIL.
IN JAIL, THERE WAS THE WHOLE EXPERIMENT THAT TURNED CARL LUCAS INTO LUKE CAGE. UNBREAKABLE SKIN, SUPER-POWERS...
...*BUT*...

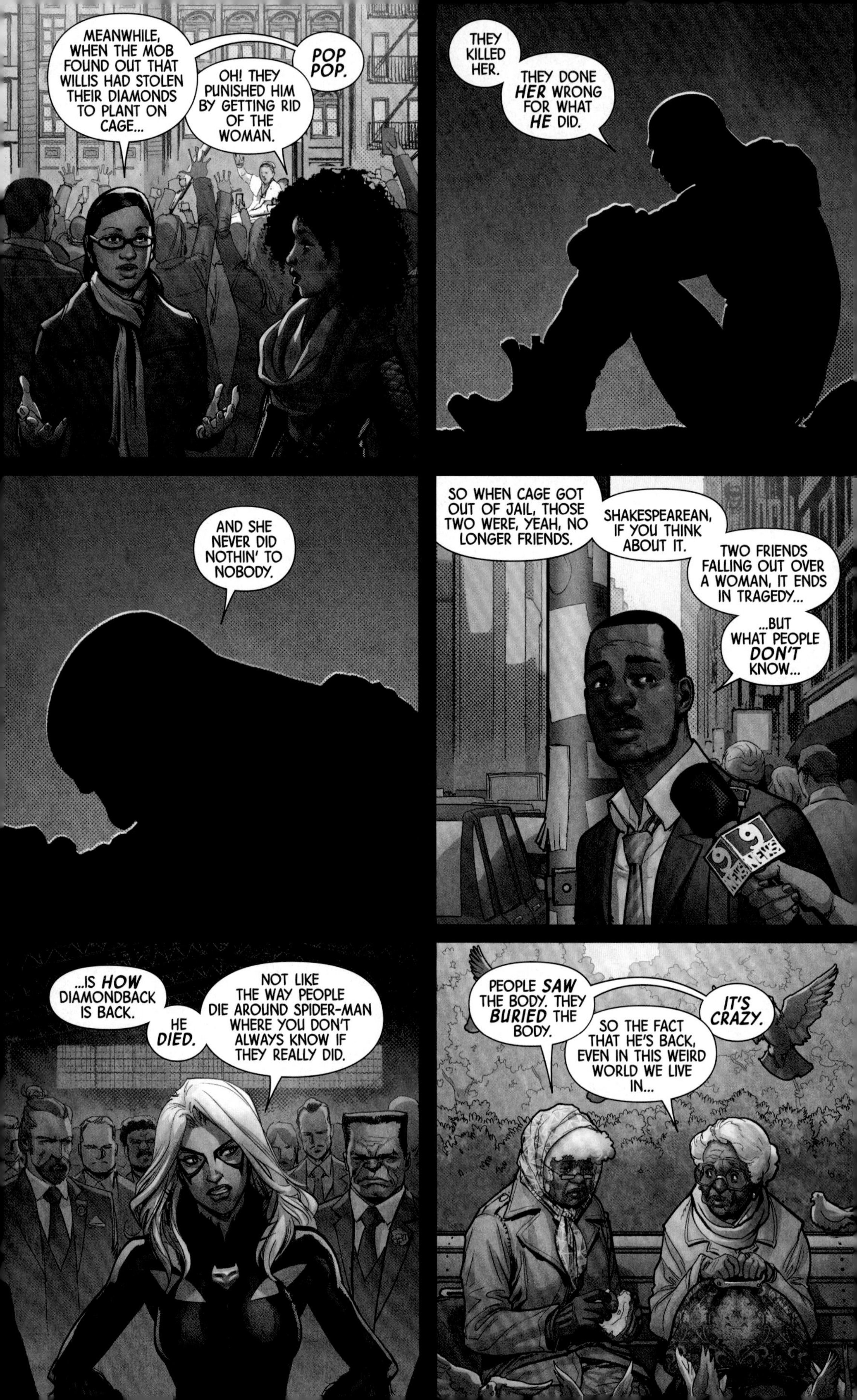
MEANWHILE, WHEN THE MOB FOUND OUT THAT WILLIS HAD STOLEN THEIR DIAMONDS TO PLANT ON CAGE...
POP POP.
OH! THEY PUNISHED HIM BY GETTING RID OF THE WOMAN.
THEY KILLED HER.
THEY DONE HER WRONG FOR WHAT HE DID.
AND SHE NEVER DID NOTHIN' TO NOBODY.
SO WHEN CAGE GOT OUT OF JAIL, THOSE TWO WERE, YEAH, NO LONGER FRIENDS.
SHAKESPEAREAN, IF YOU THINK ABOUT IT.
TWO FRIENDS FALLING OUT OVER A WOMAN, IT ENDS IN TRAGEDY...
...BUT WHAT PEOPLE DON'T KNOW...
...IS HOW DIAMONDBACK IS BACK.
HE DIED.
NOT LIKE THE WAY PEOPLE DIE AROUND SPIDER-MAN WHERE YOU DON'T ALWAYS KNOW IF THEY REALLY DID.
PEOPLE SAW THE BODY. THEY BURIED THE BODY.
IT'S CRAZY.
SO THE FACT THAT HE'S BACK, EVEN IN THIS WEIRD WORLD WE LIVE IN...

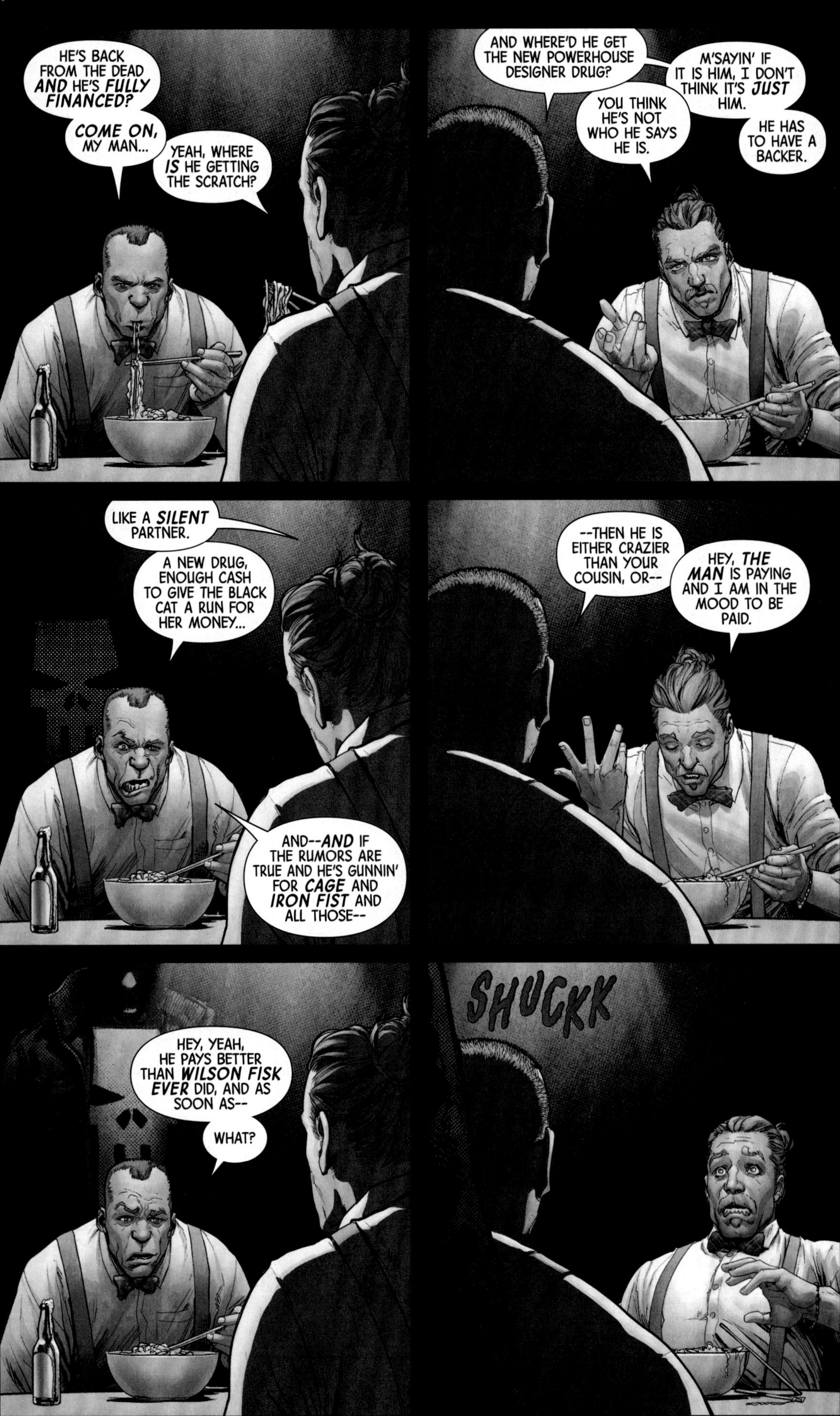
HE'S BACK FROM THE DEAD AND HE'S FULLY FINANCED?
COME ON, MY MAN...
YEAH, WHERE IS HE GETTING THE SCRATCH?
AND WHERE'D HE GET THE NEW POWERHOUSE DESIGNER DRUG?
YOU THINK HE'S NOT WHO HE SAYS HE IS.
M'SAYIN' IF IT IS HIM, I DON'T THINK IT'S JUST HIM.
HE HAS TO HAVE A BACKER.
LIKE A SILENT PARTNER.
A NEW DRUG, ENOUGH CASH TO GIVE THE BLACK CAT A RUN FOR HER MONEY...
AND--AND IF THE RUMORS ARE TRUE AND HE'S GUNNIN' FOR CAGE AND IRON FIST AND ALL THOSE--
--THEN HE IS EITHER CRAZIER THAN YOUR COUSIN, OR--
HEY, THE MAN IS PAYING AND I AM IN THE MOOD TO BE PAID.
HEY, YEAH, HE PAYS BETTER THAN WILSON FISK EVER DID, AND AS SOON AS--
WHAT?
SHUCKK

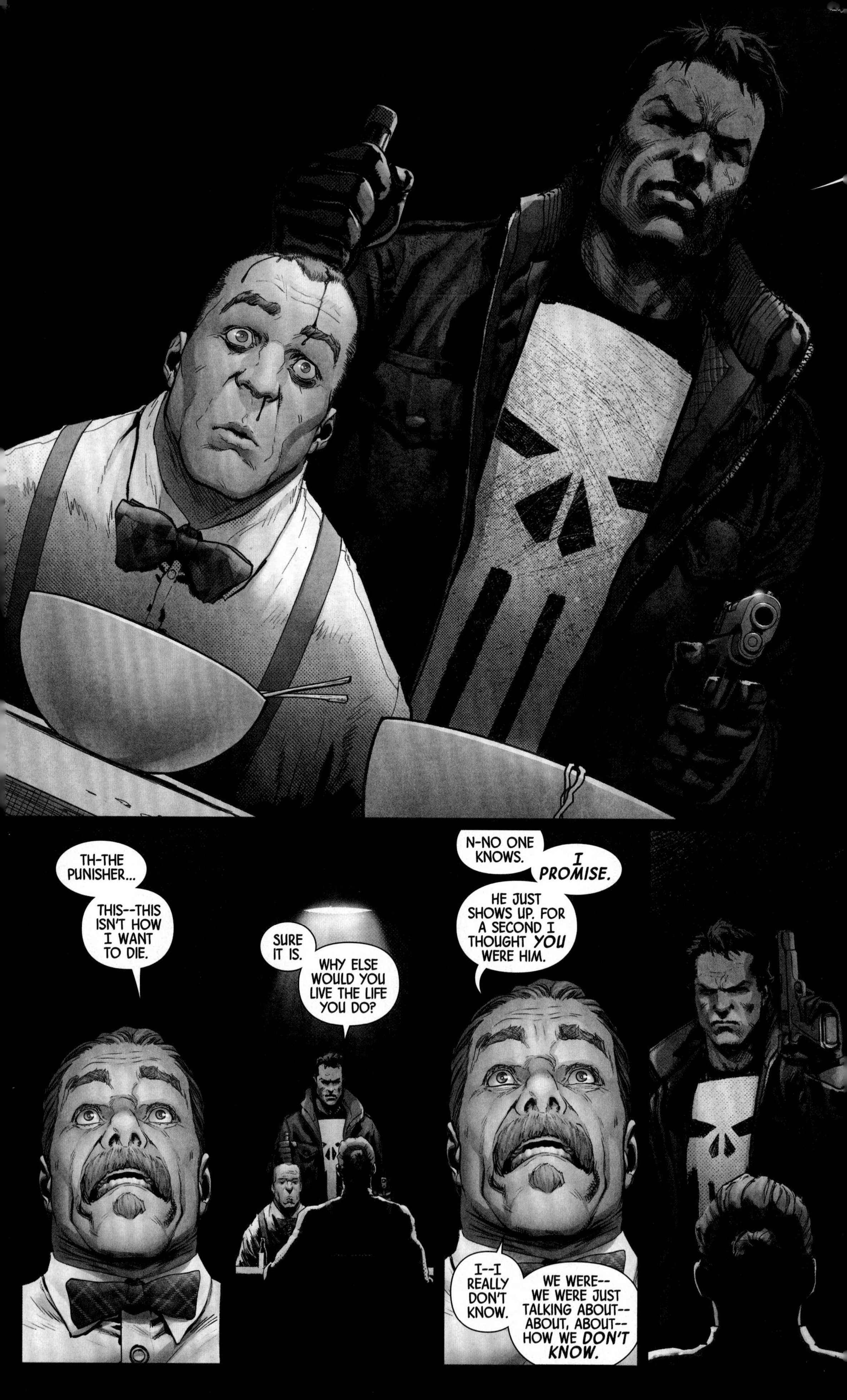
TH-THE PUNISHER...
THIS--THIS ISN'T HOW I WANT TO DIE.
SURE IT IS.
WHY ELSE WOULD YOU LIVE THE LIFE YOU DO?
N-NO ONE KNOWS.
I PROMISE.
HE JUST SHOWS UP. FOR A SECOND I THOUGHT YOU WERE HIM.
I--I REALLY DON'T KNOW.
WE WERE-- WE WERE JUST TALKING ABOUT-- ABOUT, ABOUT-- HOW WE DON'T KNOW.

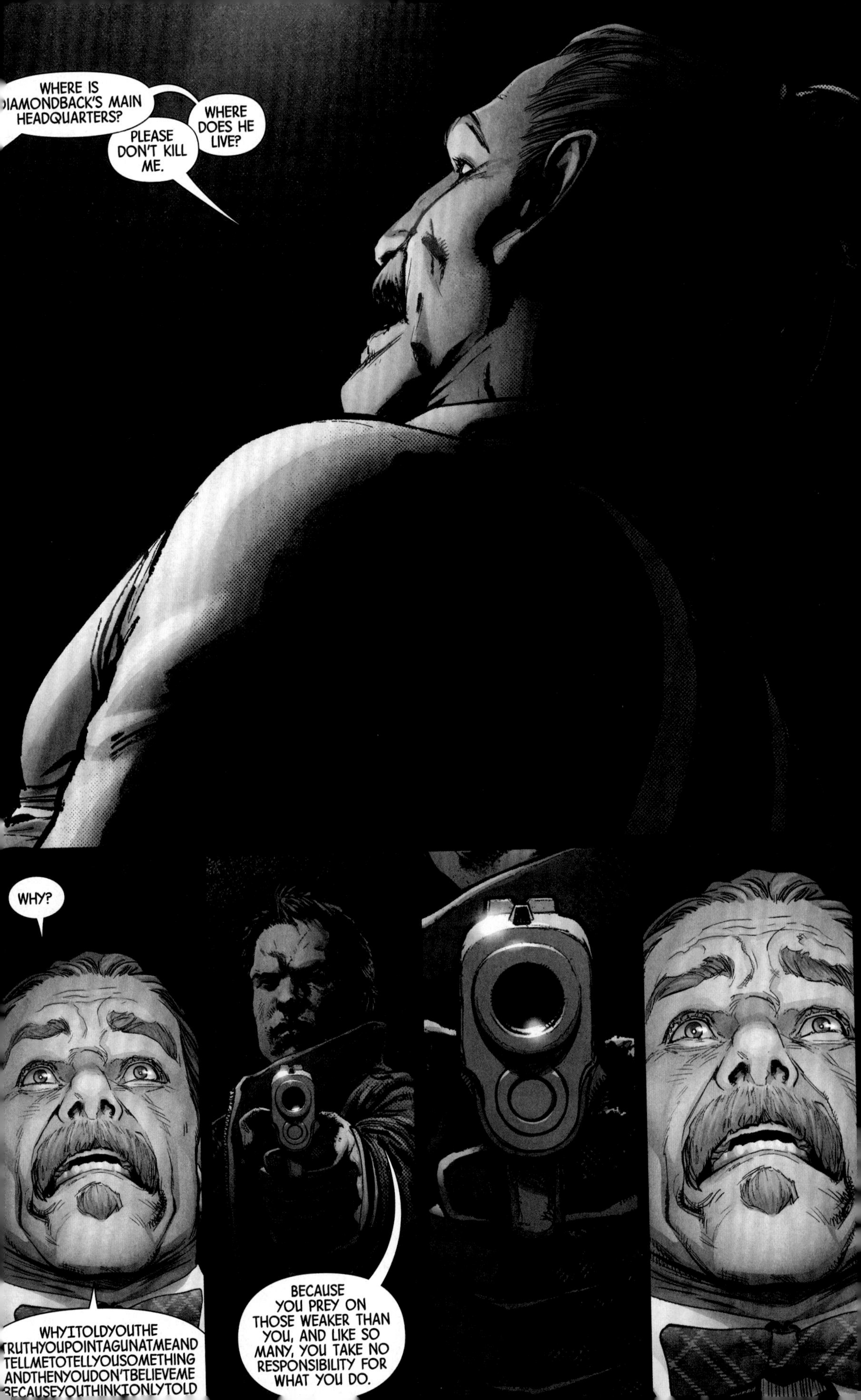
WHERE IS DIAMONDBACK'S MAIN HEADQUARTERS?
WHERE DOES HE LIVE?
PLEASE DON'T KILL ME.
WHY?
WHYITOLDYOUTHE TRUTHYOUPOINTAGUNATMEAND TELLMETOTELLYOUSOMETHING ANDTHENYOUDON'TBELIEVEME BECAUSEYOUTHINKIONLYTOLD
BECAUSE YOU PREY ON THOSE WEAKER THAN YOU, AND LIKE SO MANY, YOU TAKE NO RESPONSIBILITY FOR WHAT YOU DO.

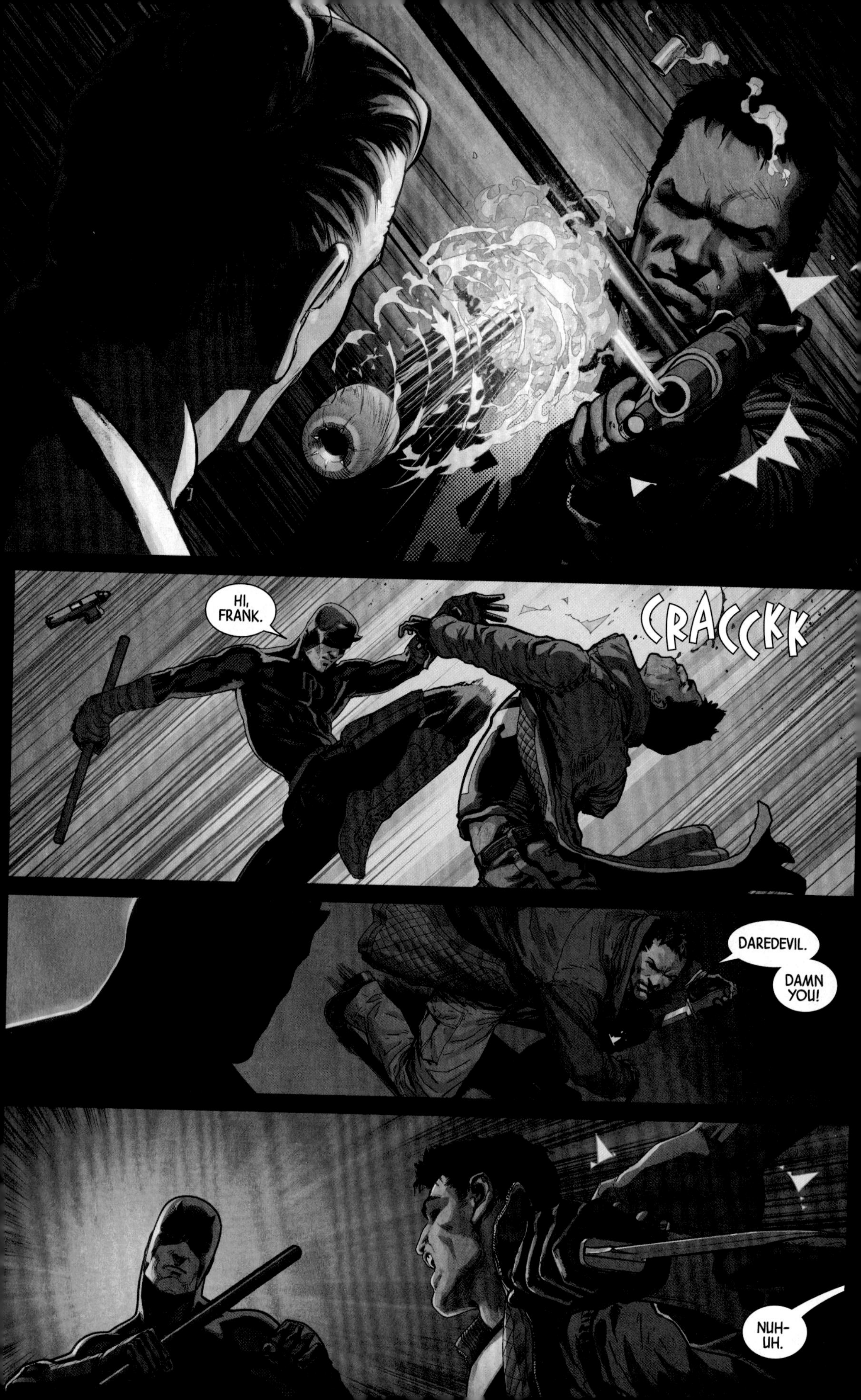
HI, FRANK.
CRACCKK
DAREDEVIL.
DAMN YOU!
NUH-UH.

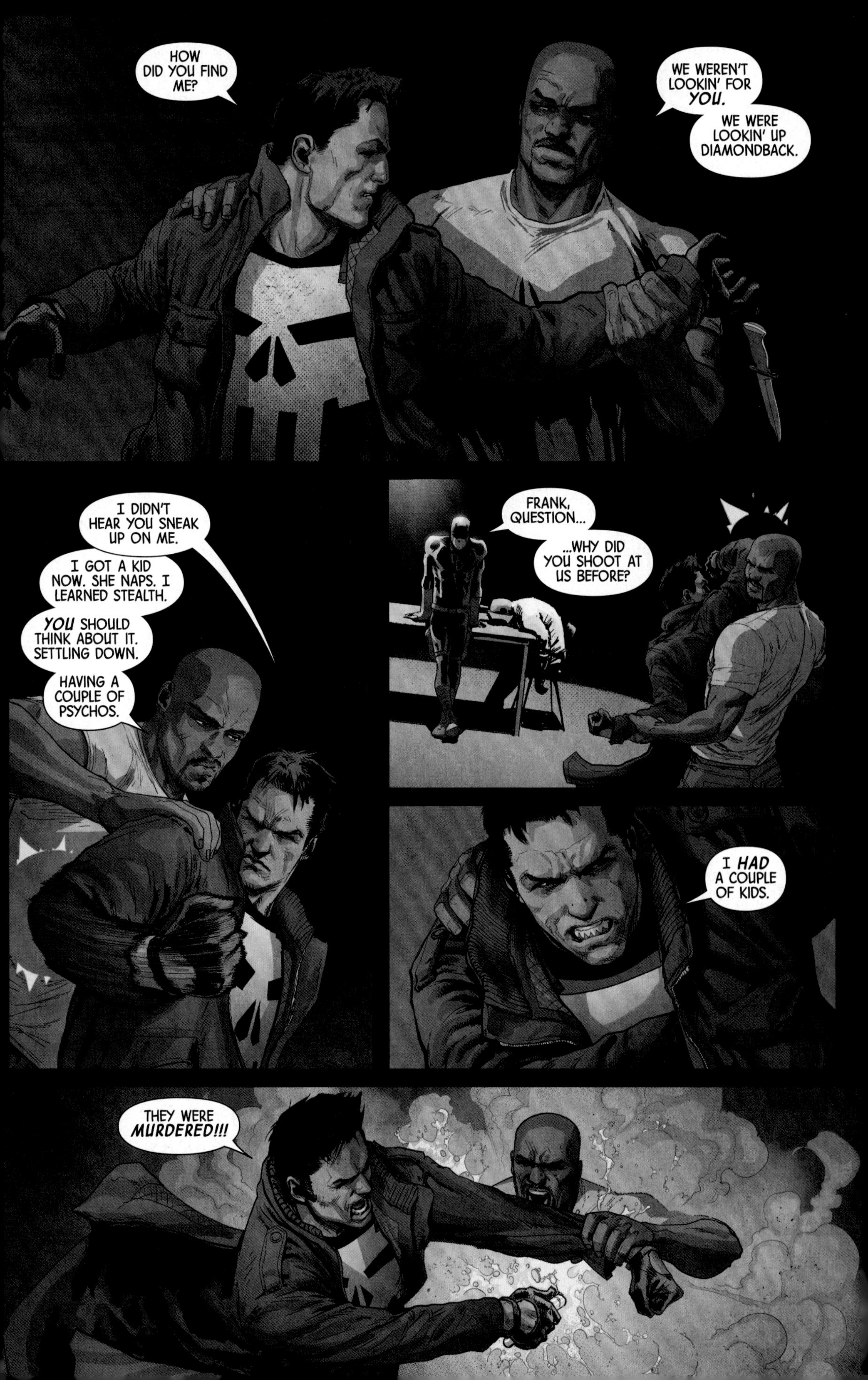
HOW DID YOU FIND ME?
WE WEREN'T LOOKIN' FOR YOU.
WE WERE LOOKIN' UP DIAMONDBACK.
I DIDN'T HEAR YOU SNEAK UP ON ME.
I GOT A KID NOW. SHE NAPS. I LEARNED STEALTH.
YOU SHOULD THINK ABOUT IT. SETTLING DOWN.
HAVING A COUPLE OF PSYCHOS.
FRANK, QUESTION...
...WHY DID YOU SHOOT AT US BEFORE?
I HAD A COUPLE OF KIDS.
THEY WERE MURDERED!!!

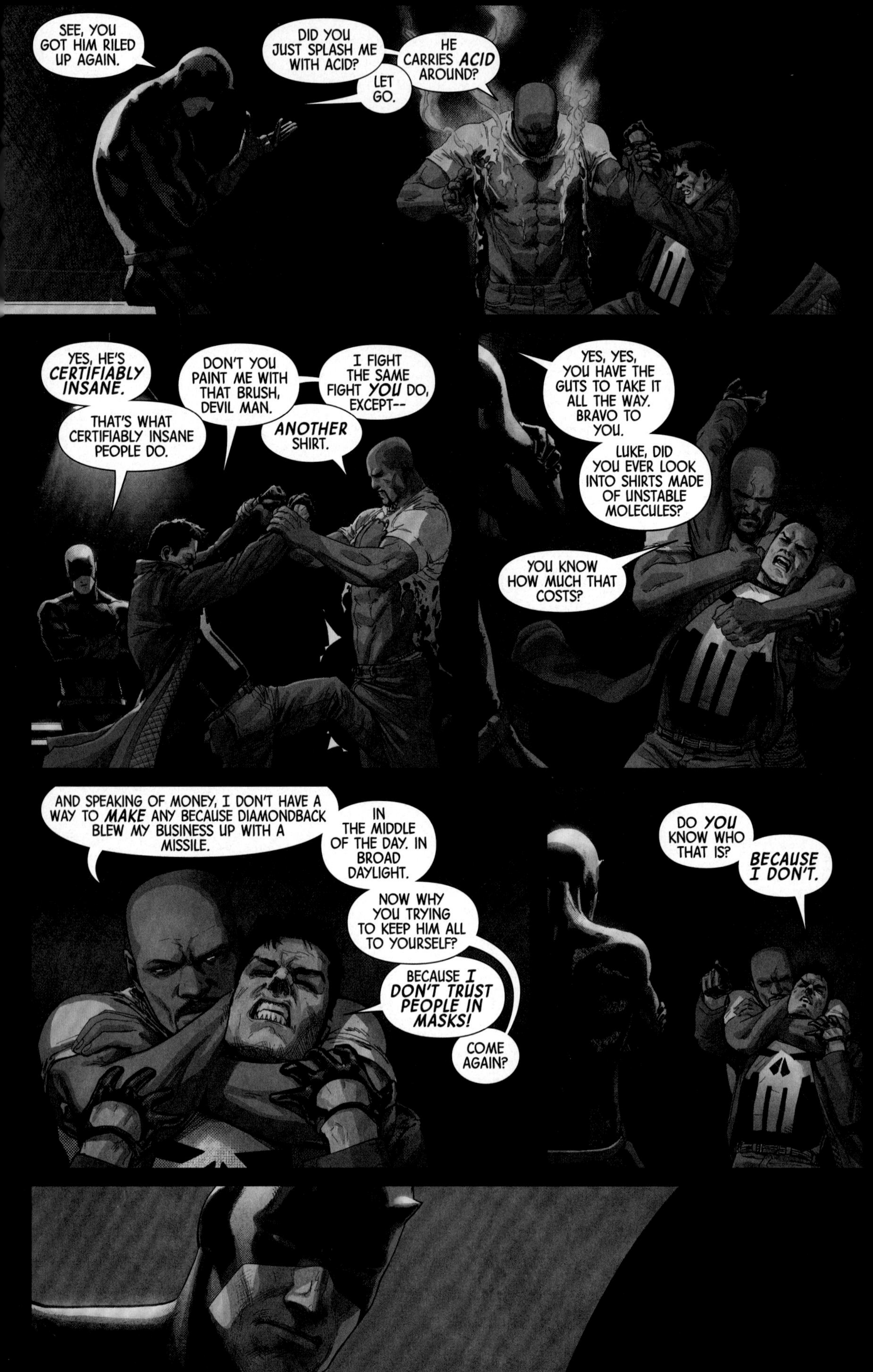
SEE, YOU GOT HIM RILED UP AGAIN.
DID YOU JUST SPLASH ME WITH ACID?
HE CARRIES ACID AROUND?
LET GO.
YES, HE'S CERTIFIABLY INSANE.
THAT'S WHAT CERTIFIABLY INSANE PEOPLE DO.
DON'T YOU PAINT ME WITH THAT BRUSH, DEVIL MAN.
I FIGHT THE SAME FIGHT YOU DO, EXCEPT--
ANOTHER SHIRT.
YES, YES, YOU HAVE THE GUTS TO TAKE IT ALL THE WAY. BRAVO TO YOU.
LUKE, DID YOU EVER LOOK INTO SHIRTS MADE OF UNSTABLE MOLECULES?
YOU KNOW HOW MUCH THAT COSTS?
AND SPEAKING OF MONEY, I DON'T HAVE A WAY TO MAKE ANY BECAUSE DIAMONDBACK BLEW MY BUSINESS UP WITH A MISSILE.
IN THE MIDDLE OF THE DAY. IN BROAD DAYLIGHT.
NOW WHY YOU TRYING TO KEEP HIM ALL TO YOURSELF?
BECAUSE I DON'T TRUST PEOPLE IN MASKS!
COME AGAIN?
DO YOU KNOW WHO THAT IS?
BECAUSE I DON'T.

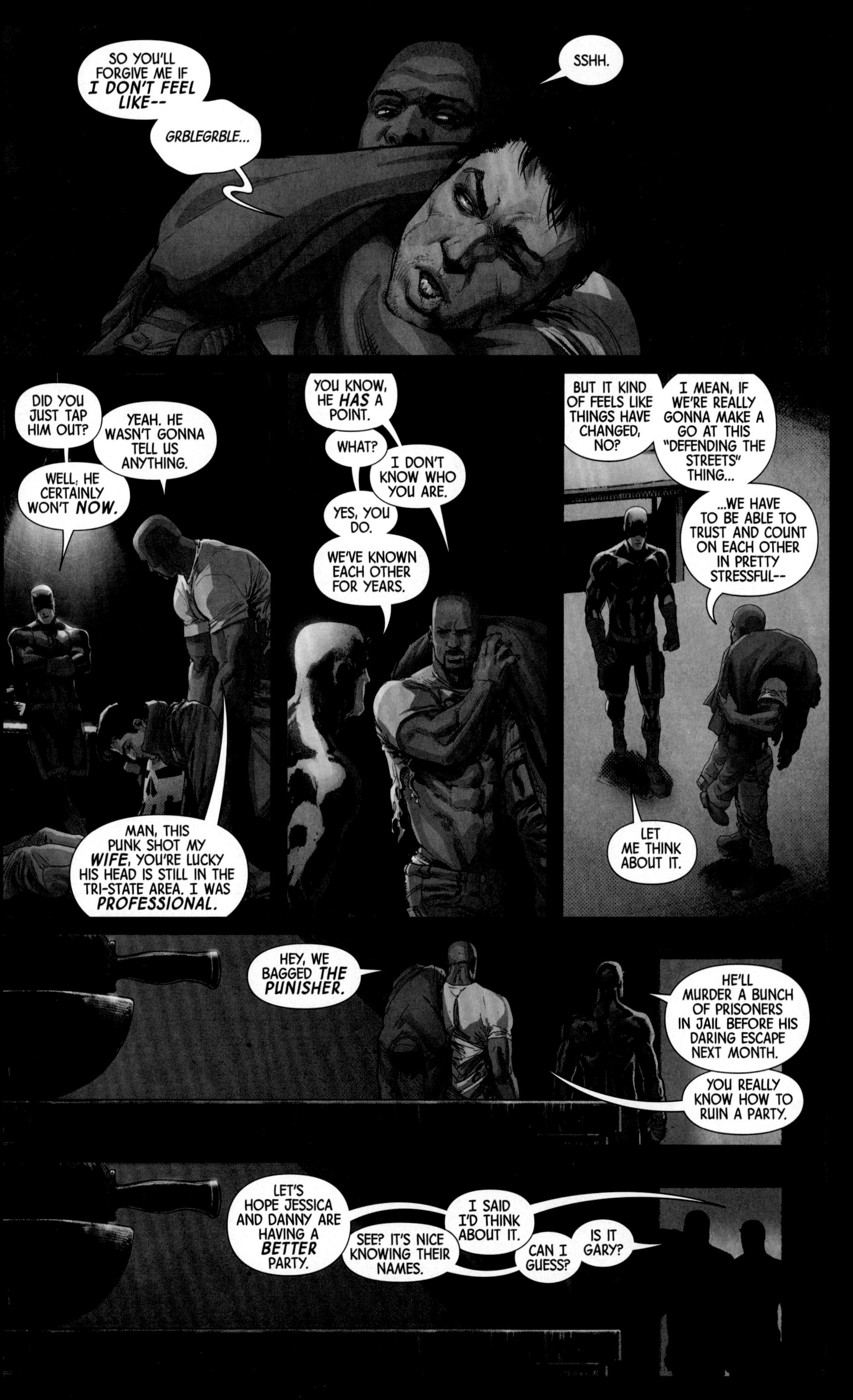
SO YOU'LL FORGIVE ME IF I DON'T FEEL LIKE--
GRBLEGRBLE...
SSHH.
DID YOU JUST TAP HIM OUT?
YEAH. HE WASN'T GONNA TELL US ANYTHING.
WELL, HE CERTAINLY WON'T NOW.
MAN, THIS PUNK SHOT MY WIFE, YOU'RE LUCKY HIS HEAD IS STILL IN THE TRI-STATE AREA. I WAS PROFESSIONAL.
YOU KNOW, HE HAS A POINT.
WHAT?
I DON'T KNOW WHO YOU ARE.
YES, YOU DO.
WE'VE KNOWN EACH OTHER FOR YEARS.
BUT IT KIND OF FEELS LIKE THINGS HAVE CHANGED, NO?
I MEAN, IF WE'RE REALLY GONNA MAKE A GO AT THIS "DEFENDING THE STREETS" THING...
...WE HAVE TO BE ABLE TO TRUST AND COUNT ON EACH OTHER IN PRETTY STRESSFUL--
LET ME THINK ABOUT IT.
HEY, WE BAGGED THE PUNISHER.
HE'LL MURDER A BUNCH OF PRISONERS IN JAIL BEFORE HIS DARING ESCAPE NEXT MONTH.
YOU REALLY KNOW HOW TO RUIN A PARTY.
LET'S HOPE JESSICA AND DANNY ARE HAVING A BETTER PARTY.
I SAID I'D THINK ABOUT IT.
SEE? IT'S NICE KNOWING THEIR NAMES.
CAN I GUESS?
IS IT GARY?

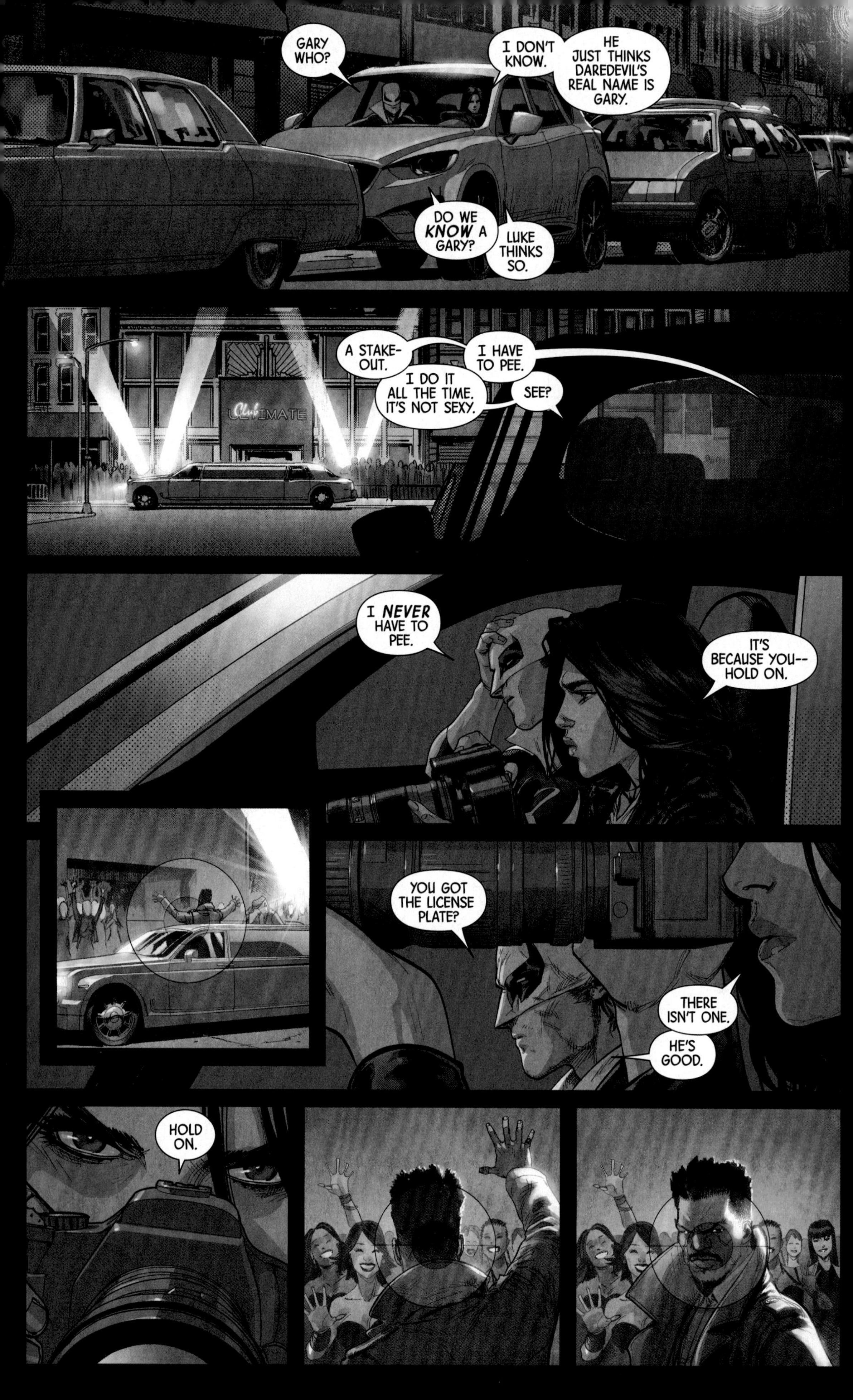
GARY WHO?
I DON'T KNOW.
HE JUST THINKS DAREDEVIL'S REAL NAME IS GARY.
DO WE KNOW A GARY?
LUKE THINKS SO.
Club ULTIMATE
A STAKE-OUT.
I HAVE TO PEE.
I DO IT ALL THE TIME. IT'S NOT SEXY.
SEE?
I NEVER HAVE TO PEE.
IT'S BECAUSE YOU-- HOLD ON.
YOU GOT THE LICENSE PLATE?
THERE ISN'T ONE.
HE'S GOOD.
HOLD ON.

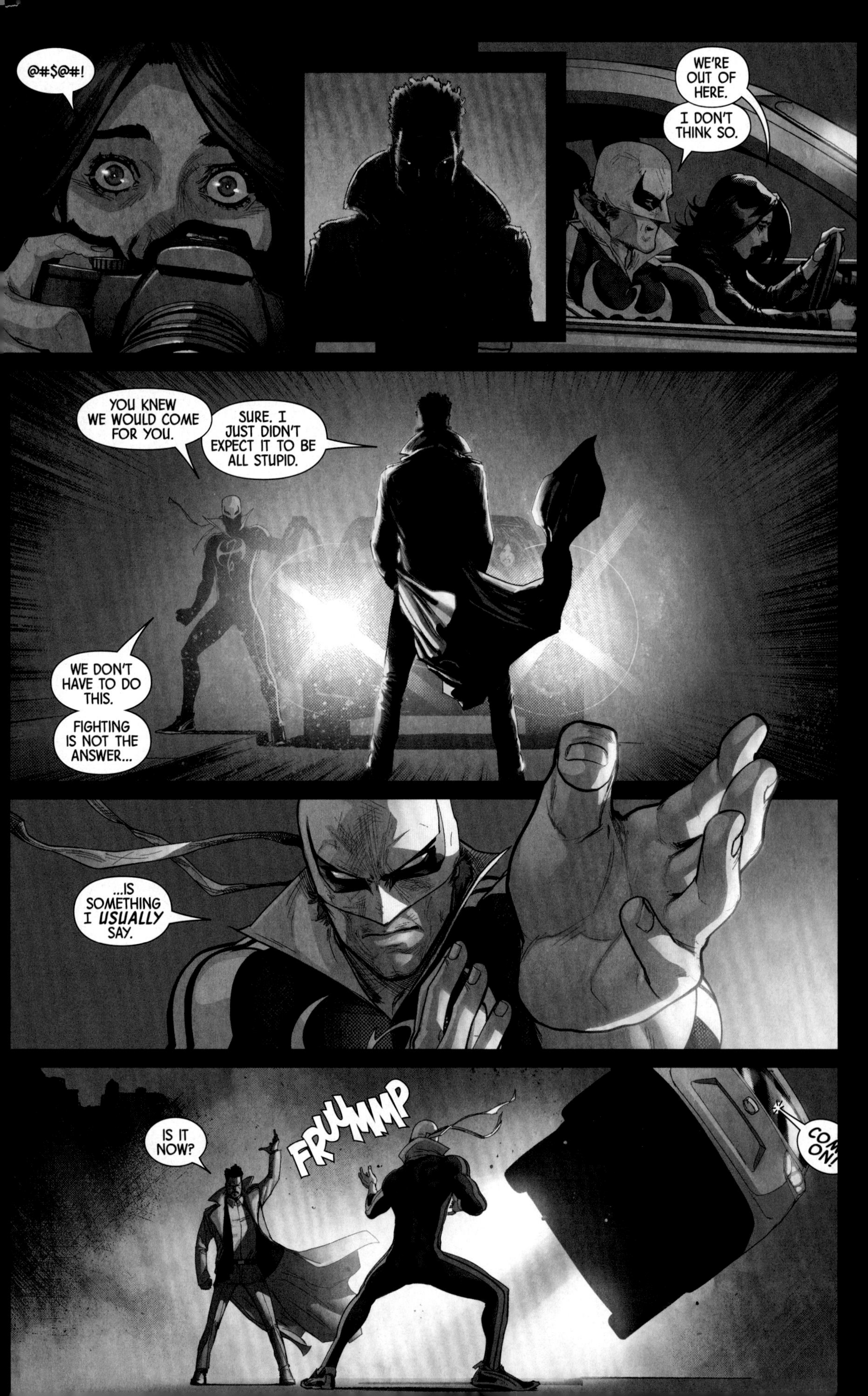
@#$@#!
WE'RE OUT OF HERE.
I DON'T THINK SO.
YOU KNEW WE WOULD COME FOR YOU.
SURE. I JUST DIDN'T EXPECT IT TO BE ALL STUPID.
WE DON'T HAVE TO DO THIS.
FIGHTING IS NOT THE ANSWER...
...IS SOMETHING I *USUALLY* SAY.
IS IT NOW?
FRUUMMP
COME ON!

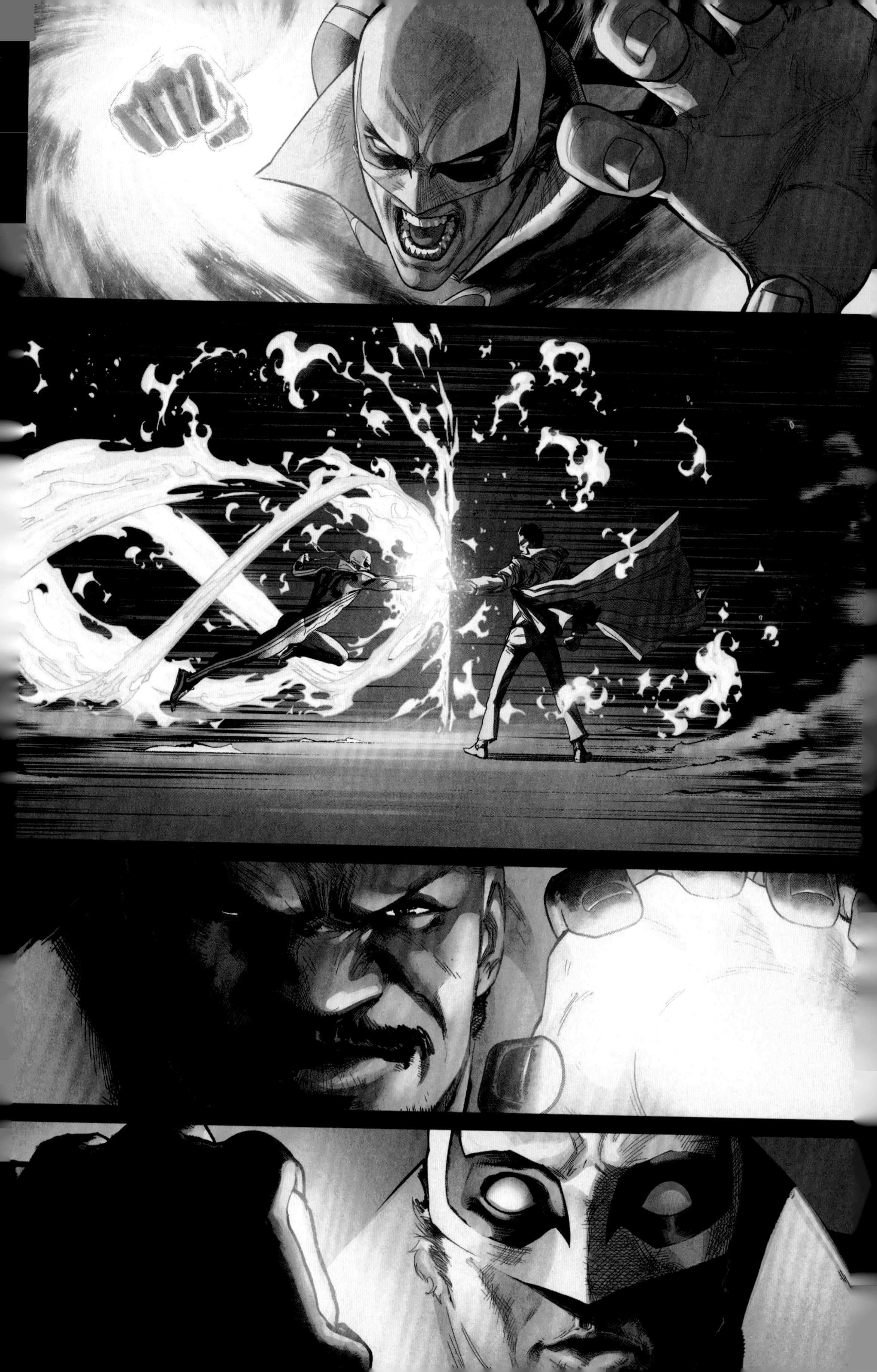

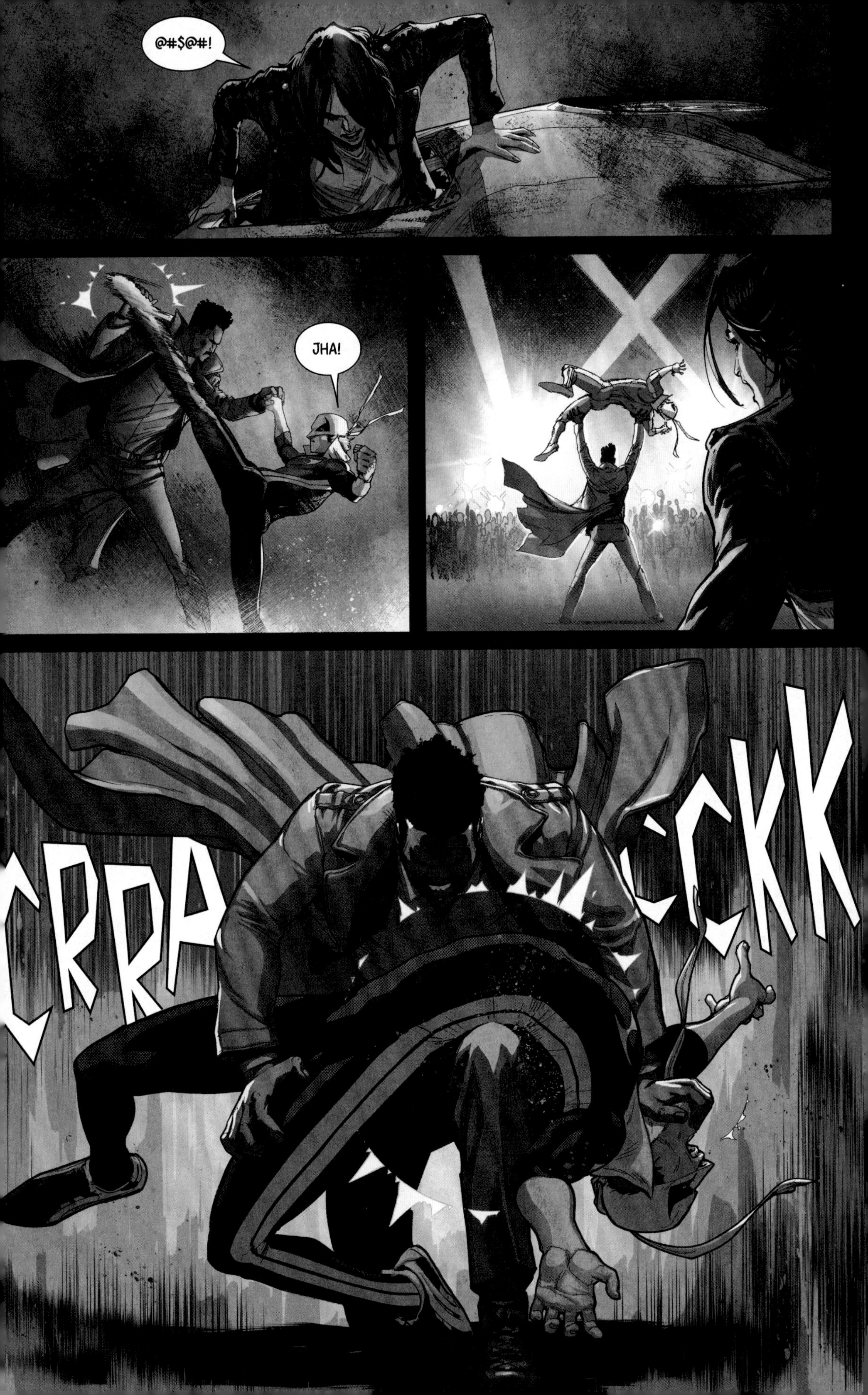
@#$@#!
JHA!
CRRA
CKK

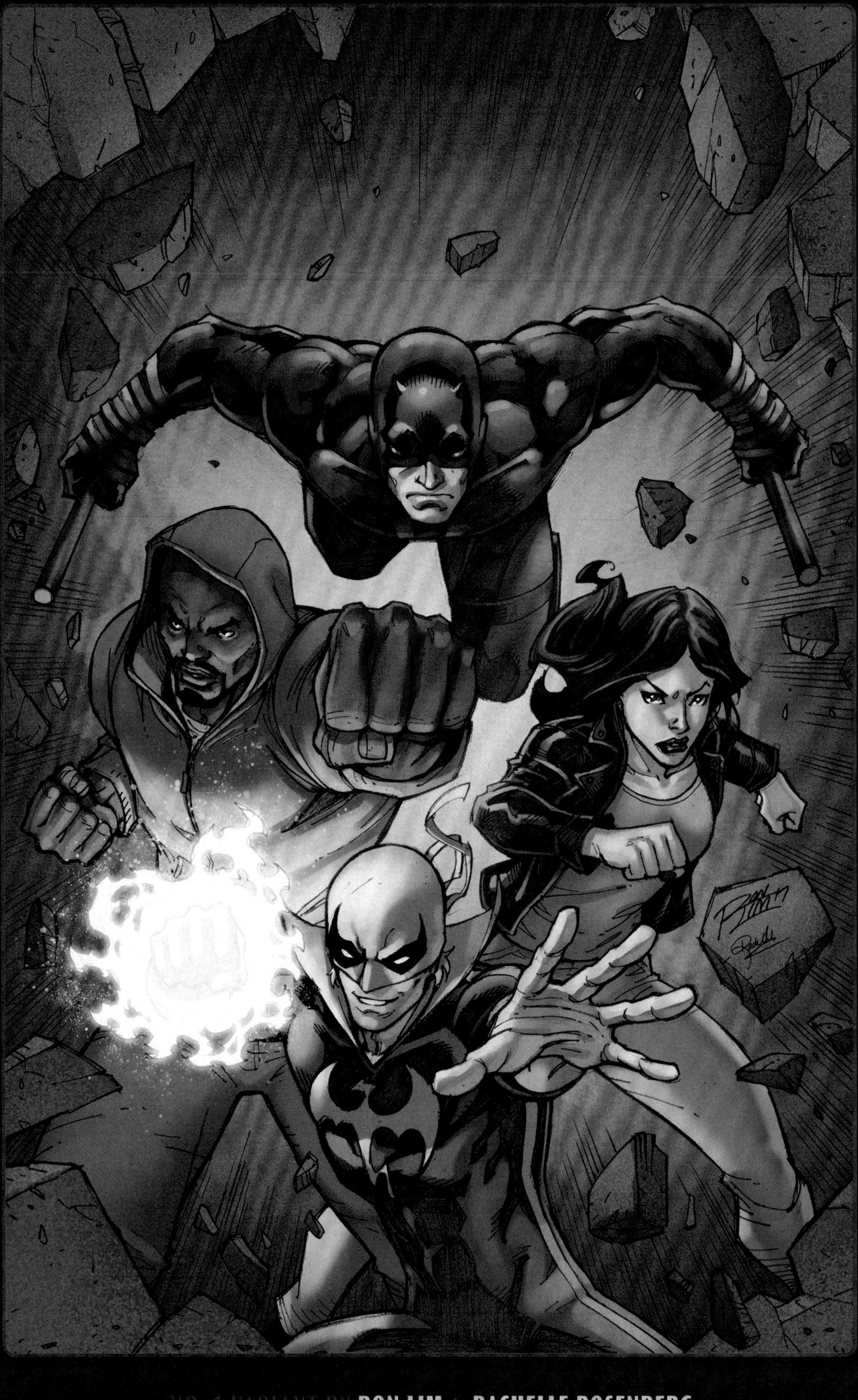

NO. 1 VARIANT BY **RON LIM** & **RACHELLE ROSENBERG**

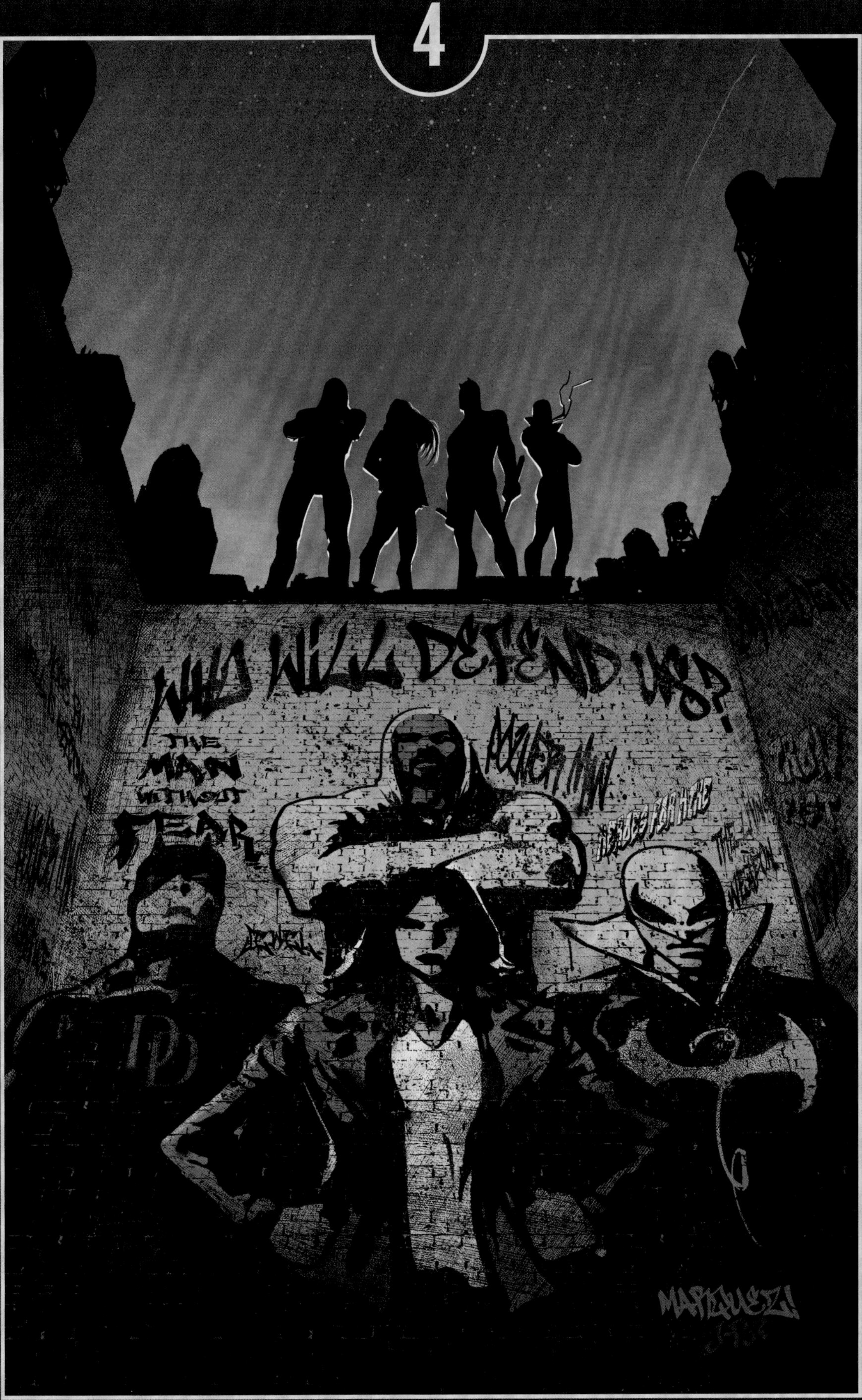
4
WHO WILL DEFEND US?
THE MAN WITHOUT FEAR
POWER MAN
HEROES FOR HIRE
JEWEL
MARQUEZ!

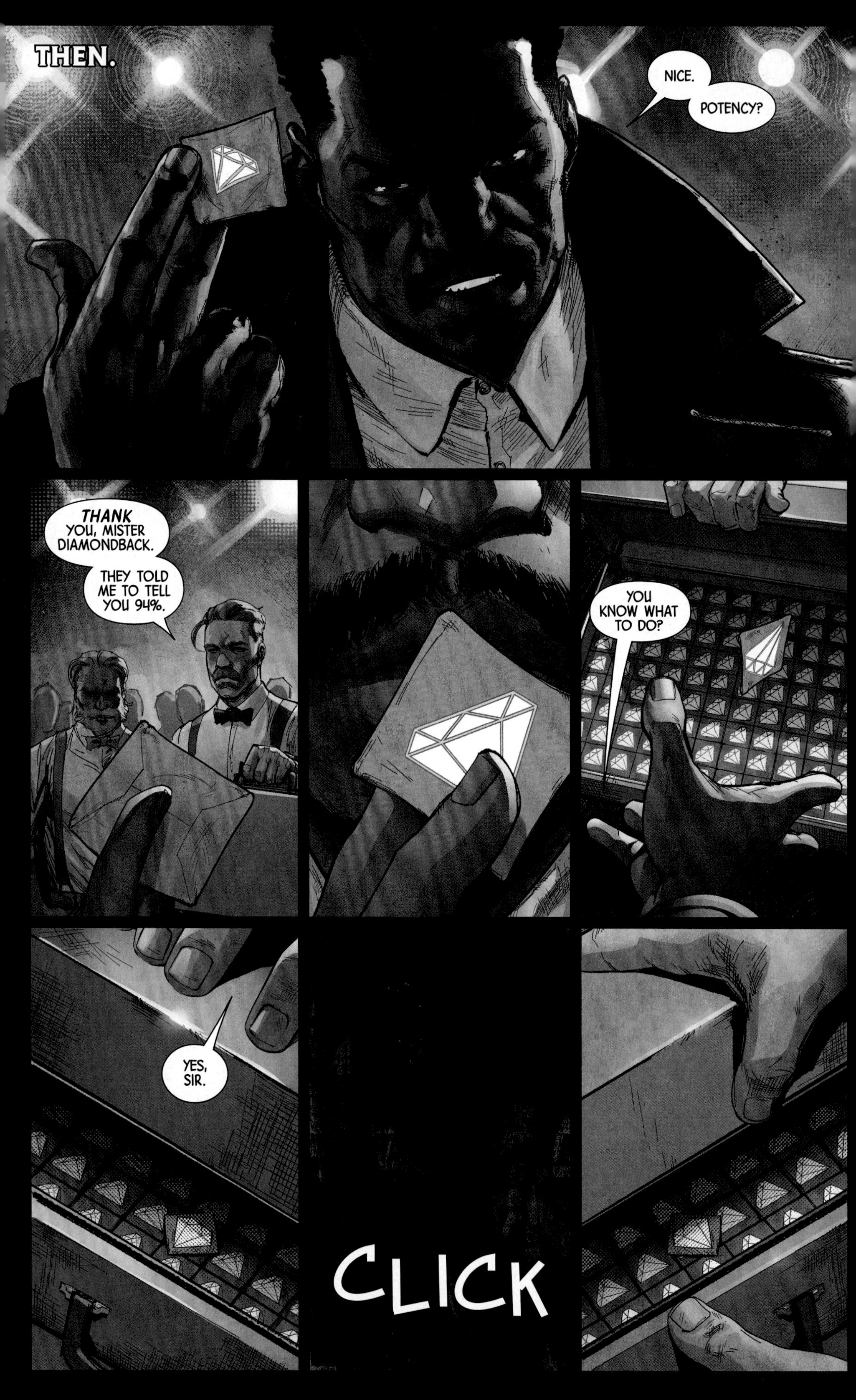
THEN.
NICE.
POTENCY?
THANK YOU, MISTER DIAMONDBACK.
THEY TOLD ME TO TELL YOU 94%.
YOU KNOW WHAT TO DO?
YES, SIR.
CLICK

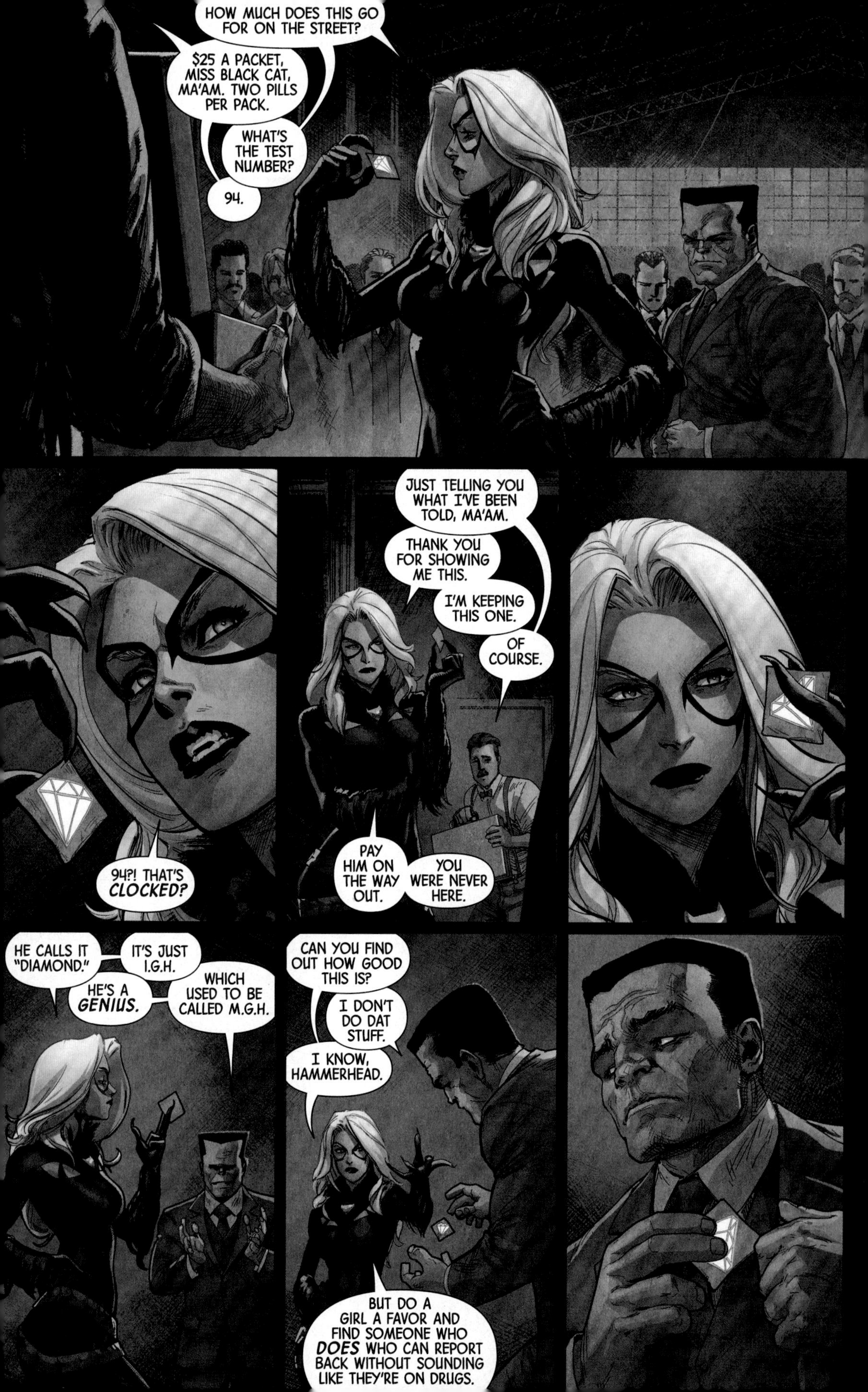

HOW MUCH DOES THIS GO FOR ON THE STREET?
$25 A PACKET, MISS BLACK CAT, MA'AM. TWO PILLS PER PACK.
WHAT'S THE TEST NUMBER?
94.
94?! THAT'S CLOCKED?
JUST TELLING YOU WHAT I'VE BEEN TOLD, MA'AM.
THANK YOU FOR SHOWING ME THIS.
I'M KEEPING THIS ONE.
OF COURSE.
PAY HIM ON THE WAY OUT.
YOU WERE NEVER HERE.
HE CALLS IT "DIAMOND."
IT'S JUST I.G.H.
HE'S A GENIUS.
WHICH USED TO BE CALLED M.G.H.
CAN YOU FIND OUT HOW GOOD THIS IS?
I DON'T DO DAT STUFF.
I KNOW, HAMMERHEAD.
BUT DO A GIRL A FAVOR AND FIND SOMEONE WHO DOES WHO CAN REPORT BACK WITHOUT SOUNDING LIKE THEY'RE ON DRUGS.

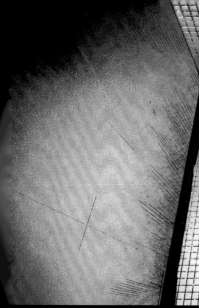

Y'R BETTER DEN DAT, BIG GUY.

ROMAN.

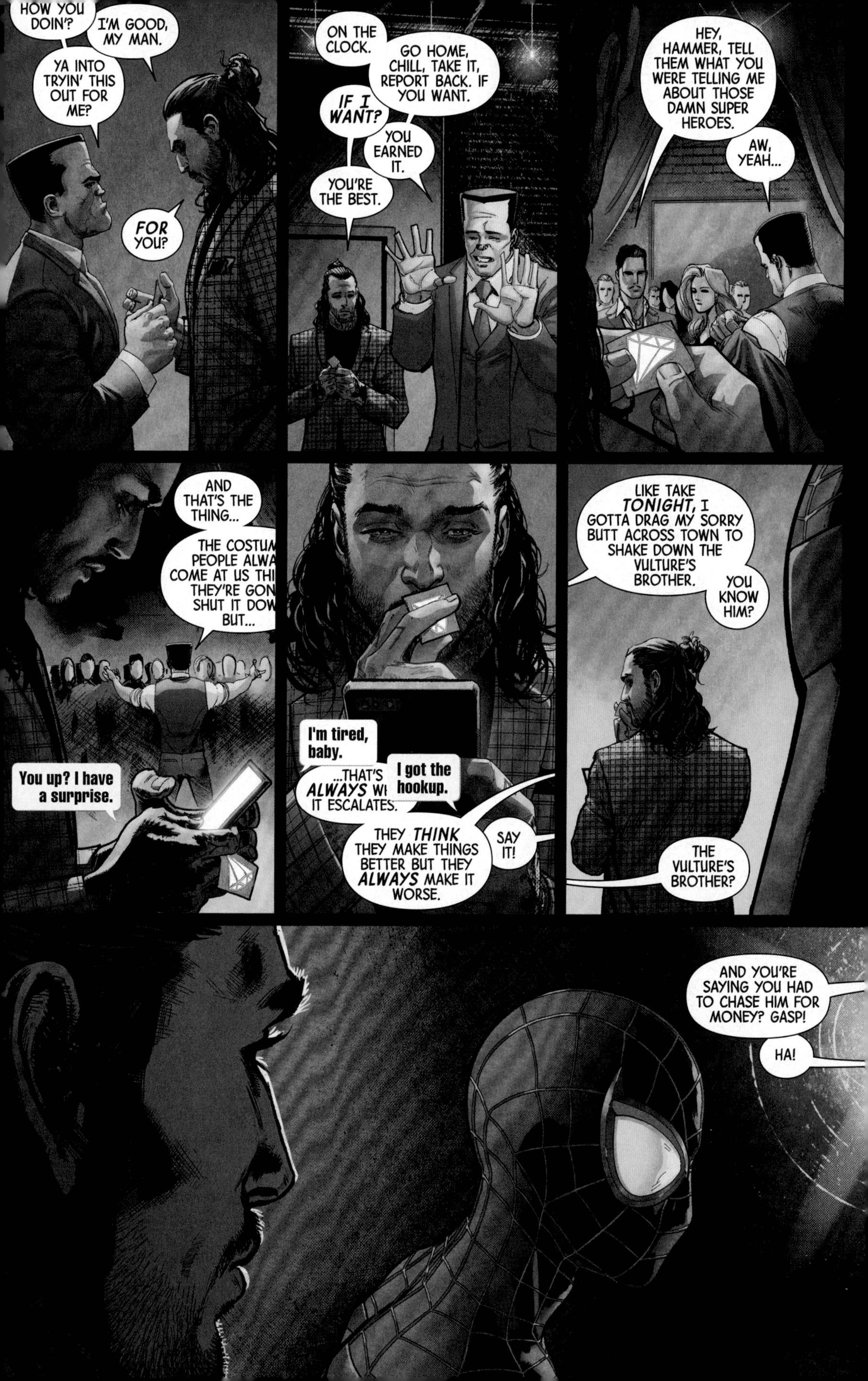
HOW YOU DOIN'?
I'M GOOD, MY MAN.
YA INTO TRYIN' THIS OUT FOR ME?
FOR YOU?
ON THE CLOCK.
GO HOME, CHILL, TAKE IT, REPORT BACK. IF YOU WANT.
IF I WANT?
YOU EARNED IT.
YOU'RE THE BEST.
HEY, HAMMER, TELL THEM WHAT YOU WERE TELLING ME ABOUT THOSE DAMN SUPER HEROES.
AW, YEAH...
AND THAT'S THE THING...
THE COSTUM PEOPLE ALWA COME AT US THI THEY'RE GON SHUT IT DOW BUT...
You up? I have a surprise.
I'm tired, baby.
...THAT'S ALWAYS WH IT ESCALATES.
I got the hookup.
THEY THINK THEY MAKE THINGS BETTER BUT THEY ALWAYS MAKE IT WORSE.
SAY IT!
LIKE TAKE TONIGHT, I GOTTA DRAG MY SORRY BUTT ACROSS TOWN TO SHAKE DOWN THE VULTURE'S BROTHER.
YOU KNOW HIM?
THE VULTURE'S BROTHER?
AND YOU'RE SAYING YOU HAD TO CHASE HIM FOR MONEY? GASP!
HA!

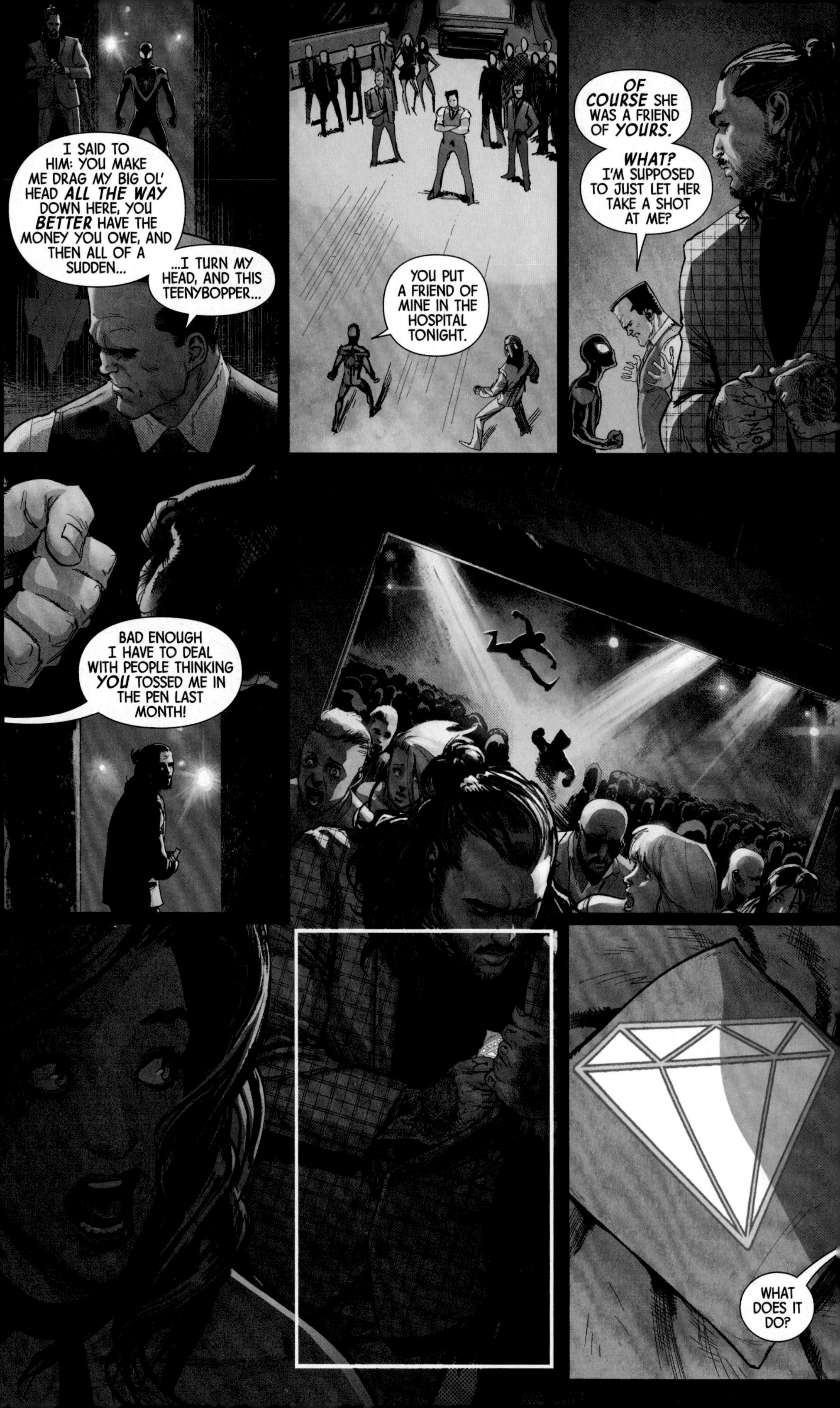
I SAID TO HIM: YOU MAKE ME DRAG MY BIG OL' HEAD ALL THE WAY DOWN HERE, YOU BETTER HAVE THE MONEY YOU OWE, AND THEN ALL OF A SUDDEN...
...I TURN MY HEAD, AND THIS TEENYBOPPER...
YOU PUT A FRIEND OF MINE IN THE HOSPITAL TONIGHT.
OF COURSE SHE WAS A FRIEND OF YOURS.
WHAT? I'M SUPPOSED TO JUST LET HER TAKE A SHOT AT ME?
BAD ENOUGH I HAVE TO DEAL WITH PEOPLE THINKING YOU TOSSED ME IN THE PEN LAST MONTH!
WHAT DOES IT DO?

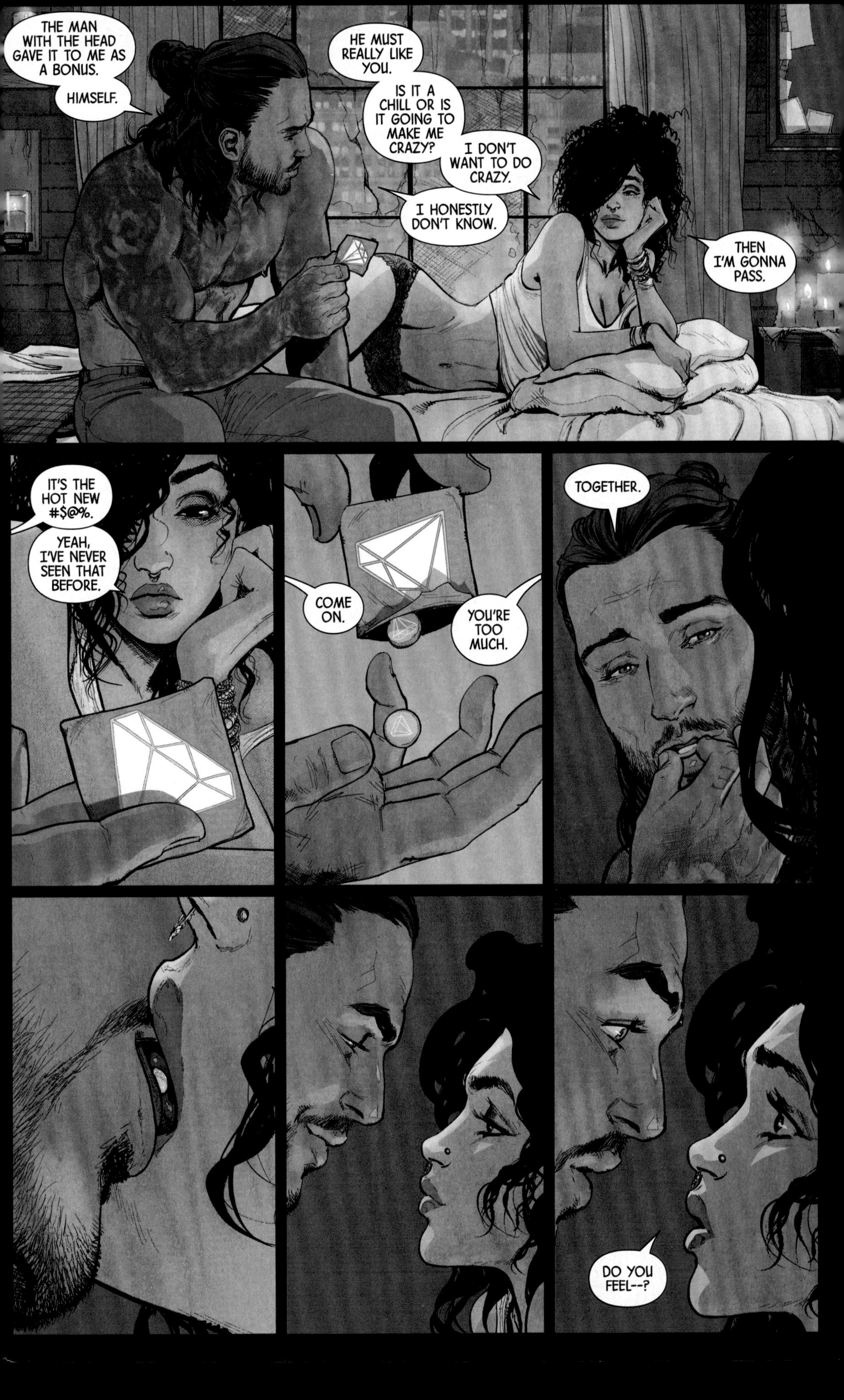
THE MAN WITH THE HEAD GAVE IT TO ME AS A BONUS.
HIMSELF.
HE MUST REALLY LIKE YOU.
IS IT A CHILL OR IS IT GOING TO MAKE ME CRAZY?
I DON'T WANT TO DO CRAZY.
I HONESTLY DON'T KNOW.
THEN I'M GONNA PASS.
IT'S THE HOT NEW #$@%.
YEAH, I'VE NEVER SEEN THAT BEFORE.
COME ON.
YOU'RE TOO MUCH.
TOGETHER.
DO YOU FEEL--?

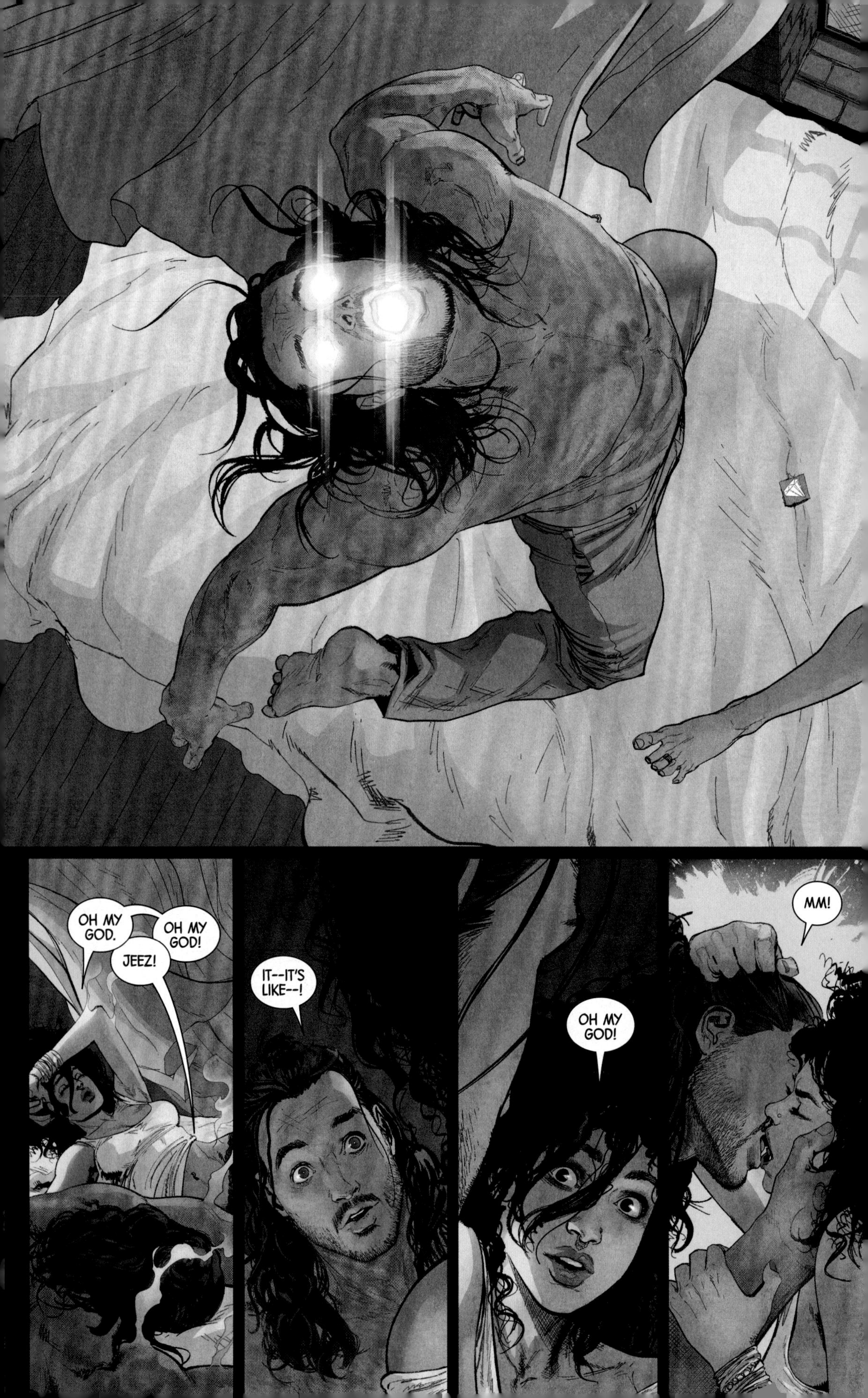
OH MY GOD.
OH MY GOD!
JEEZ!
IT--IT'S LIKE--!
OH MY GOD!
MM!

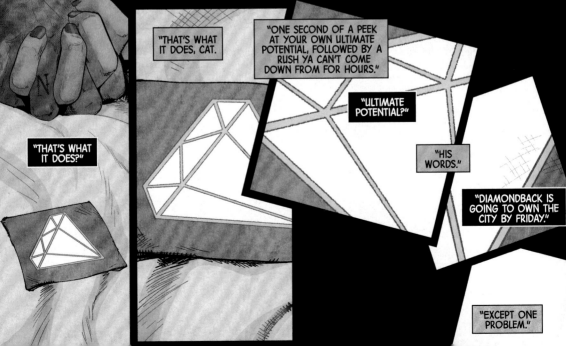

"THAT'S WHAT IT DOES, CAT.

"ONE SECOND OF A PEEK AT YOUR OWN ULTIMATE POTENTIAL, FOLLOWED BY A RUSH YA CAN'T COME DOWN FROM FOR HOURS."

"ULTIMATE POTENTIAL?"

"THAT'S WHAT IT DOES?"

"HIS WORDS."

"DIAMONDBACK IS GOING TO OWN THE CITY BY FRIDAY."

"EXCEPT ONE PROBLEM."

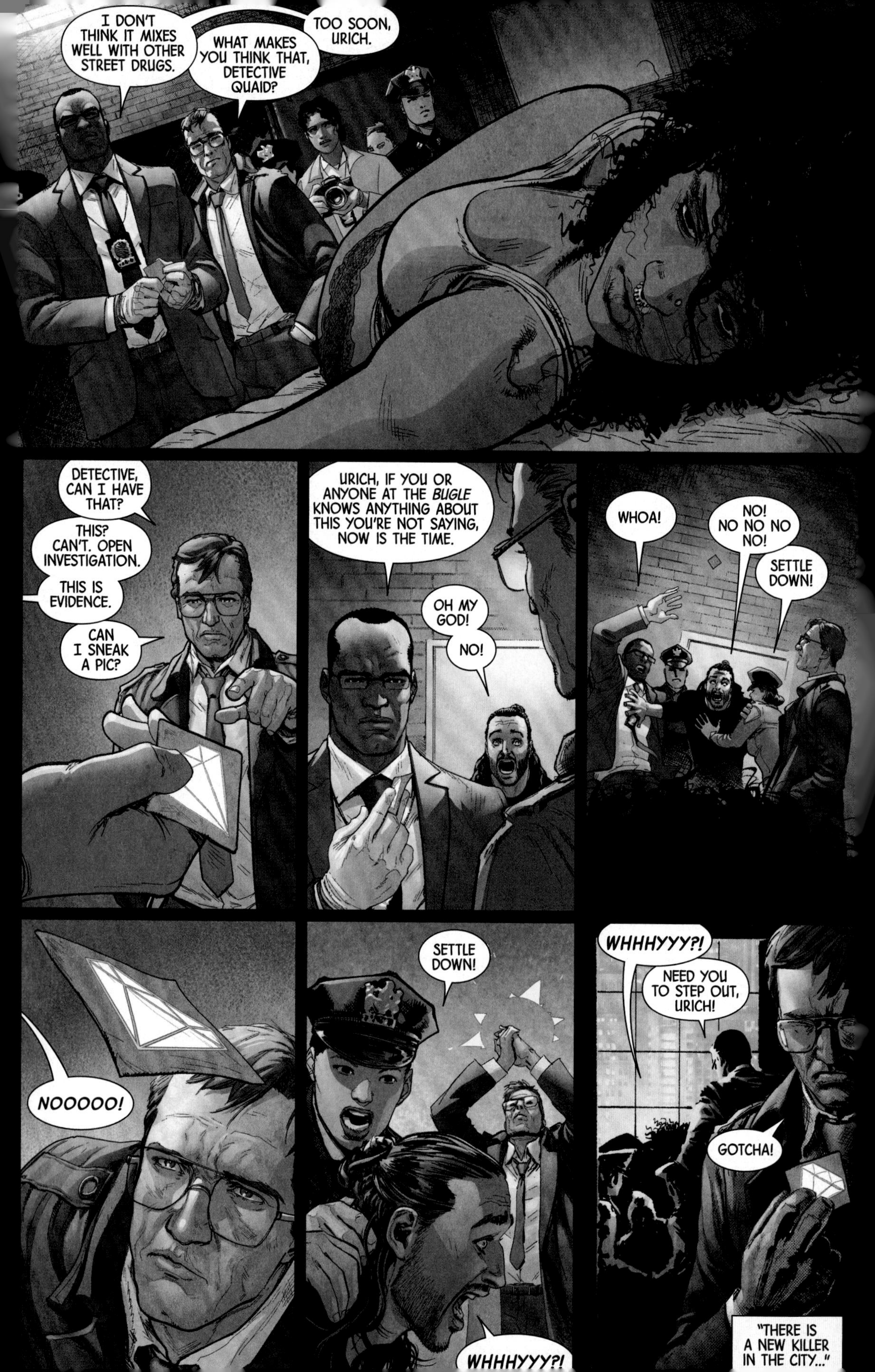
I DON'T THINK IT MIXES WELL WITH OTHER STREET DRUGS.
WHAT MAKES YOU THINK THAT, DETECTIVE QUAID?
TOO SOON, URICH.
DETECTIVE, CAN I HAVE THAT?
THIS? CAN'T. OPEN INVESTIGATION.
THIS IS EVIDENCE.
CAN I SNEAK A PIC?
URICH, IF YOU OR ANYONE AT THE *BUGLE* KNOWS ANYTHING ABOUT THIS YOU'RE NOT SAYING, NOW IS THE TIME.
OH MY GOD!
NO!
WHOA!
NO! NO NO NO NO!
SETTLE DOWN!
NOOOOO!
SETTLE DOWN!
WHHHYYY?!
WHHHYYY?!
NEED YOU TO STEP OUT, URICH!
GOTCHA!
"THERE IS A NEW KILLER IN THE CITY..."

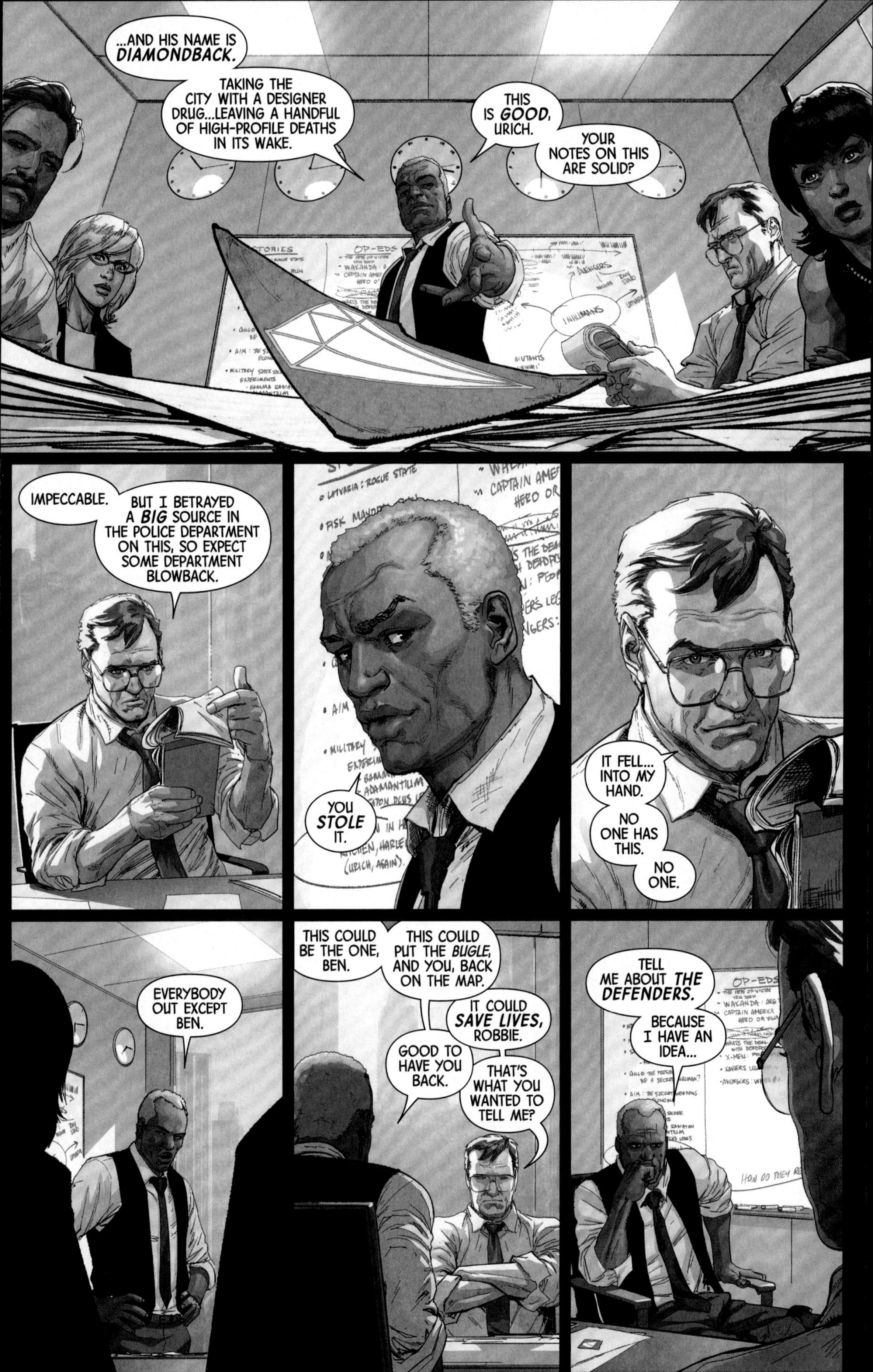
...AND HIS NAME IS *DIAMONDBACK.*
TAKING THE CITY WITH A DESIGNER DRUG...LEAVING A HANDFUL OF HIGH-PROFILE DEATHS IN ITS WAKE.
THIS IS *GOOD*, URICH.
YOUR NOTES ON THIS ARE SOLID?
IMPECCABLE.
BUT I BETRAYED A *BIG* SOURCE IN THE POLICE DEPARTMENT ON THIS, SO EXPECT SOME DEPARTMENT BLOWBACK.
YOU *STOLE* IT.
IT FELL... INTO MY HAND.
NO ONE HAS THIS.
NO ONE.
EVERYBODY OUT EXCEPT BEN.
THIS COULD BE THE ONE, BEN.
THIS COULD PUT THE *BUGLE*, AND YOU, BACK ON THE MAP.
IT COULD *SAVE LIVES,* ROBBIE.
GOOD TO HAVE YOU BACK.
THAT'S WHAT YOU WANTED TO TELL ME?
TELL ME ABOUT *THE DEFENDERS.*
BECAUSE I HAVE AN IDEA...

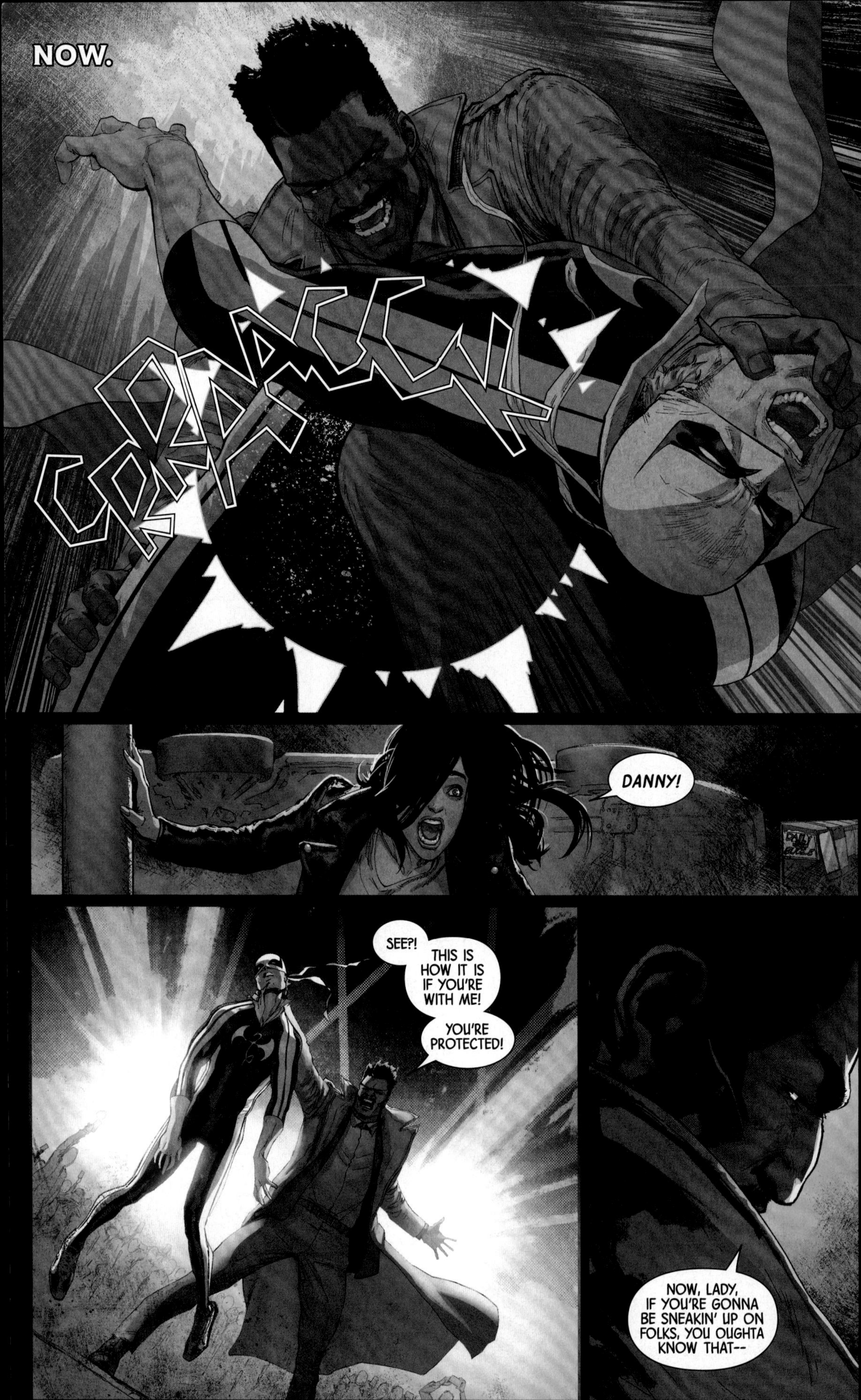
NOW.
CRRAACCK
DANNY!
SEE?!
THIS IS HOW IT IS IF YOU'RE WITH ME!
YOU'RE PROTECTED!
NOW, LADY, IF YOU'RE GONNA BE SNEAKIN' UP ON FOLKS, YOU OUGHTA KNOW THAT--

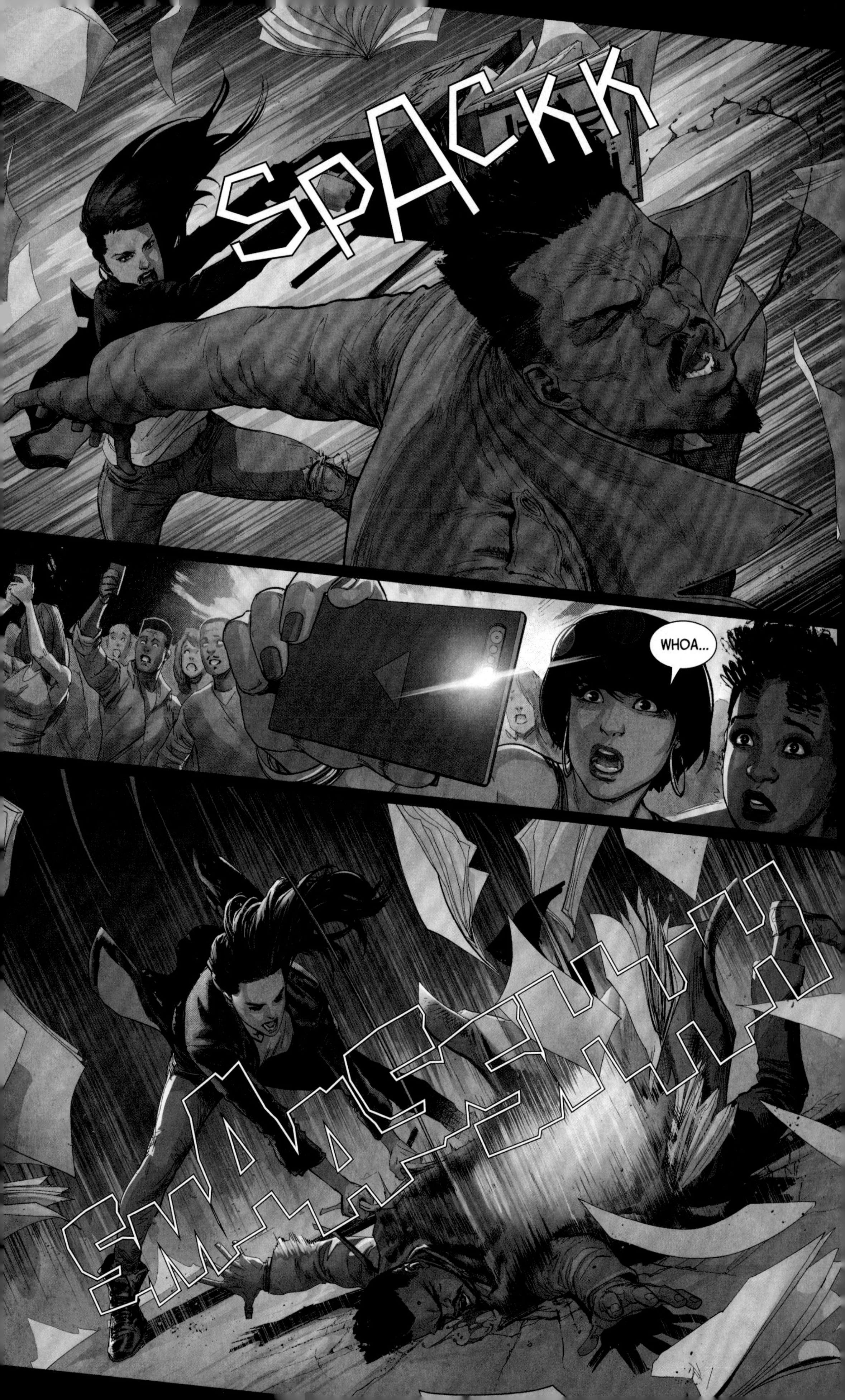
SPACKK
WHOA...
SMASSHHH

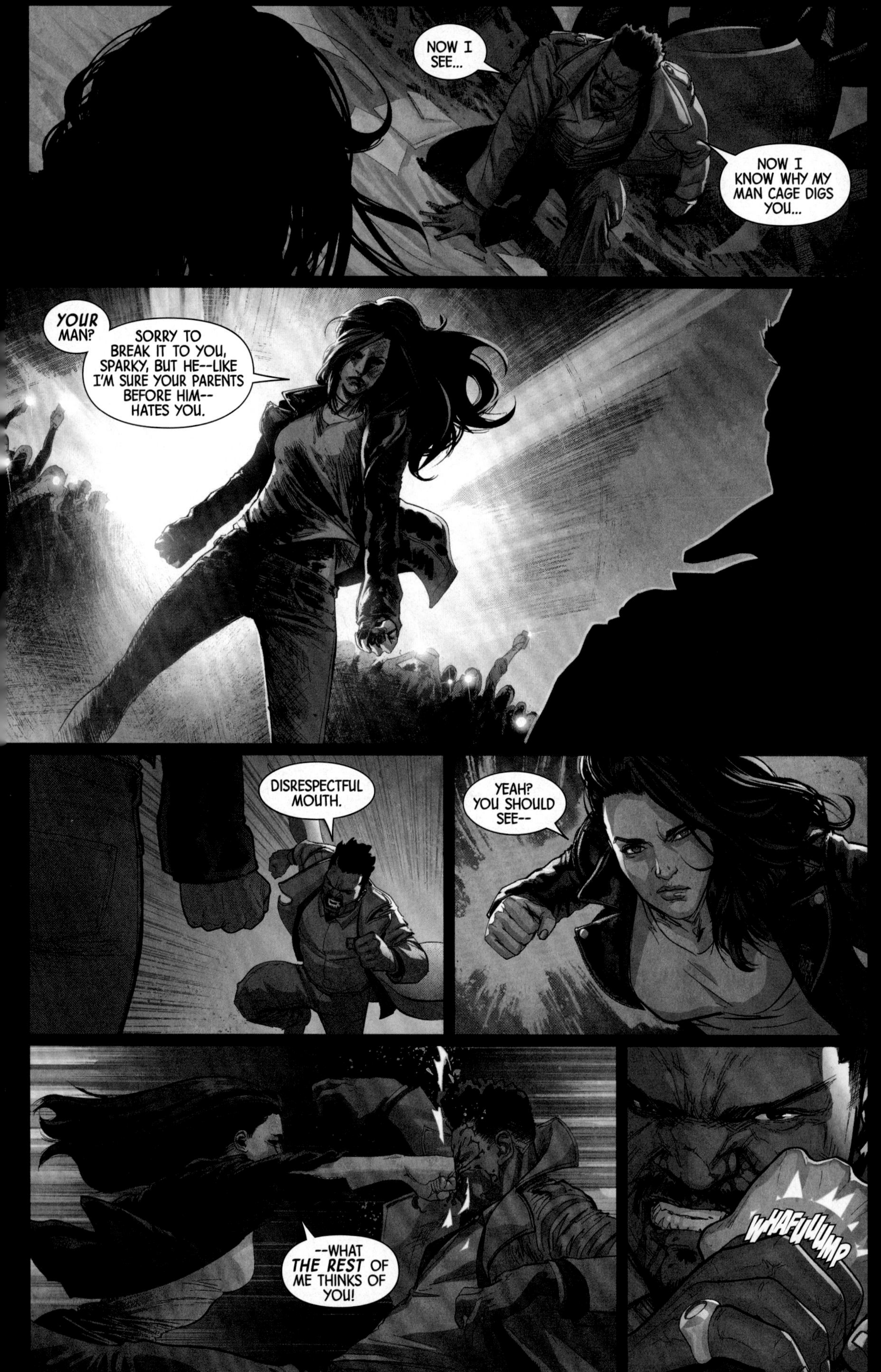
NOW I SEE...
NOW I KNOW WHY MY MAN CAGE DIGS YOU...
YOUR MAN?
SORRY TO BREAK IT TO YOU, SPARKY, BUT HE--LIKE I'M SURE YOUR PARENTS BEFORE HIM--HATES YOU.
DISRESPECTFUL MOUTH.
YEAH? YOU SHOULD SEE--
--WHAT THE REST OF ME THINKS OF YOU!
WHAFUUUMP

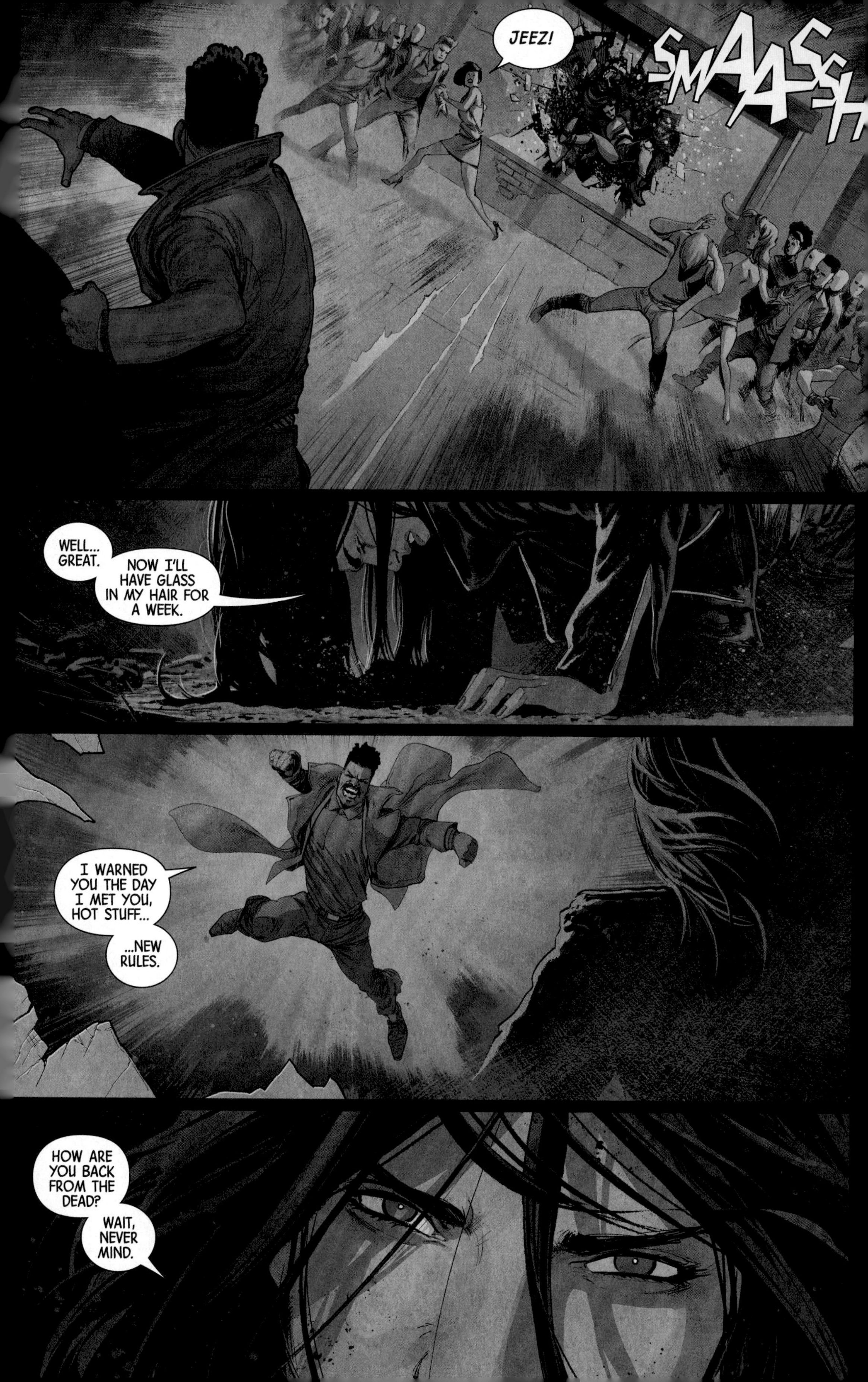
JEEZ!
SMAASSH
WELL... GREAT.
NOW I'LL HAVE GLASS IN MY HAIR FOR A WEEK.
I WARNED YOU THE DAY I MET YOU, HOT STUFF...
...NEW RULES.
HOW ARE YOU BACK FROM THE DEAD?
WAIT, NEVER MIND.

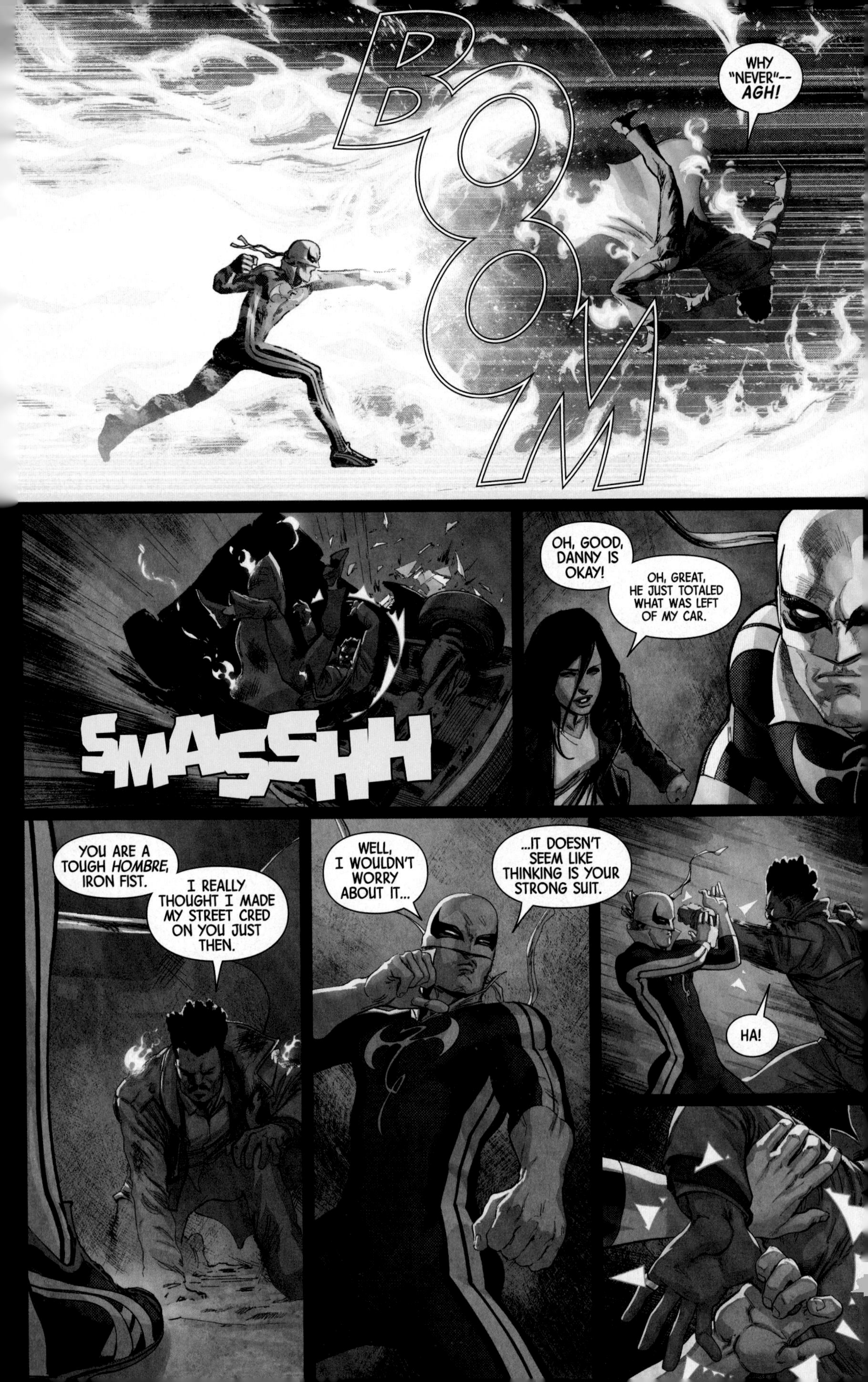
BOOM
WHY "NEVER"-- AGH!
SMASSHH
OH, GOOD, DANNY IS OKAY!
OH, GREAT, HE JUST TOTALED WHAT WAS LEFT OF MY CAR.
YOU ARE A TOUGH *HOMBRE*, IRON FIST.
I REALLY THOUGHT I MADE MY STREET CRED ON YOU JUST THEN.
WELL, I WOULDN'T WORRY ABOUT IT...
...IT DOESN'T SEEM LIKE THINKING IS YOUR STRONG SUIT.
HA!

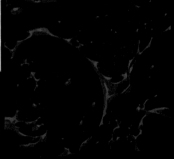

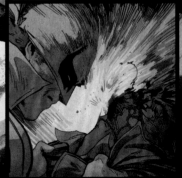

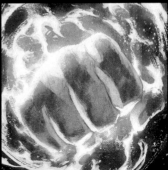

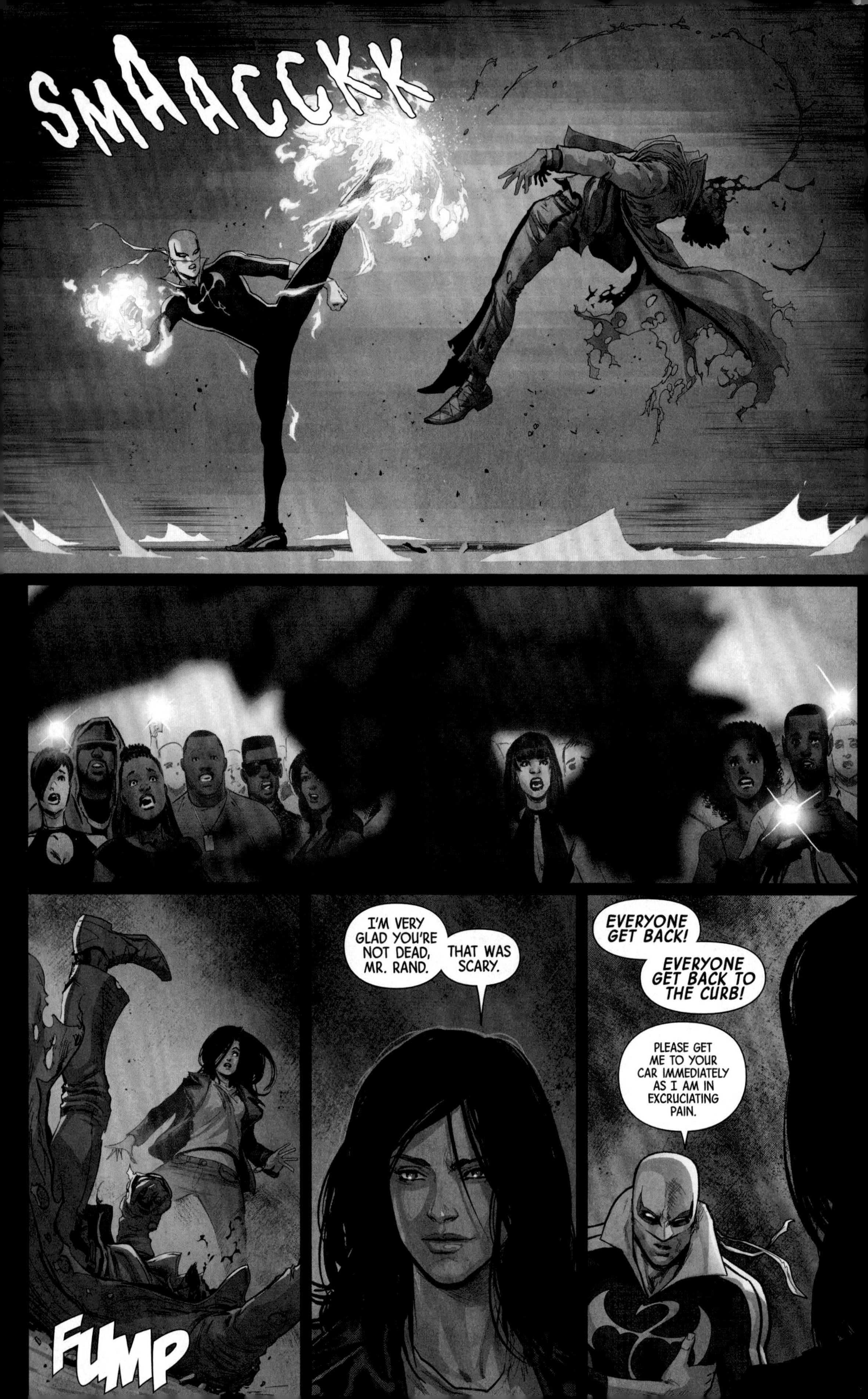
SMAACCKK
FUMP
I'M VERY GLAD YOU'RE NOT DEAD, MR. RAND.
THAT WAS SCARY.
EVERYONE GET BACK!
EVERYONE GET BACK TO THE CURB!
PLEASE GET ME TO YOUR CAR IMMEDIATELY AS I AM IN EXCRUCIATING PAIN.

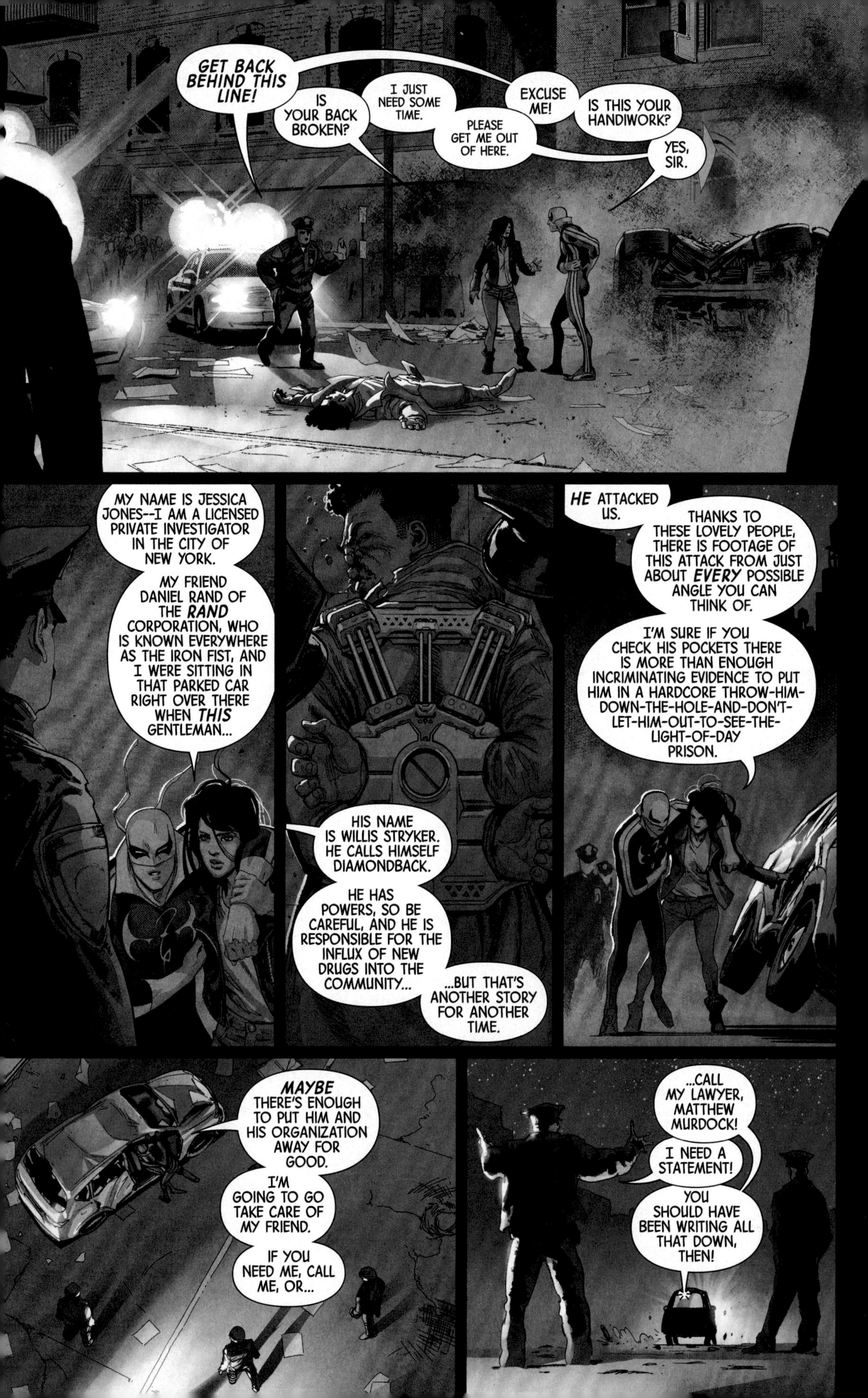
GET BACK BEHIND THIS LINE!
IS YOUR BACK BROKEN?
I JUST NEED SOME TIME.
PLEASE GET ME OUT OF HERE.
EXCUSE ME!
IS THIS YOUR HANDIWORK?
YES, SIR.
MY NAME IS JESSICA JONES--I AM A LICENSED PRIVATE INVESTIGATOR IN THE CITY OF NEW YORK.
MY FRIEND DANIEL RAND OF THE RAND CORPORATION, WHO IS KNOWN EVERYWHERE AS THE IRON FIST, AND I WERE SITTING IN THAT PARKED CAR RIGHT OVER THERE WHEN THIS GENTLEMAN...
HIS NAME IS WILLIS STRYKER. HE CALLS HIMSELF DIAMONDBACK.
HE HAS POWERS, SO BE CAREFUL, AND HE IS RESPONSIBLE FOR THE INFLUX OF NEW DRUGS INTO THE COMMUNITY...
...BUT THAT'S ANOTHER STORY FOR ANOTHER TIME.
HE ATTACKED US.
THANKS TO THESE LOVELY PEOPLE, THERE IS FOOTAGE OF THIS ATTACK FROM JUST ABOUT EVERY POSSIBLE ANGLE YOU CAN THINK OF.
I'M SURE IF YOU CHECK HIS POCKETS THERE IS MORE THAN ENOUGH INCRIMINATING EVIDENCE TO PUT HIM IN A HARDCORE THROW-HIM-DOWN-THE-HOLE-AND-DON'T-LET-HIM-OUT-TO-SEE-THE-LIGHT-OF-DAY PRISON.
MAYBE THERE'S ENOUGH TO PUT HIM AND HIS ORGANIZATION AWAY FOR GOOD.
I'M GOING TO GO TAKE CARE OF MY FRIEND.
IF YOU NEED ME, CALL ME, OR...
...CALL MY LAWYER, MATTHEW MURDOCK!
I NEED A STATEMENT!
YOU SHOULD HAVE BEEN WRITING ALL THAT DOWN, THEN!

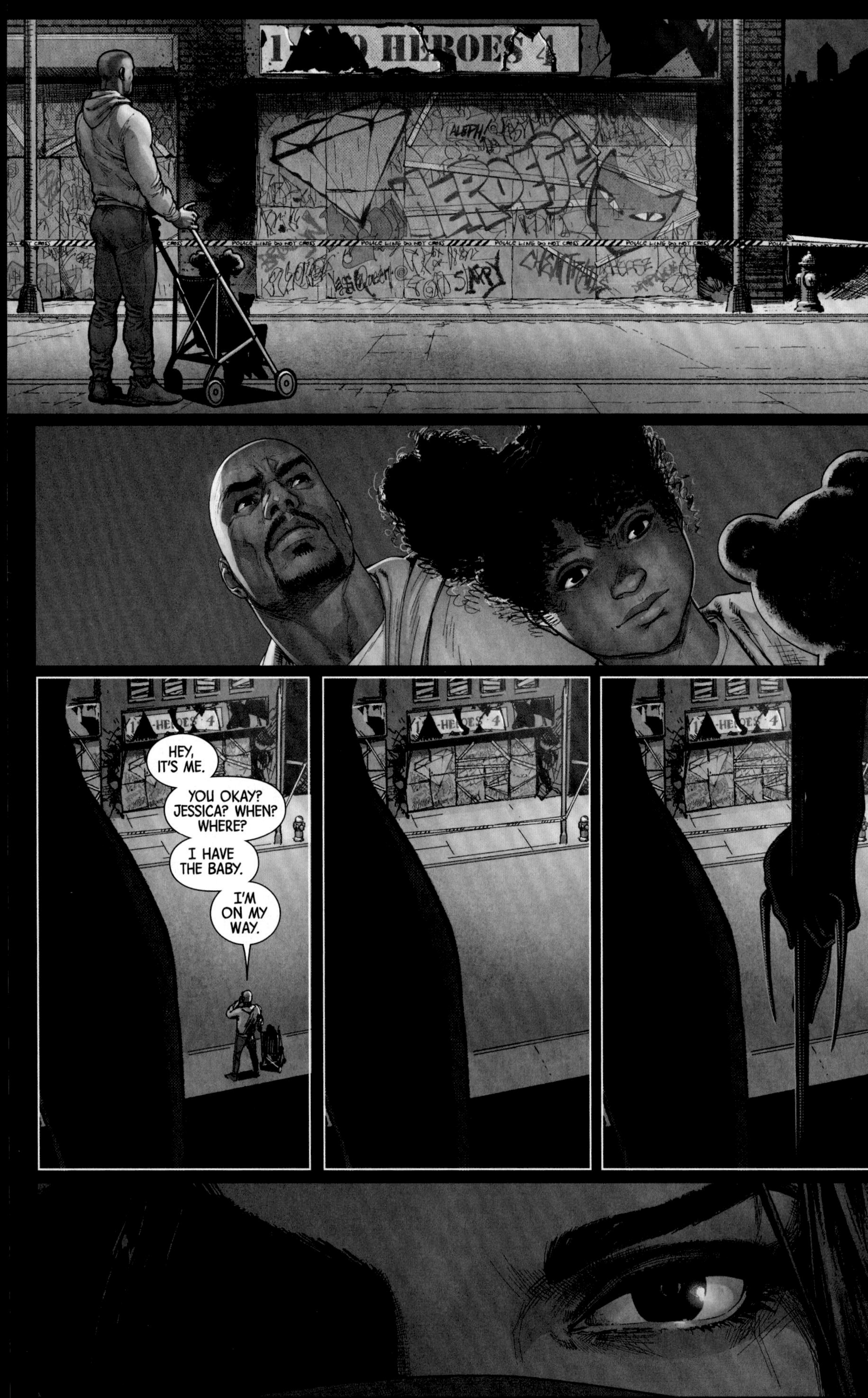
HEROES 4
HEY, IT'S ME.
YOU OKAY? JESSICA? WHEN? WHERE?
I HAVE THE BABY.
I'M ON MY WAY.

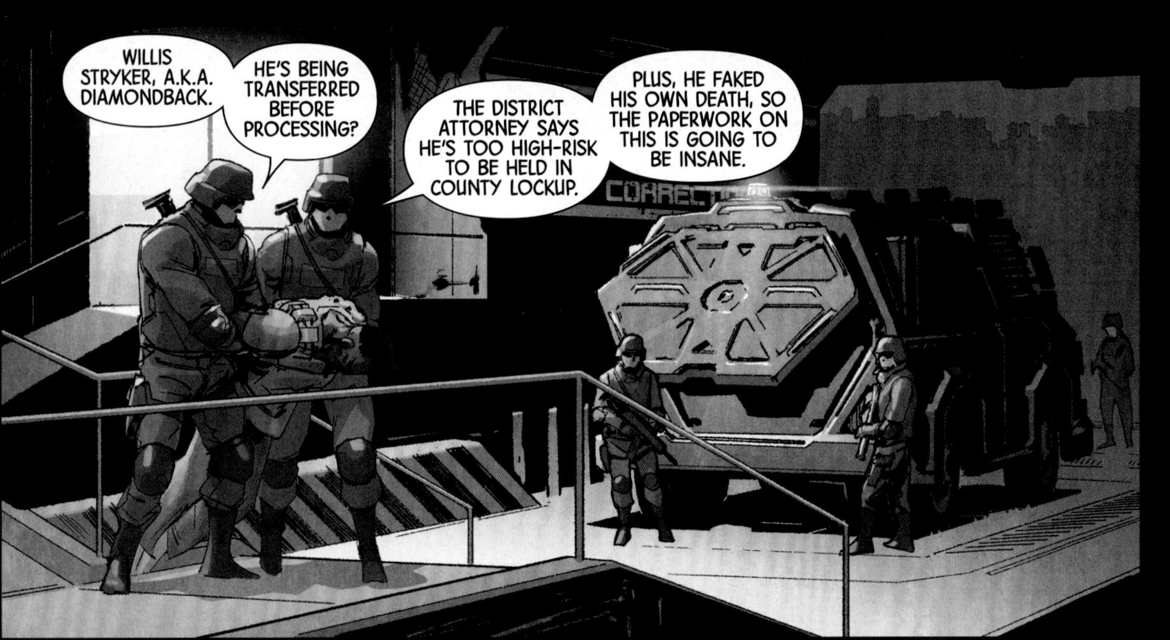
WILLIS STRYKER, A.K.A. DIAMONDBACK.
HE'S BEING TRANSFERRED BEFORE PROCESSING?
THE DISTRICT ATTORNEY SAYS HE'S TOO HIGH-RISK TO BE HELD IN COUNTY LOCKUP.
PLUS, HE FAKED HIS OWN DEATH, SO THE PAPERWORK ON THIS IS GOING TO BE INSANE.

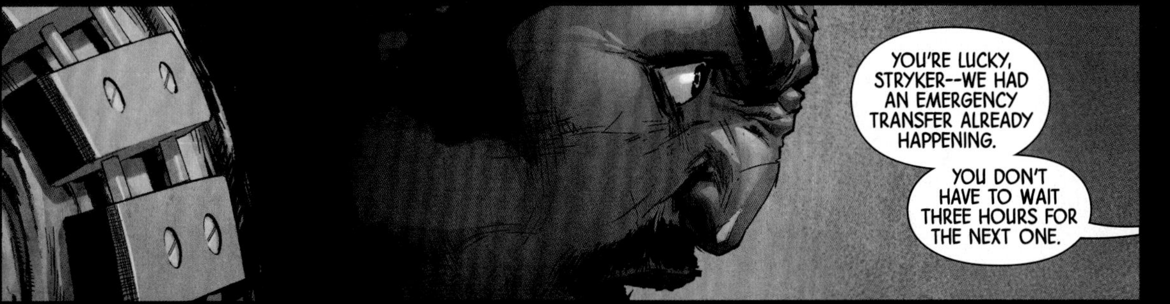
YOU'RE LUCKY, STRYKER--WE HAD AN EMERGENCY TRANSFER ALREADY HAPPENING.
YOU DON'T HAVE TO WAIT THREE HOURS FOR THE NEXT ONE.

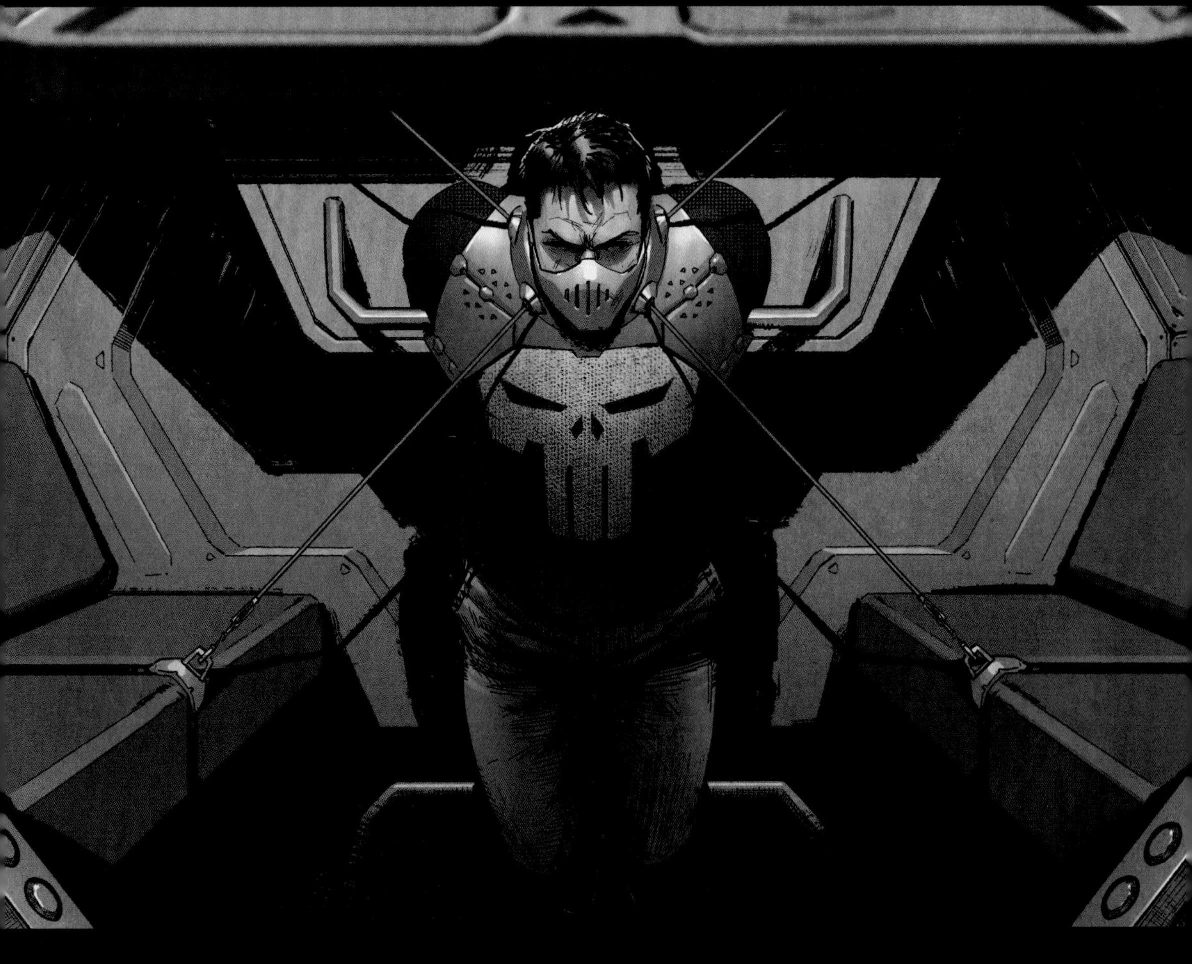

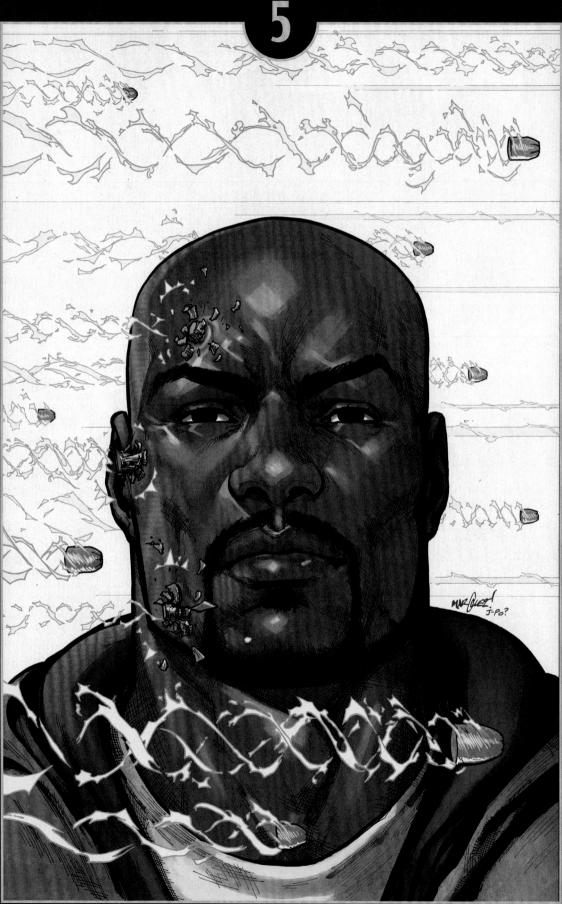

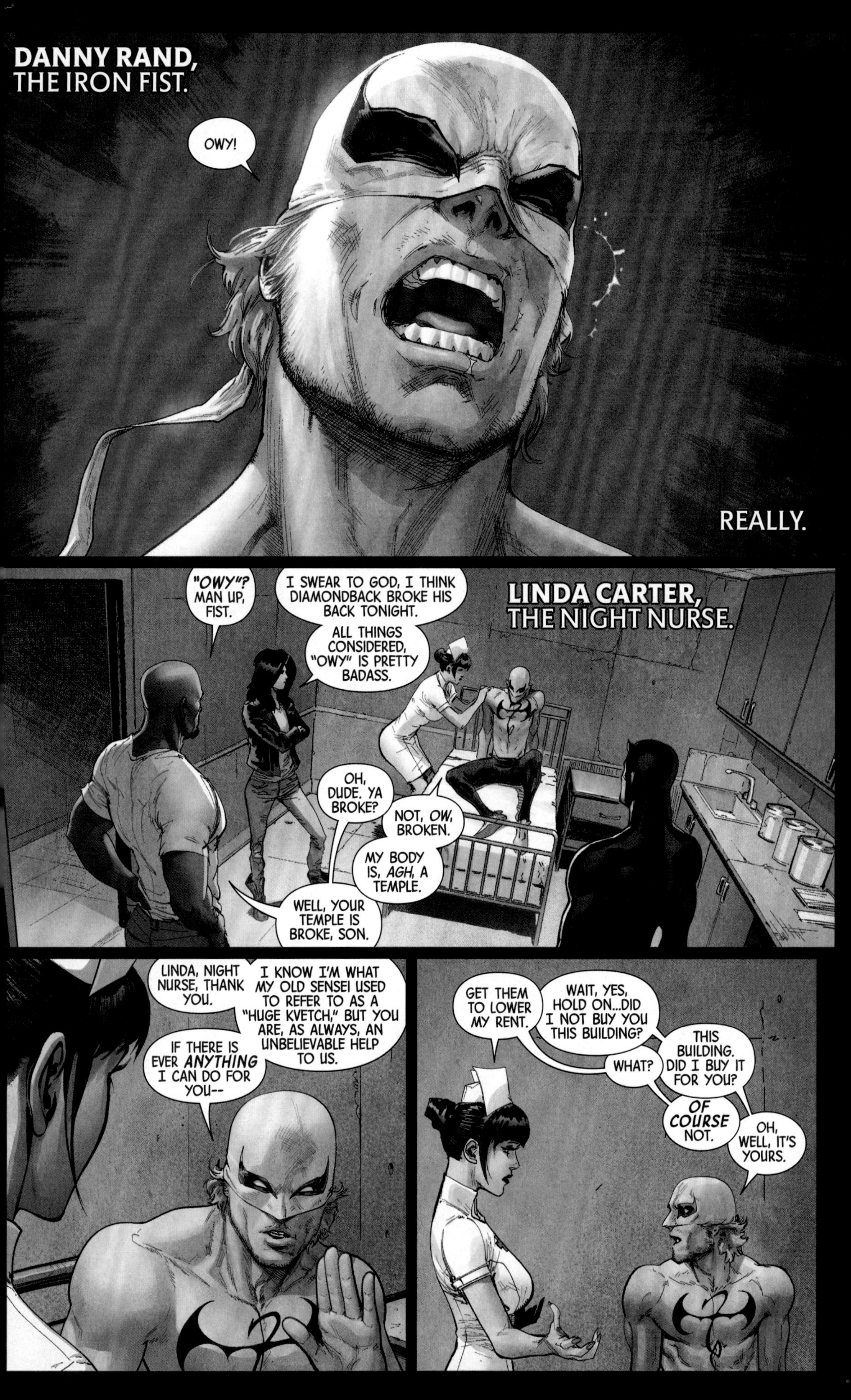
DANNY RAND, THE IRON FIST.
OWY!
REALLY.
"OWY"? MAN UP, FIST.
I SWEAR TO GOD, I THINK DIAMONDBACK BROKE HIS BACK TONIGHT.
ALL THINGS CONSIDERED, "OWY" IS PRETTY BADASS.
LINDA CARTER, THE NIGHT NURSE.
OH, DUDE. YA BROKE?
NOT, OW, BROKEN.
MY BODY IS, AGH, A TEMPLE.
WELL, YOUR TEMPLE IS BROKE, SON.
LINDA, NIGHT NURSE, THANK YOU.
I KNOW I'M WHAT MY OLD SENSEI USED TO REFER TO AS A "HUGE KVETCH," BUT YOU ARE, AS ALWAYS, AN UNBELIEVABLE HELP TO US.
IF THERE IS EVER ANYTHING I CAN DO FOR YOU--
GET THEM TO LOWER MY RENT.
WAIT, YES, HOLD ON...DID I NOT BUY YOU THIS BUILDING?
WHAT?
THIS BUILDING. DID I BUY IT FOR YOU?
OF COURSE NOT.
OH, WELL, IT'S YOURS.

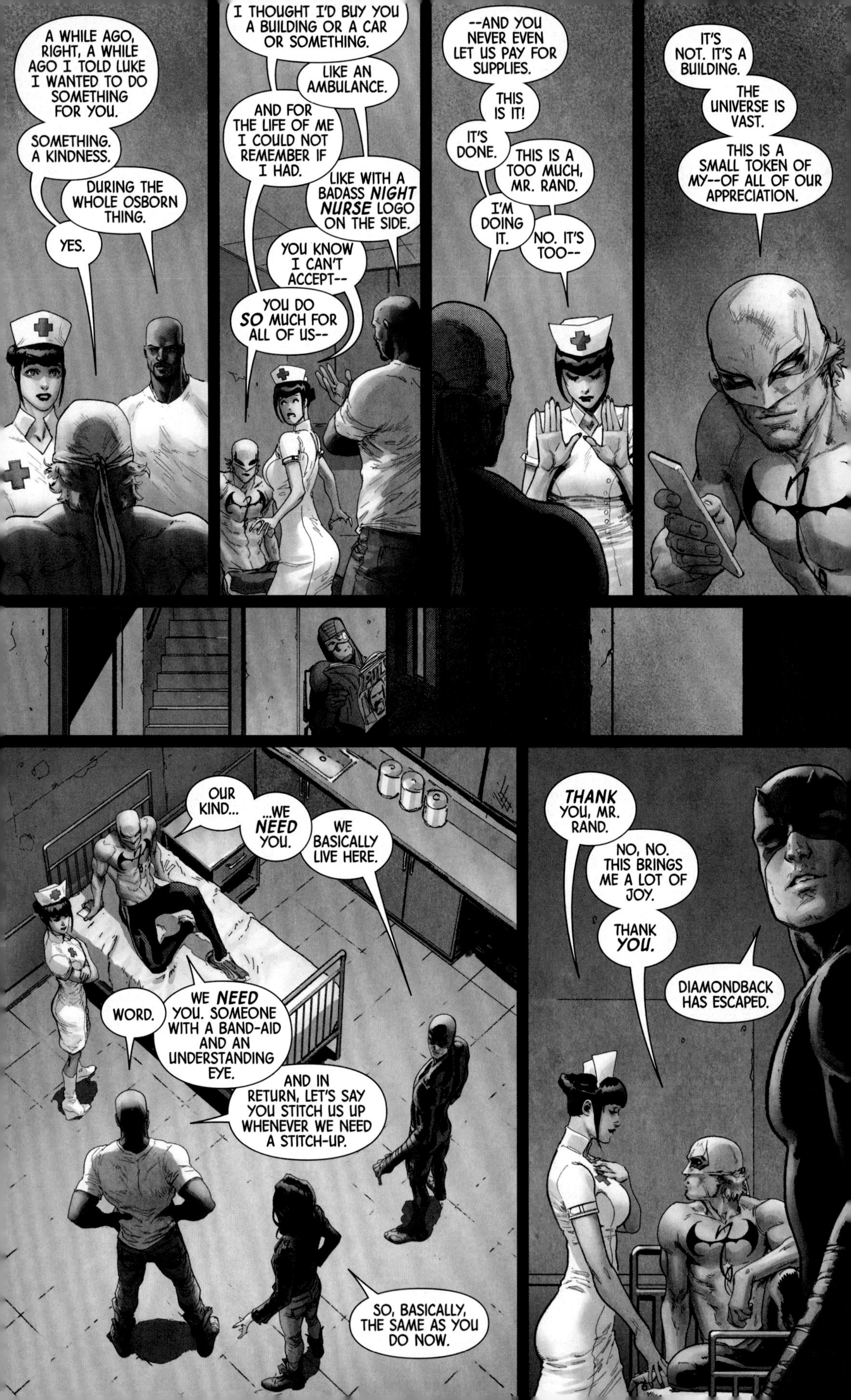
A WHILE AGO, RIGHT, A WHILE AGO I TOLD LUKE I WANTED TO DO SOMETHING FOR YOU.
SOMETHING. A KINDNESS.
DURING THE WHOLE OSBORN THING.
YES.
I THOUGHT I'D BUY YOU A BUILDING OR A CAR OR SOMETHING.
LIKE AN AMBULANCE.
AND FOR THE LIFE OF ME I COULD NOT REMEMBER IF I HAD.
LIKE WITH A BADASS **NIGHT NURSE** LOGO ON THE SIDE.
YOU KNOW I CAN'T ACCEPT--
YOU DO **SO** MUCH FOR ALL OF US--
--AND YOU NEVER EVEN LET US PAY FOR SUPPLIES.
THIS IS IT!
IT'S DONE.
THIS IS A TOO MUCH, MR. RAND.
I'M DOING IT.
NO. IT'S TOO--
IT'S NOT. IT'S A BUILDING.
THE UNIVERSE IS VAST.
THIS IS A SMALL TOKEN OF MY--OF ALL OF OUR APPRECIATION.
OUR KIND...
...WE **NEED** YOU.
WE BASICALLY LIVE HERE.
WORD.
WE **NEED** YOU. SOMEONE WITH A BAND-AID AND AN UNDERSTANDING EYE.
AND IN RETURN, LET'S SAY YOU STITCH US UP WHENEVER WE NEED A STITCH-UP.
SO, BASICALLY, THE SAME AS YOU DO NOW.
THANK YOU, MR. RAND.
NO, NO. THIS BRINGS ME A LOT OF JOY.
THANK **YOU.**
DIAMONDBACK HAS ESCAPED.

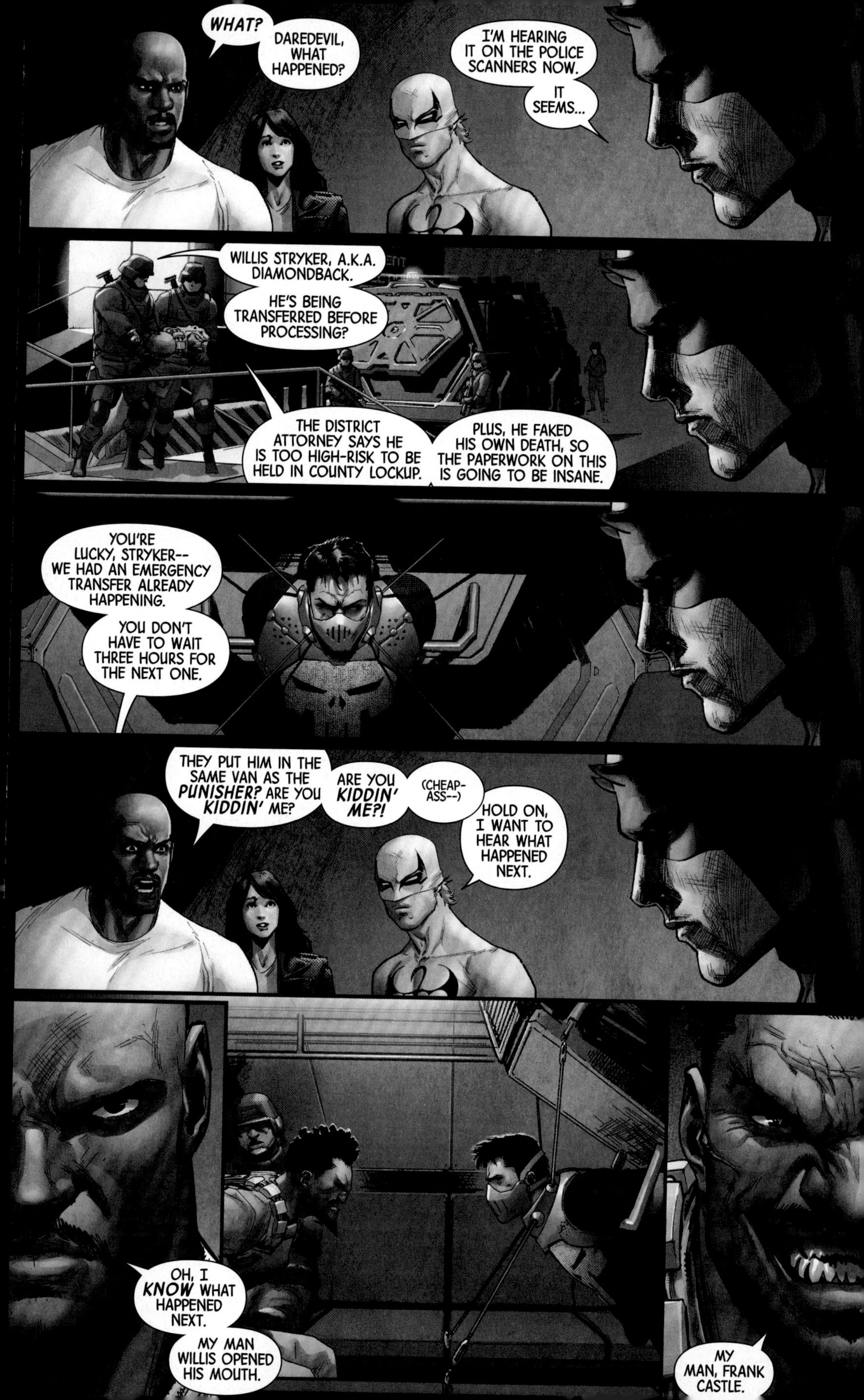

WHAT?
DAREDEVIL, WHAT HAPPENED?
I'M HEARING IT ON THE POLICE SCANNERS NOW.
IT SEEMS...
WILLIS STRYKER, A.K.A. DIAMONDBACK.
HE'S BEING TRANSFERRED BEFORE PROCESSING?
THE DISTRICT ATTORNEY SAYS HE IS TOO HIGH-RISK TO BE HELD IN COUNTY LOCKUP.
PLUS, HE FAKED HIS OWN DEATH, SO THE PAPERWORK ON THIS IS GOING TO BE INSANE.
YOU'RE LUCKY, STRYKER-- WE HAD AN EMERGENCY TRANSFER ALREADY HAPPENING.
YOU DON'T HAVE TO WAIT THREE HOURS FOR THE NEXT ONE.
THEY PUT HIM IN THE SAME VAN AS THE *PUNISHER?* ARE YOU *KIDDIN'* ME?
ARE YOU *KIDDIN' ME?!*
(CHEAP-ASS--)
HOLD ON, I WANT TO HEAR WHAT HAPPENED NEXT.
OH, I *KNOW* WHAT HAPPENED NEXT.
MY MAN WILLIS OPENED HIS MOUTH.
MY MAN, FRANK CASTLE.

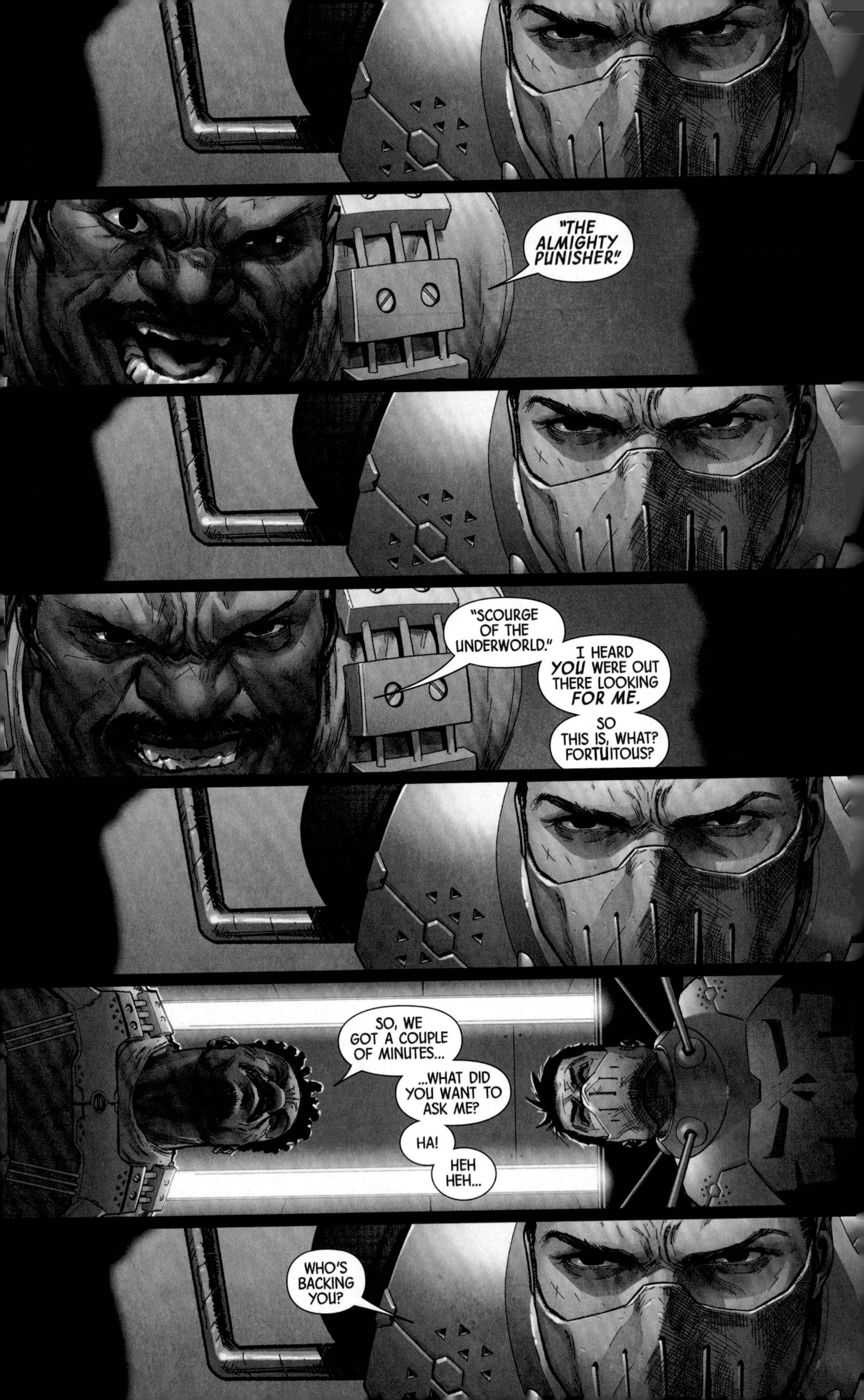
"THE ALMIGHTY PUNISHER!"
"SCOURGE OF THE UNDERWORLD."
I HEARD YOU WERE OUT THERE LOOKING FOR ME.
SO THIS IS, WHAT? FORTUITOUS?
SO, WE GOT A COUPLE OF MINUTES...
...WHAT DID YOU WANT TO ASK ME?
HA!
HEH HEH...
WHO'S BACKING YOU?

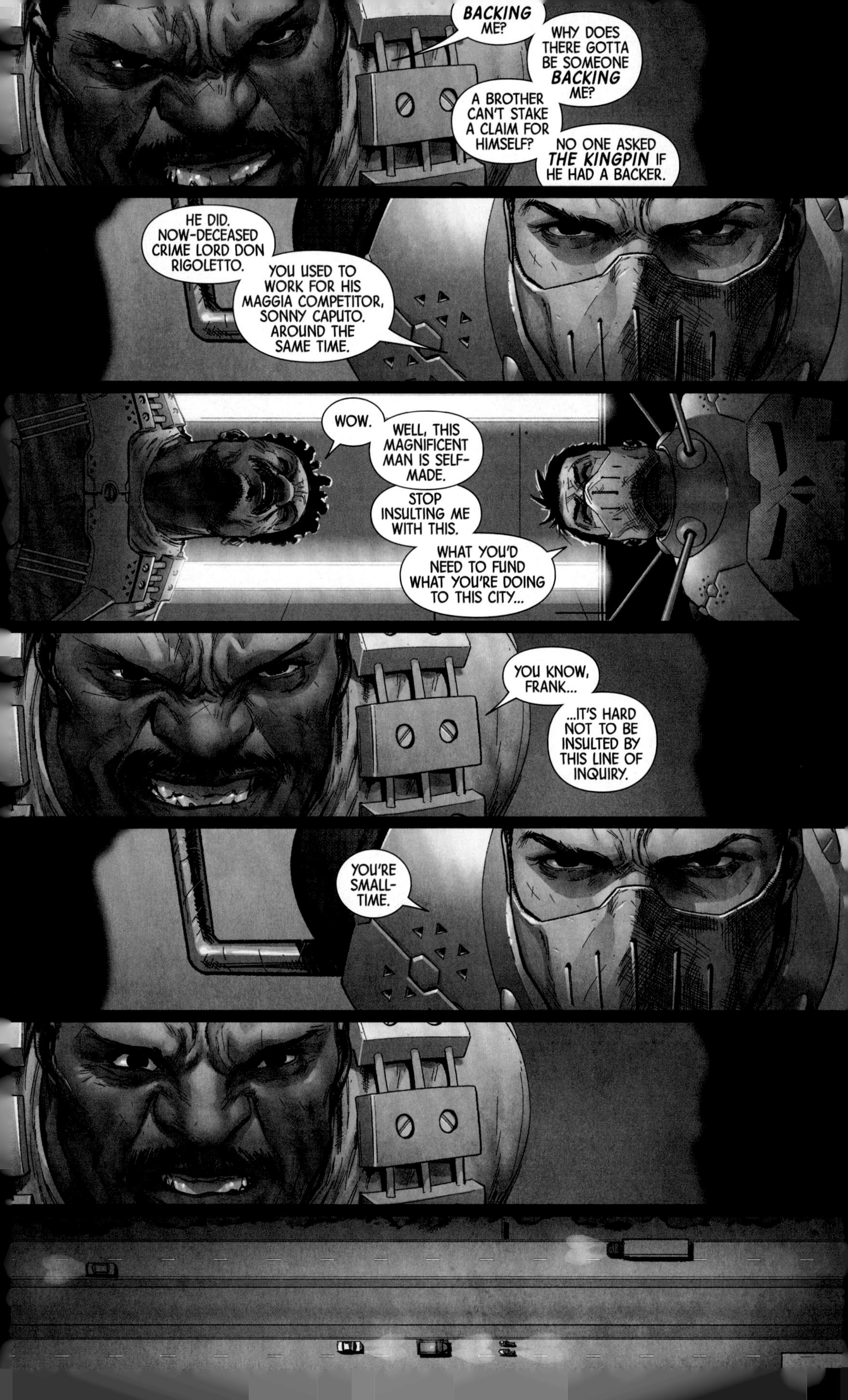
BACKING ME?
WHY DOES THERE GOTTA BE SOMEONE BACKING ME?
A BROTHER CAN'T STAKE A CLAIM FOR HIMSELF?
NO ONE ASKED THE KINGPIN IF HE HAD A BACKER.
HE DID. NOW-DECEASED CRIME LORD DON RIGOLETTO.
YOU USED TO WORK FOR HIS MAGGIA COMPETITOR, SONNY CAPUTO. AROUND THE SAME TIME.
WOW.
WELL, THIS MAGNIFICENT MAN IS SELF-MADE.
STOP INSULTING ME WITH THIS.
WHAT YOU'D NEED TO FUND WHAT YOU'RE DOING TO THIS CITY...
YOU KNOW, FRANK...
...IT'S HARD NOT TO BE INSULTED BY THIS LINE OF INQUIRY.
YOU'RE SMALL-TIME.

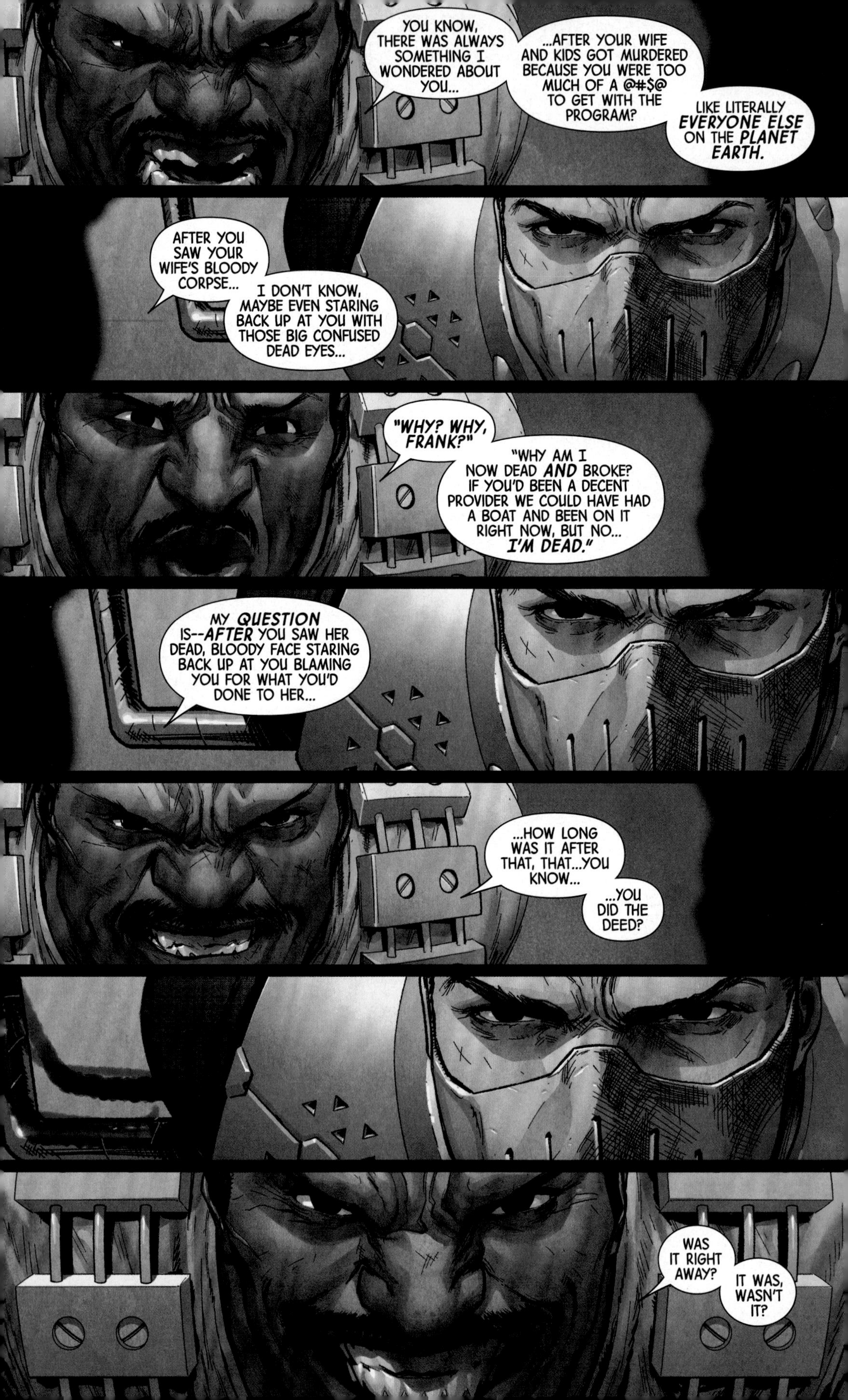
YOU KNOW, THERE WAS ALWAYS SOMETHING I WONDERED ABOUT YOU...
...AFTER YOUR WIFE AND KIDS GOT MURDERED BECAUSE YOU WERE TOO MUCH OF A @#$@ TO GET WITH THE PROGRAM?
LIKE LITERALLY EVERYONE ELSE ON THE PLANET EARTH.
AFTER YOU SAW YOUR WIFE'S BLOODY CORPSE...
I DON'T KNOW, MAYBE EVEN STARING BACK UP AT YOU WITH THOSE BIG CONFUSED DEAD EYES...
"WHY? WHY, FRANK?"
"WHY AM I NOW DEAD AND BROKE? IF YOU'D BEEN A DECENT PROVIDER WE COULD HAVE HAD A BOAT AND BEEN ON IT RIGHT NOW, BUT NO... I'M DEAD."
MY QUESTION IS--AFTER YOU SAW HER DEAD, BLOODY FACE STARING BACK UP AT YOU BLAMING YOU FOR WHAT YOU'D DONE TO HER...
...HOW LONG WAS IT AFTER THAT, THAT...YOU KNOW...
...YOU DID THE DEED?
WAS IT RIGHT AWAY?
IT WAS, WASN'T IT?

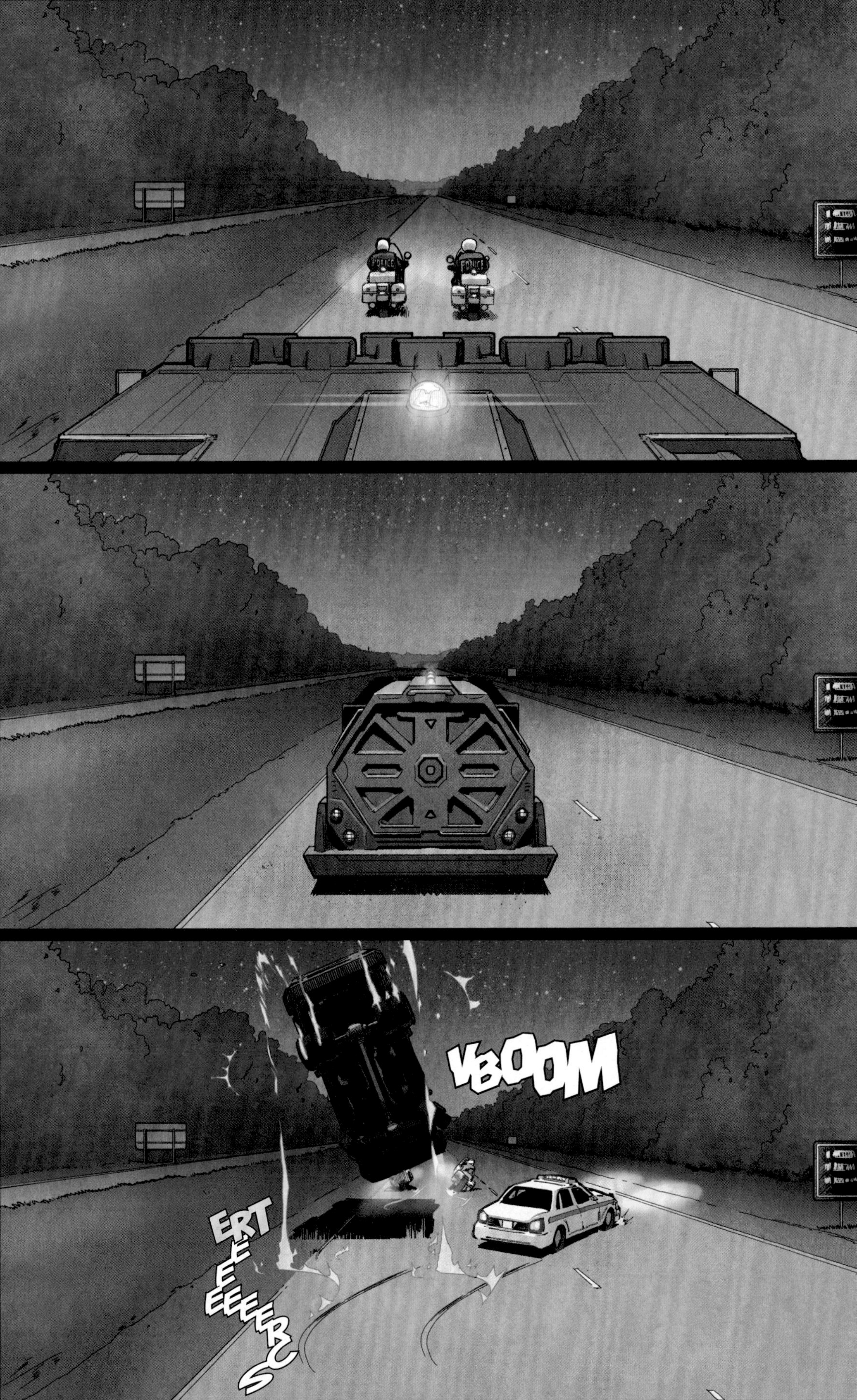
VBOOM
SCREEEEEEERT

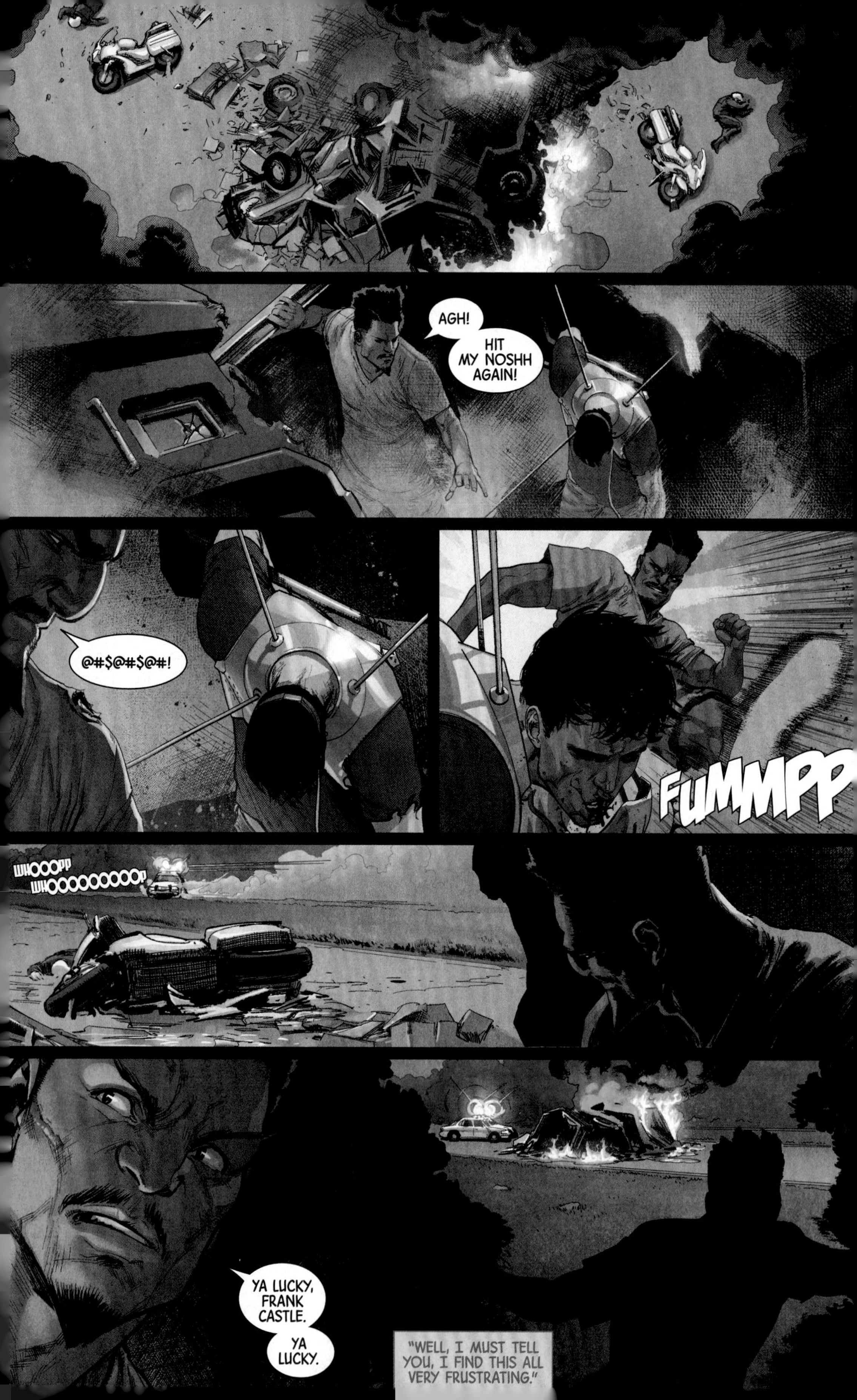
AGH!
HIT MY NOSHH AGAIN!
@#$@#$@#!
FUMMPP
WHOOOPP
WHOOOOOOOOOOP
YA LUCKY, FRANK CASTLE.
YA LUCKY.
"WELL, I MUST TELL YOU, I FIND THIS ALL VERY FRUSTRATING."

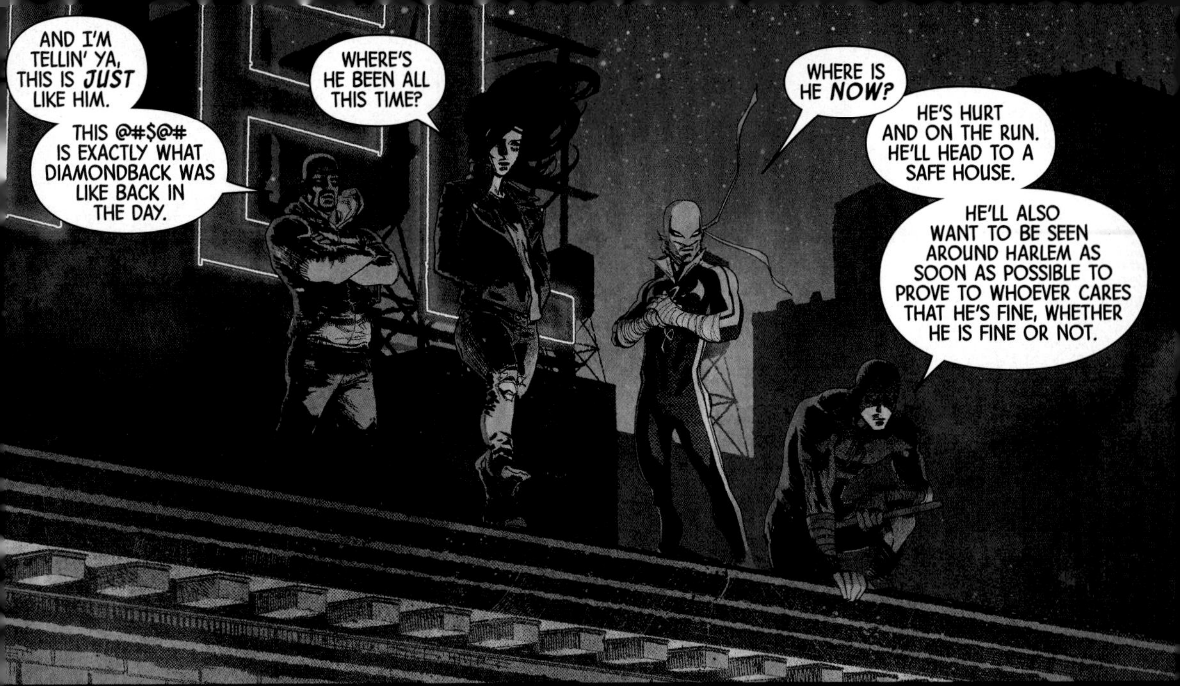
AND I'M TELLIN' YA, THIS IS JUST LIKE HIM.
THIS @#$@# IS EXACTLY WHAT DIAMONDBACK WAS LIKE BACK IN THE DAY.
WHERE'S HE BEEN ALL THIS TIME?
WHERE IS HE NOW?
HE'S HURT AND ON THE RUN. HE'LL HEAD TO A SAFE HOUSE.
HE'LL ALSO WANT TO BE SEEN AROUND HARLEM AS SOON AS POSSIBLE TO PROVE TO WHOEVER CARES THAT HE'S FINE, WHETHER HE IS FINE OR NOT.

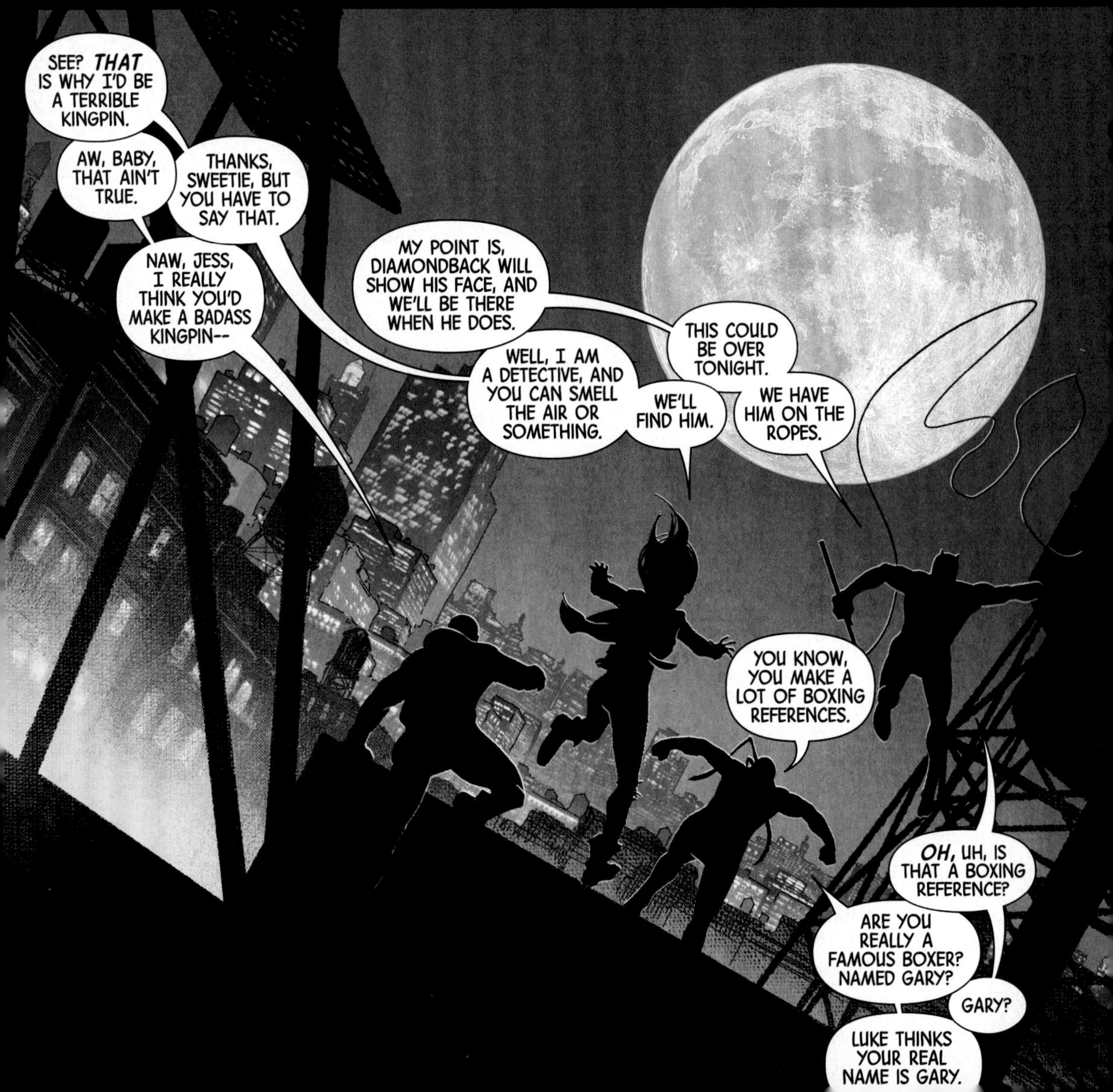
SEE? THAT IS WHY I'D BE A TERRIBLE KINGPIN.
AW, BABY, THAT AIN'T TRUE.
THANKS, SWEETIE, BUT YOU HAVE TO SAY THAT.
NAW, JESS, I REALLY THINK YOU'D MAKE A BADASS KINGPIN--
MY POINT IS, DIAMONDBACK WILL SHOW HIS FACE, AND WE'LL BE THERE WHEN HE DOES.
WELL, I AM A DETECTIVE, AND YOU CAN SMELL THE AIR OR SOMETHING.
THIS COULD BE OVER TONIGHT.
WE'LL FIND HIM.
WE HAVE HIM ON THE ROPES.
YOU KNOW, YOU MAKE A LOT OF BOXING REFERENCES.
OH, UH, IS THAT A BOXING REFERENCE?
ARE YOU REALLY A FAMOUS BOXER? NAMED GARY?
GARY?
LUKE THINKS YOUR REAL NAME IS GARY.

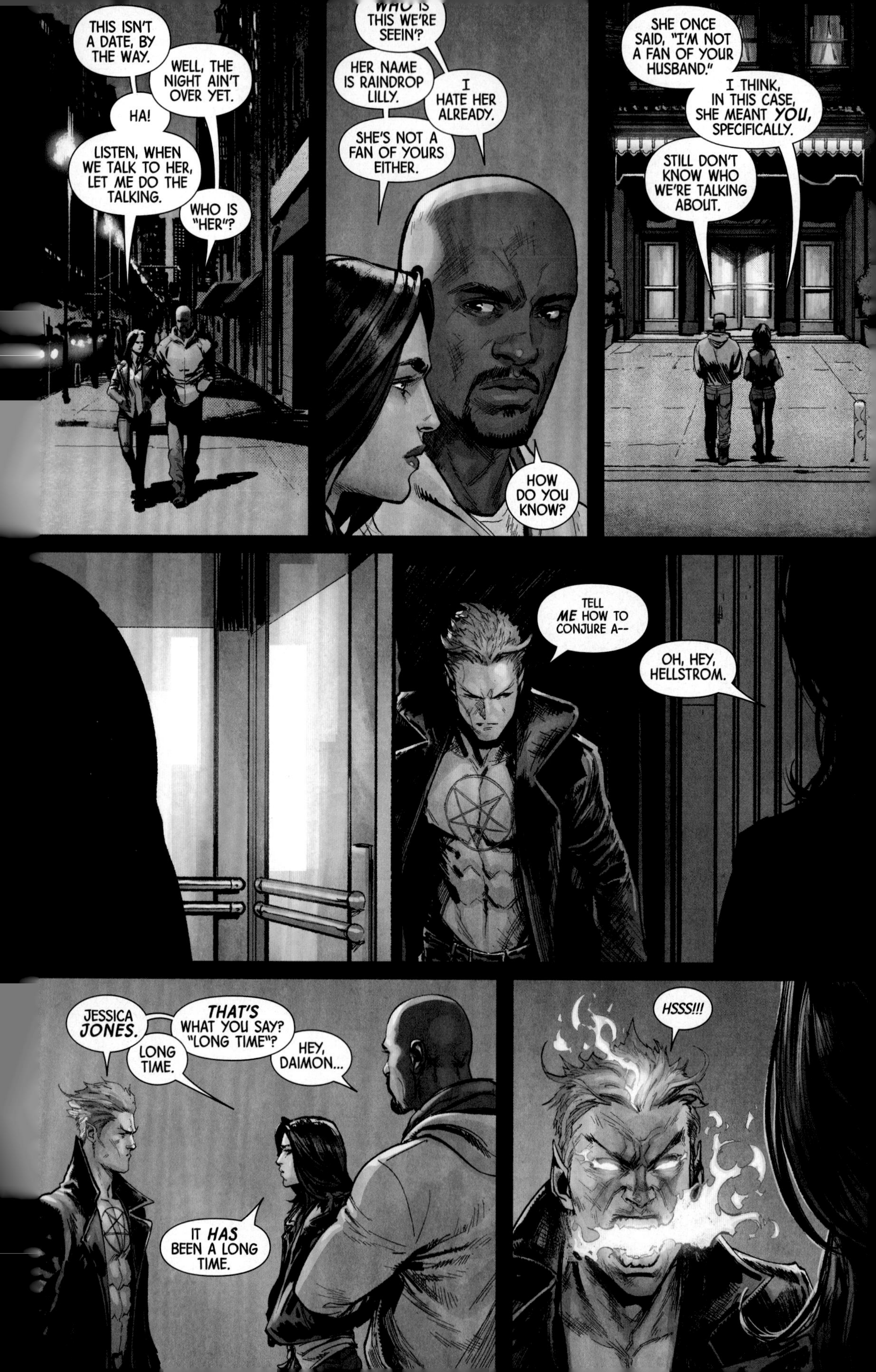
THIS ISN'T A DATE, BY THE WAY.
WELL, THE NIGHT AIN'T OVER YET.
HA!
LISTEN, WHEN WE TALK TO HER, LET ME DO THE TALKING.
WHO IS "HER"?
WHO IS THIS WE'RE SEEIN'?
HER NAME IS RAINDROP LILLY.
I HATE HER ALREADY.
SHE'S NOT A FAN OF YOURS EITHER.
HOW DO YOU KNOW?
SHE ONCE SAID, "I'M NOT A FAN OF YOUR HUSBAND."
I THINK, IN THIS CASE, SHE MEANT YOU, SPECIFICALLY.
STILL DON'T KNOW WHO WE'RE TALKING ABOUT.
TELL ME HOW TO CONJURE A--
OH, HEY, HELLSTROM.
JESSICA JONES.
LONG TIME.
THAT'S WHAT YOU SAY? "LONG TIME"?
HEY, DAIMON...
IT HAS BEEN A LONG TIME.
HSSS!!!

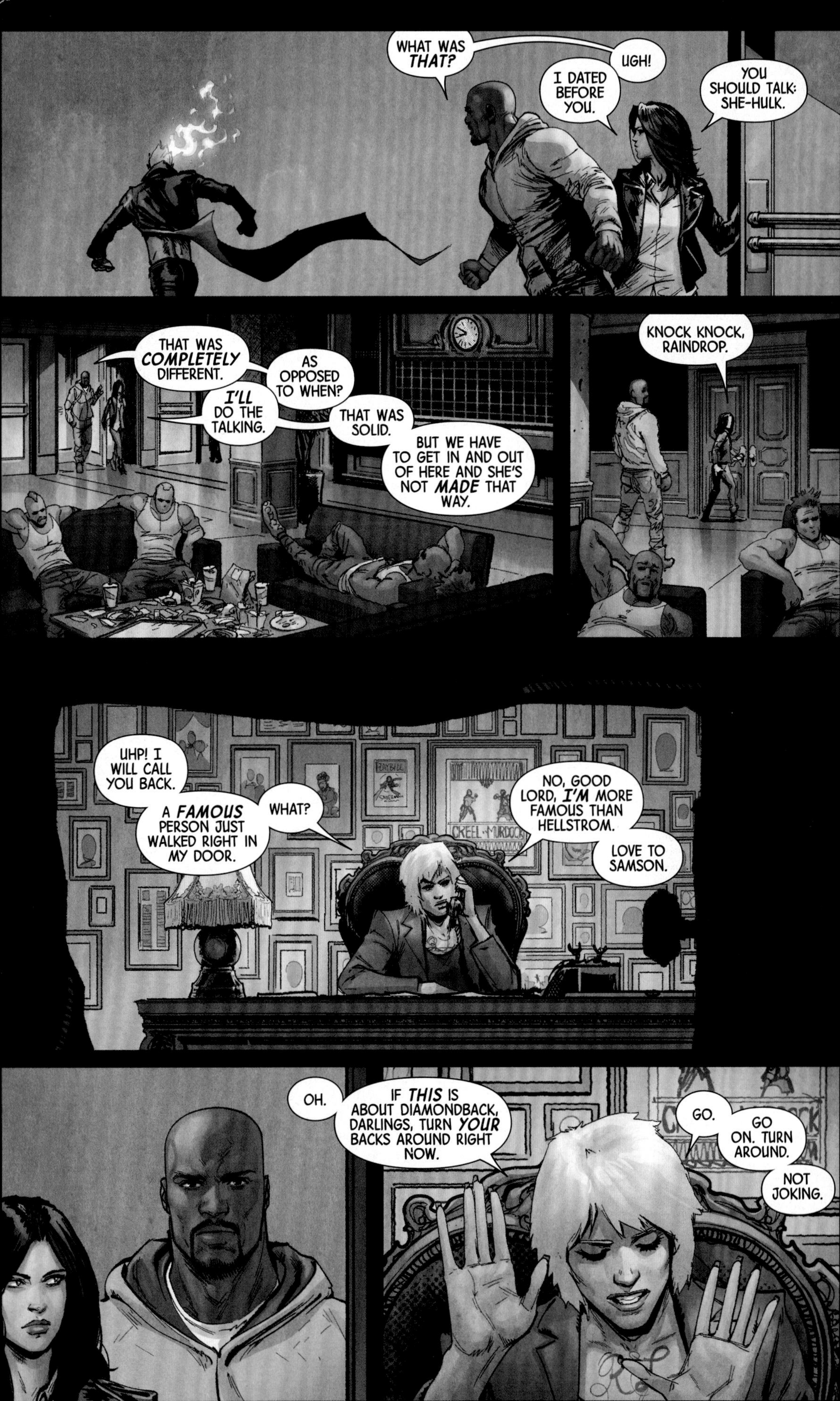
WHAT WAS *THAT?*
UGH!
I DATED BEFORE YOU.
YOU SHOULD TALK: SHE-HULK.
THAT WAS *COMPLETELY* DIFFERENT.
AS OPPOSED TO WHEN?
I'LL DO THE TALKING.
THAT WAS SOLID.
BUT WE HAVE TO GET IN AND OUT OF HERE AND SHE'S NOT *MADE* THAT WAY.
KNOCK KNOCK, RAINDROP.
UHP! I WILL CALL YOU BACK.
A *FAMOUS* PERSON JUST WALKED RIGHT IN MY DOOR.
WHAT?
NO, GOOD LORD, *I'M* MORE FAMOUS THAN HELLSTROM.
LOVE TO SAMSON.
CREEL • MURDOCK
OH.
IF *THIS* IS ABOUT DIAMONDBACK, DARLINGS, TURN *YOUR* BACKS AROUND RIGHT NOW.
GO.
GO ON. TURN AROUND.
NOT JOKING.

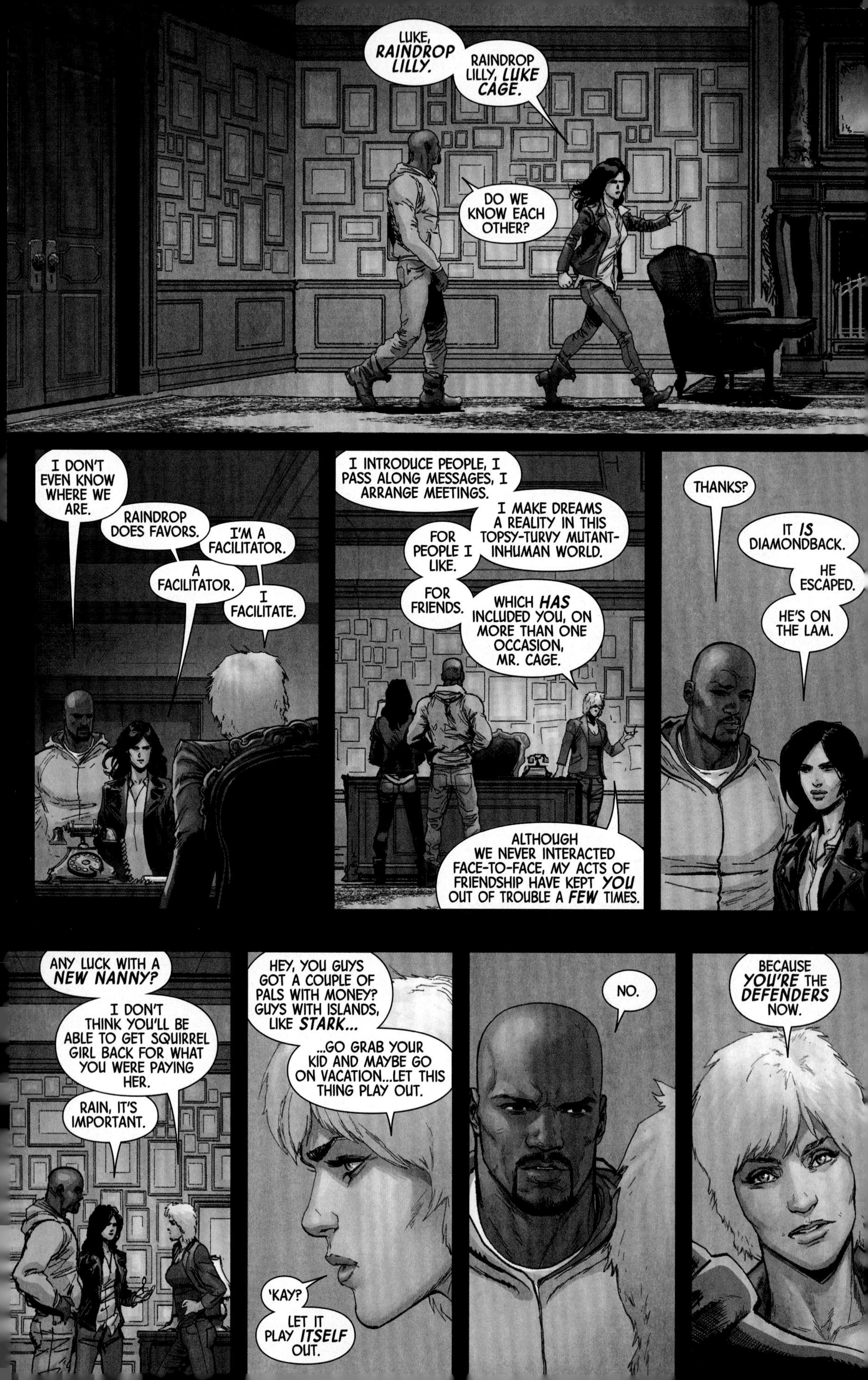

LUKE, RAINDROP LILLY.
RAINDROP LILLY, LUKE CAGE.
DO WE KNOW EACH OTHER?
I DON'T EVEN KNOW WHERE WE ARE.
RAINDROP DOES FAVORS.
I'M A FACILITATOR.
A FACILITATOR.
I FACILITATE.
I INTRODUCE PEOPLE, I PASS ALONG MESSAGES, I ARRANGE MEETINGS.
I MAKE DREAMS A REALITY IN THIS TOPSY-TURVY MUTANT-INHUMAN WORLD.
FOR PEOPLE I LIKE.
FOR FRIENDS.
WHICH HAS INCLUDED YOU, ON MORE THAN ONE OCCASION, MR. CAGE.
ALTHOUGH WE NEVER INTERACTED FACE-TO-FACE, MY ACTS OF FRIENDSHIP HAVE KEPT YOU OUT OF TROUBLE A FEW TIMES.
THANKS?
IT IS DIAMONDBACK.
HE ESCAPED.
HE'S ON THE LAM.
ANY LUCK WITH A NEW NANNY?
I DON'T THINK YOU'LL BE ABLE TO GET SQUIRREL GIRL BACK FOR WHAT YOU WERE PAYING HER.
RAIN, IT'S IMPORTANT.
HEY, YOU GUYS GOT A COUPLE OF PALS WITH MONEY? GUYS WITH ISLANDS, LIKE STARK...
...GO GRAB YOUR KID AND MAYBE GO ON VACATION...LET THIS THING PLAY OUT.
'KAY?
LET IT PLAY ITSELF OUT.
NO.
BECAUSE YOU'RE THE DEFENDERS NOW.

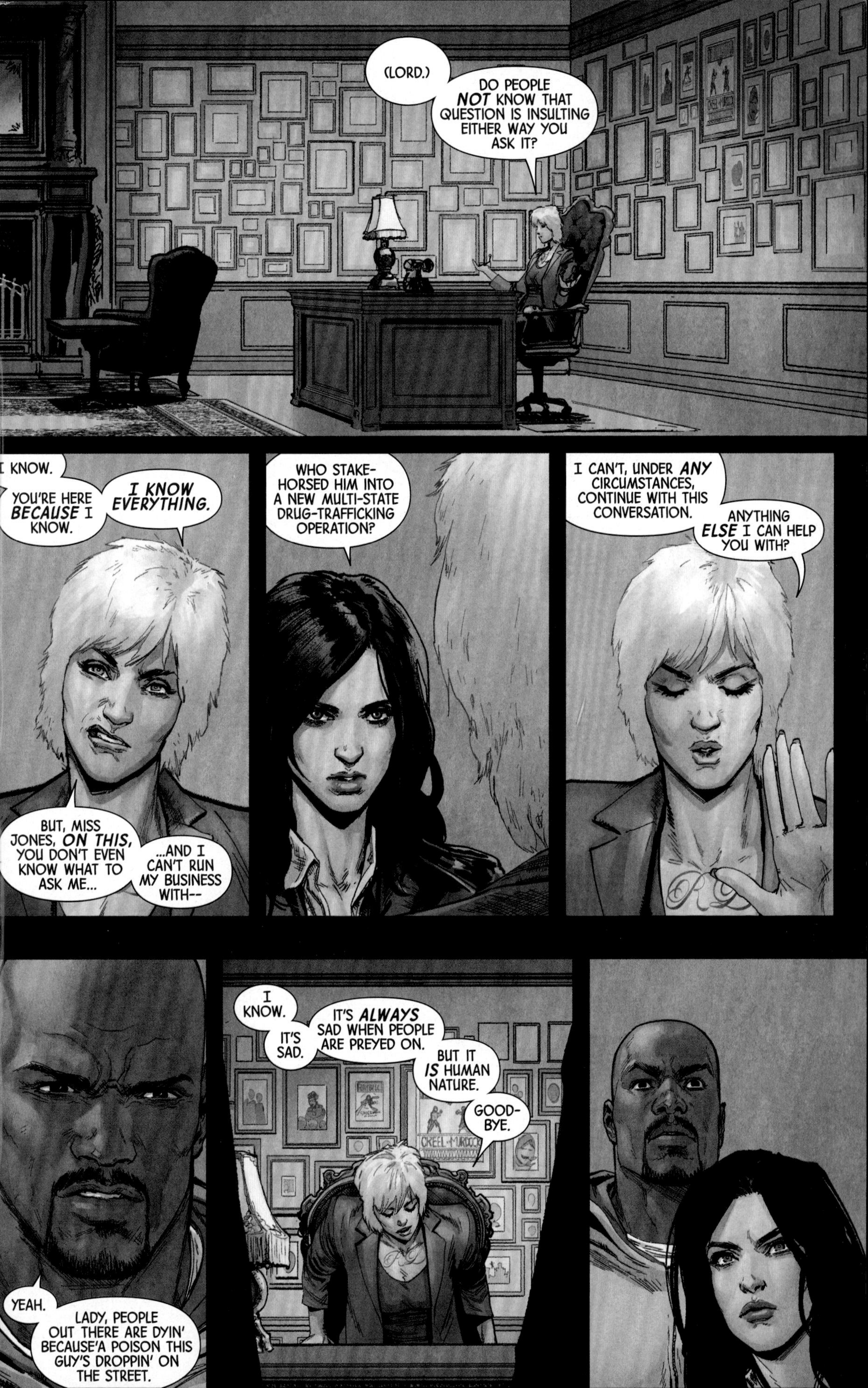

(LORD.)
DO PEOPLE NOT KNOW THAT QUESTION IS INSULTING EITHER WAY YOU ASK IT?
I KNOW.
YOU'RE HERE BECAUSE I KNOW.
I KNOW EVERYTHING.
BUT, MISS JONES, ON THIS, YOU DON'T EVEN KNOW WHAT TO ASK ME...
...AND I CAN'T RUN MY BUSINESS WITH--
WHO STAKE-HORSED HIM INTO A NEW MULTI-STATE DRUG-TRAFFICKING OPERATION?
I CAN'T, UNDER ANY CIRCUMSTANCES, CONTINUE WITH THIS CONVERSATION.
ANYTHING ELSE I CAN HELP YOU WITH?
YEAH.
LADY, PEOPLE OUT THERE ARE DYIN' BECAUSE'A POISON THIS GUY'S DROPPIN' ON THE STREET.
I KNOW.
IT'S SAD.
IT'S ALWAYS SAD WHEN PEOPLE ARE PREYED ON.
BUT IT IS HUMAN NATURE.
GOOD-BYE.

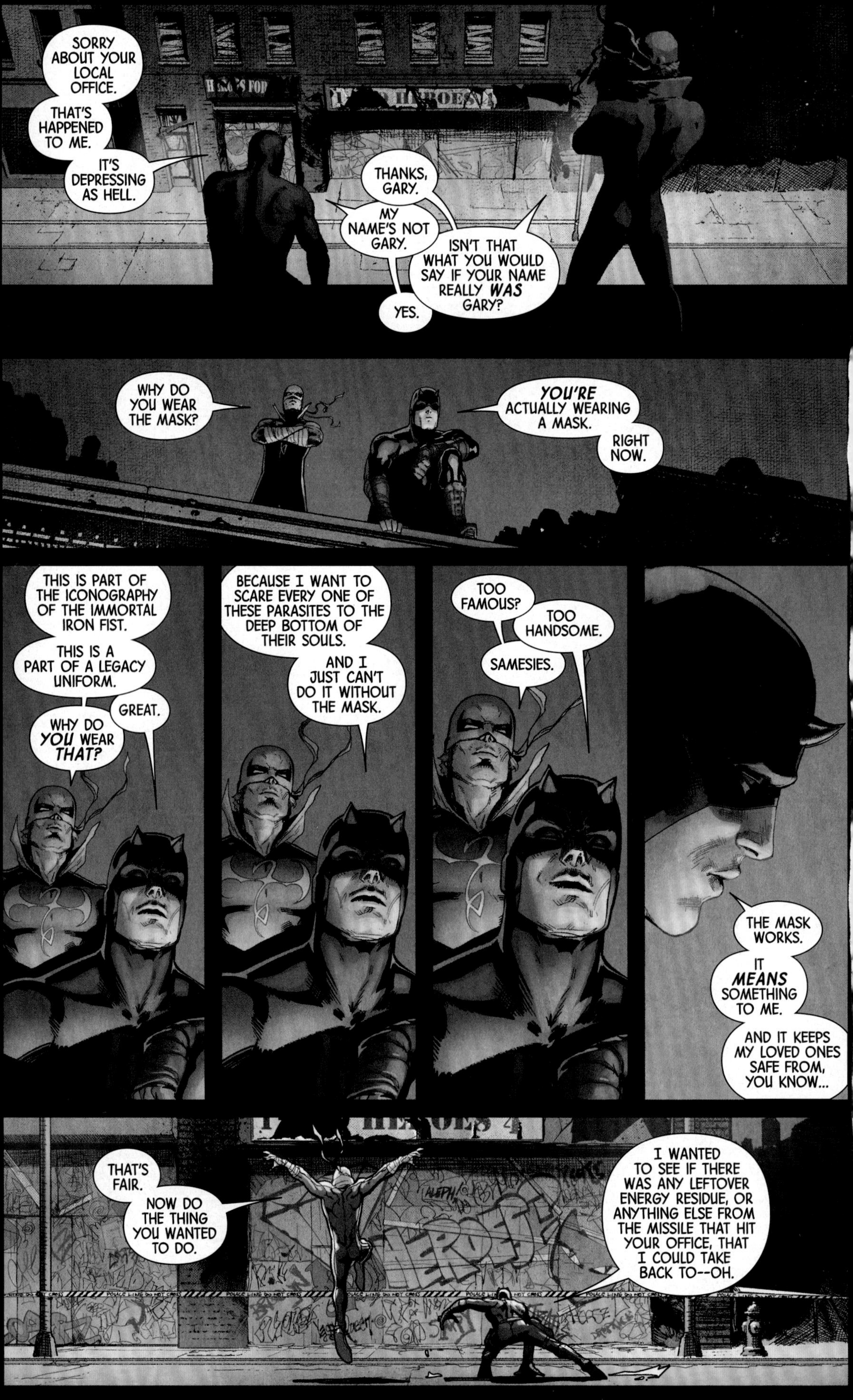
SORRY ABOUT YOUR LOCAL OFFICE.
THAT'S HAPPENED TO ME.
IT'S DEPRESSING AS HELL.
THANKS, GARY.
MY NAME'S NOT GARY.
ISN'T THAT WHAT YOU WOULD SAY IF YOUR NAME REALLY *WAS* GARY?
YES.
WHY DO YOU WEAR THE MASK?
YOU'RE ACTUALLY WEARING A MASK.
RIGHT NOW.
THIS IS PART OF THE ICONOGRAPHY OF THE IMMORTAL IRON FIST.
THIS IS A PART OF A LEGACY UNIFORM.
GREAT.
WHY DO *YOU* WEAR *THAT?*
BECAUSE I WANT TO SCARE EVERY ONE OF THESE PARASITES TO THE DEEP BOTTOM OF THEIR SOULS.
AND I JUST CAN'T DO IT WITHOUT THE MASK.
TOO FAMOUS?
TOO HANDSOME.
SAMESIES.
THE MASK WORKS.
IT *MEANS* SOMETHING TO ME.
AND IT KEEPS MY LOVED ONES SAFE FROM, YOU KNOW...
THAT'S FAIR.
NOW DO THE THING YOU WANTED TO DO.
I WANTED TO SEE IF THERE WAS ANY LEFTOVER ENERGY RESIDUE, OR ANYTHING ELSE FROM THE MISSILE THAT HIT YOUR OFFICE, THAT I COULD TAKE BACK TO--OH.

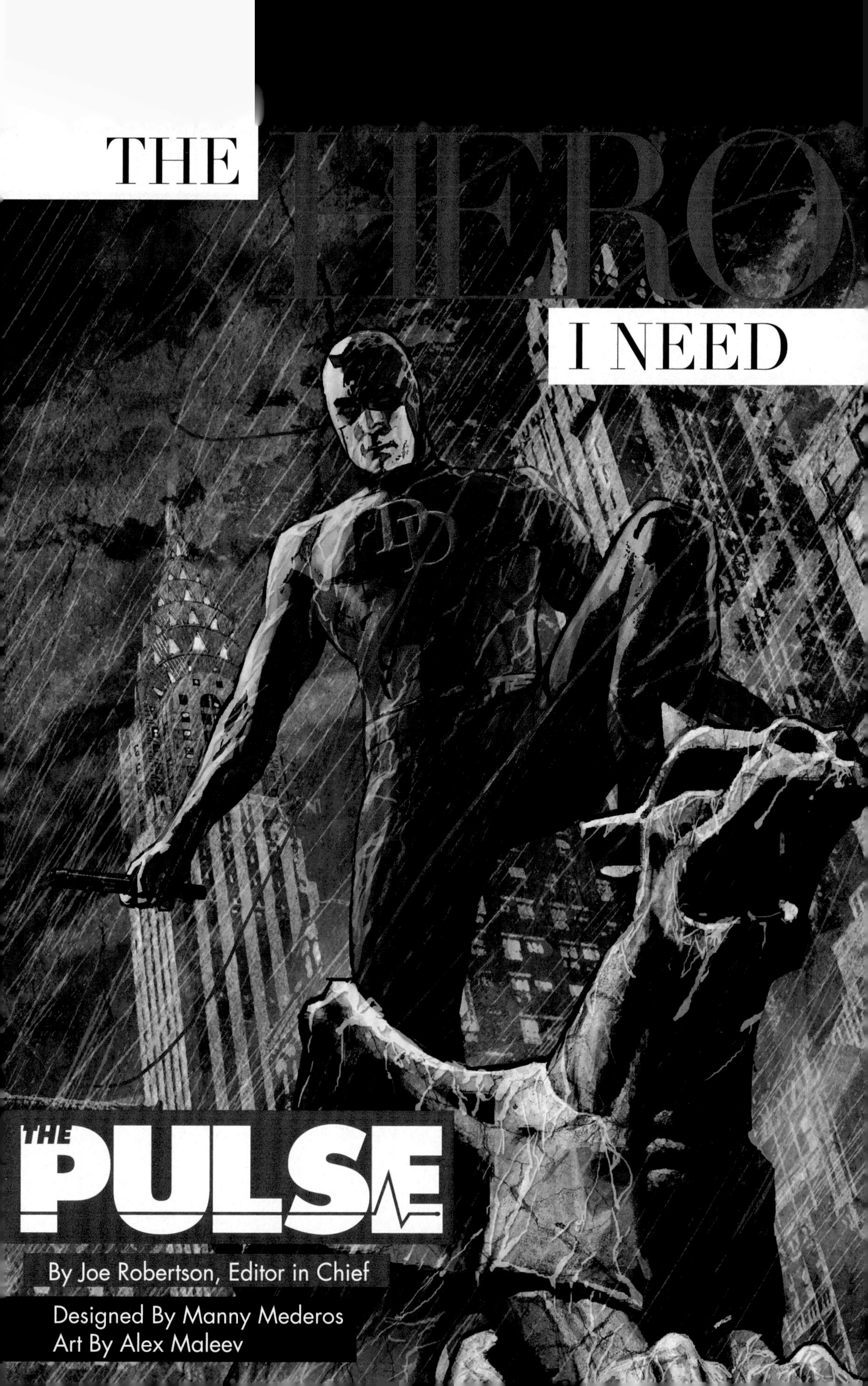

THE HERO I NEED

THE PULSE

By Joe Robertson, Editor in Chief

Designed By Manny Mederos
Art By Alex Maleev

NO. 3 VARIANT BY **W. SCOTT FORBES**

NO. 5 VENOMIZED VILLAINS VARIANT BY **DAVID MARQUEZ** & **RACHELLE ROSENBERG**

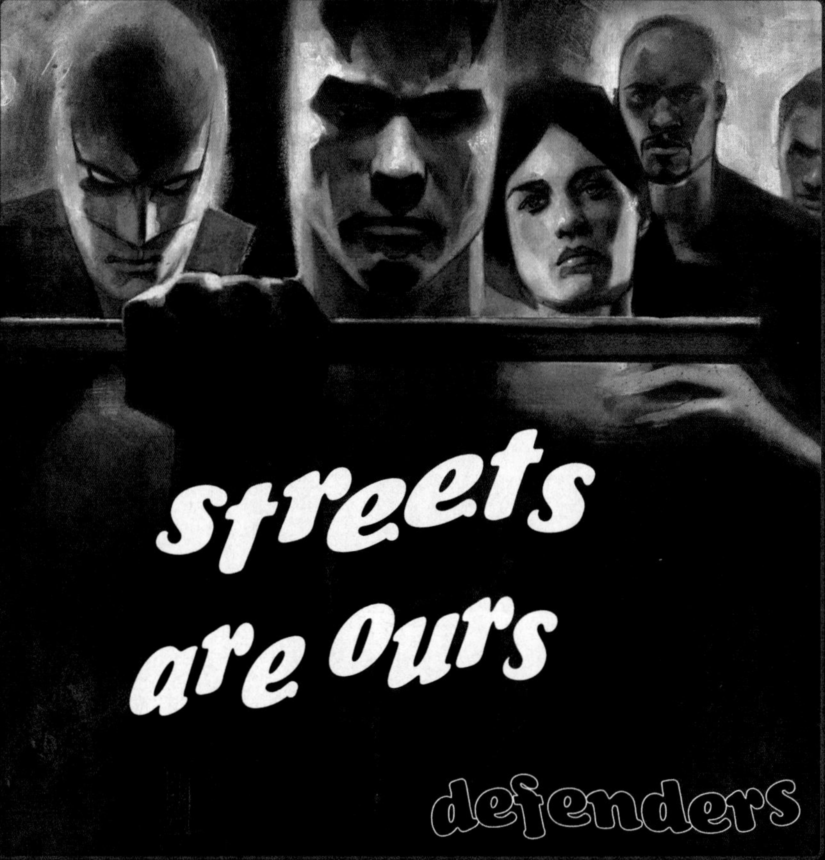
streets
are ours
defenders

NO. 1 HIP-HOP VARIANT BY **ALEX MALEEV**

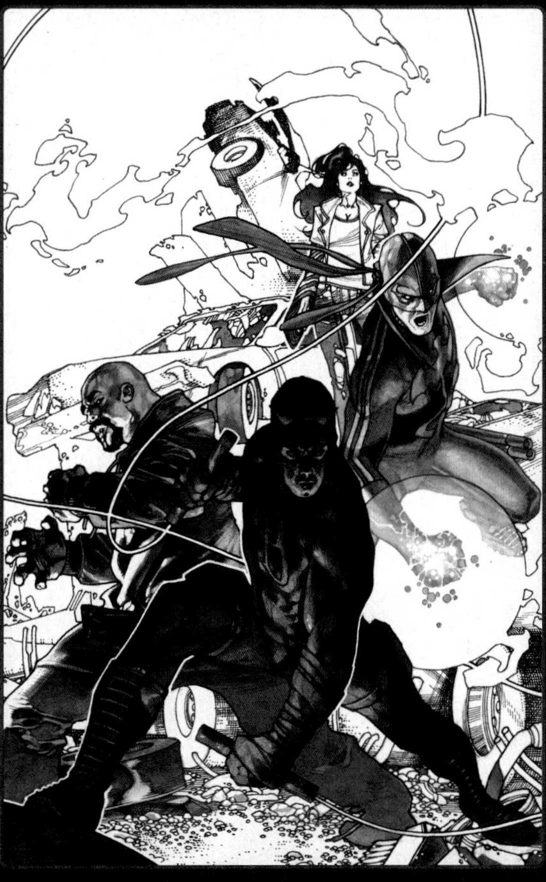

NO. 2 VARIANT BY **SIMONE BIANCHI**

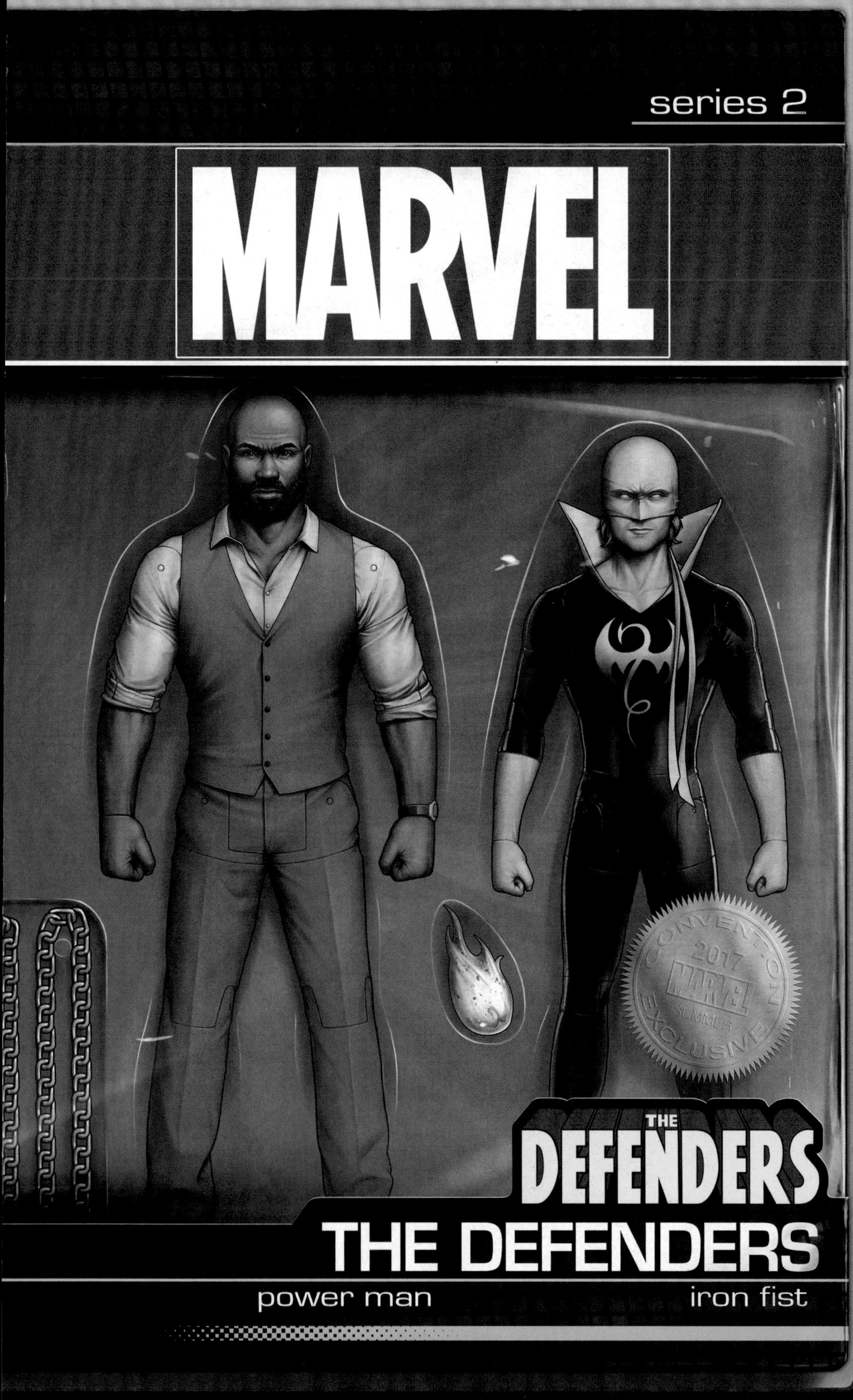
series 2
MARVEL
CONVENTION 2017 MARVEL SUMMER EXCLUSIVE
THE DEFENDERS
THE DEFENDERS
power man
iron fist

NO. 1 ACTION FIGURE VARIANT BY JOHN TYLER CHRISTOPHER

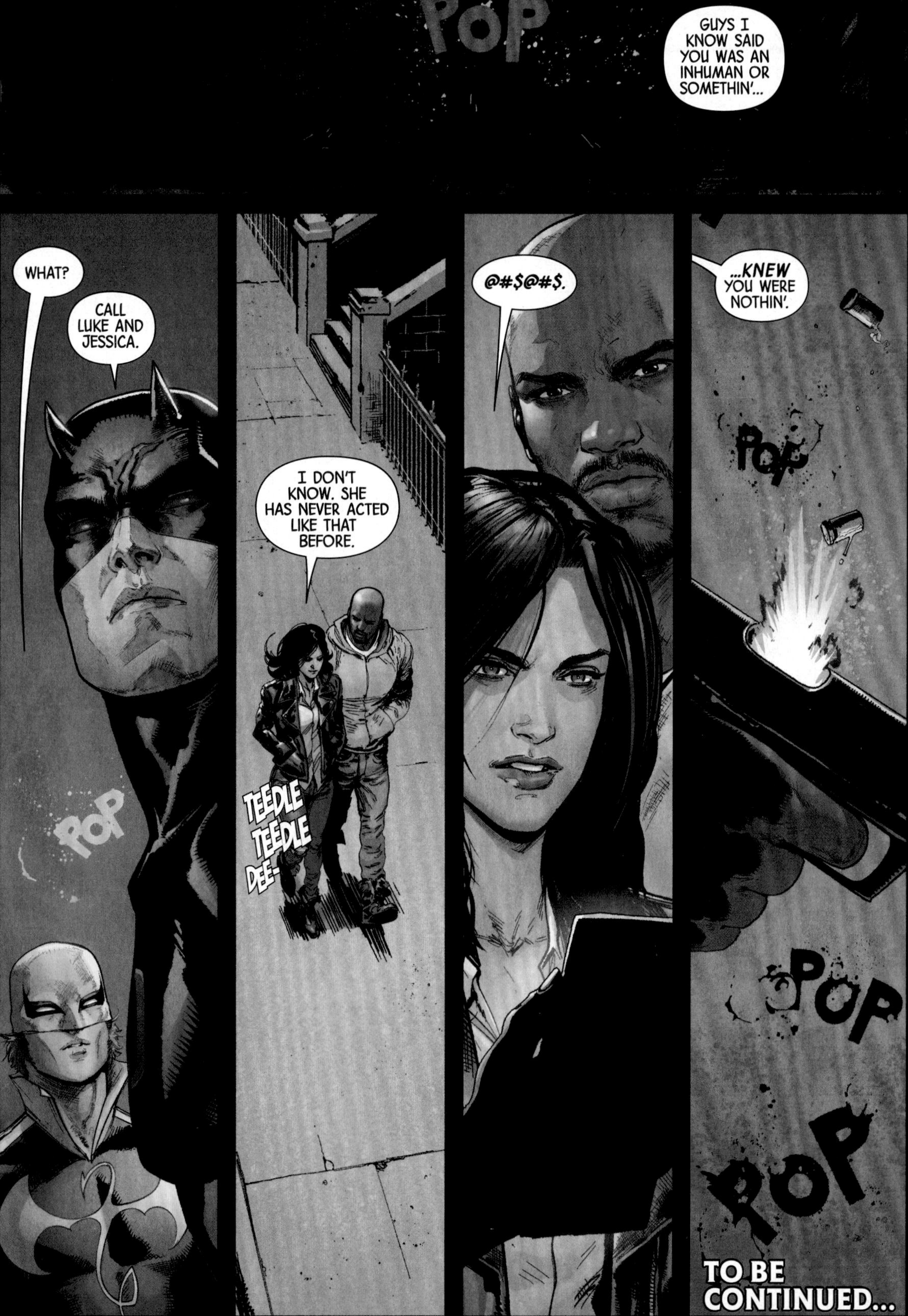
POP
GUYS I KNOW SAID YOU WAS AN INHUMAN OR SOMETHIN'...
WHAT?
CALL LUKE AND JESSICA.
POP
I DON'T KNOW. SHE HAS NEVER ACTED LIKE THAT BEFORE.
TEEDLE TEEDLE DEE-
@#$@#$.
...KNEW YOU WERE NOTHIN'.
POP
POP
POP
TO BE CONTINUED...

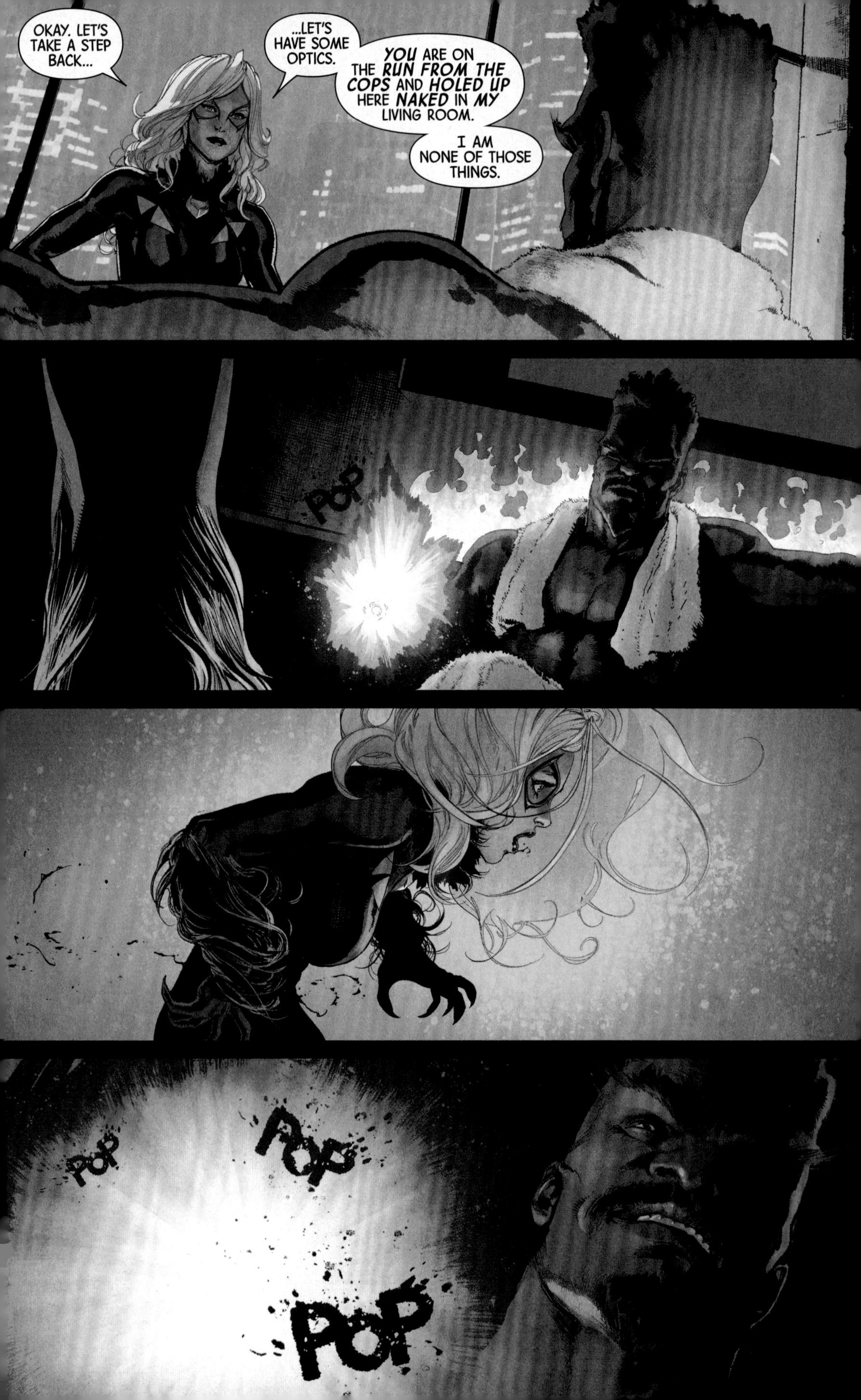
OKAY. LET'S TAKE A STEP BACK...
...LET'S HAVE SOME OPTICS.
YOU ARE ON THE RUN FROM THE COPS AND HOLED UP HERE NAKED IN MY LIVING ROOM.
I AM NONE OF THOSE THINGS.
POP
POP
POP
POP

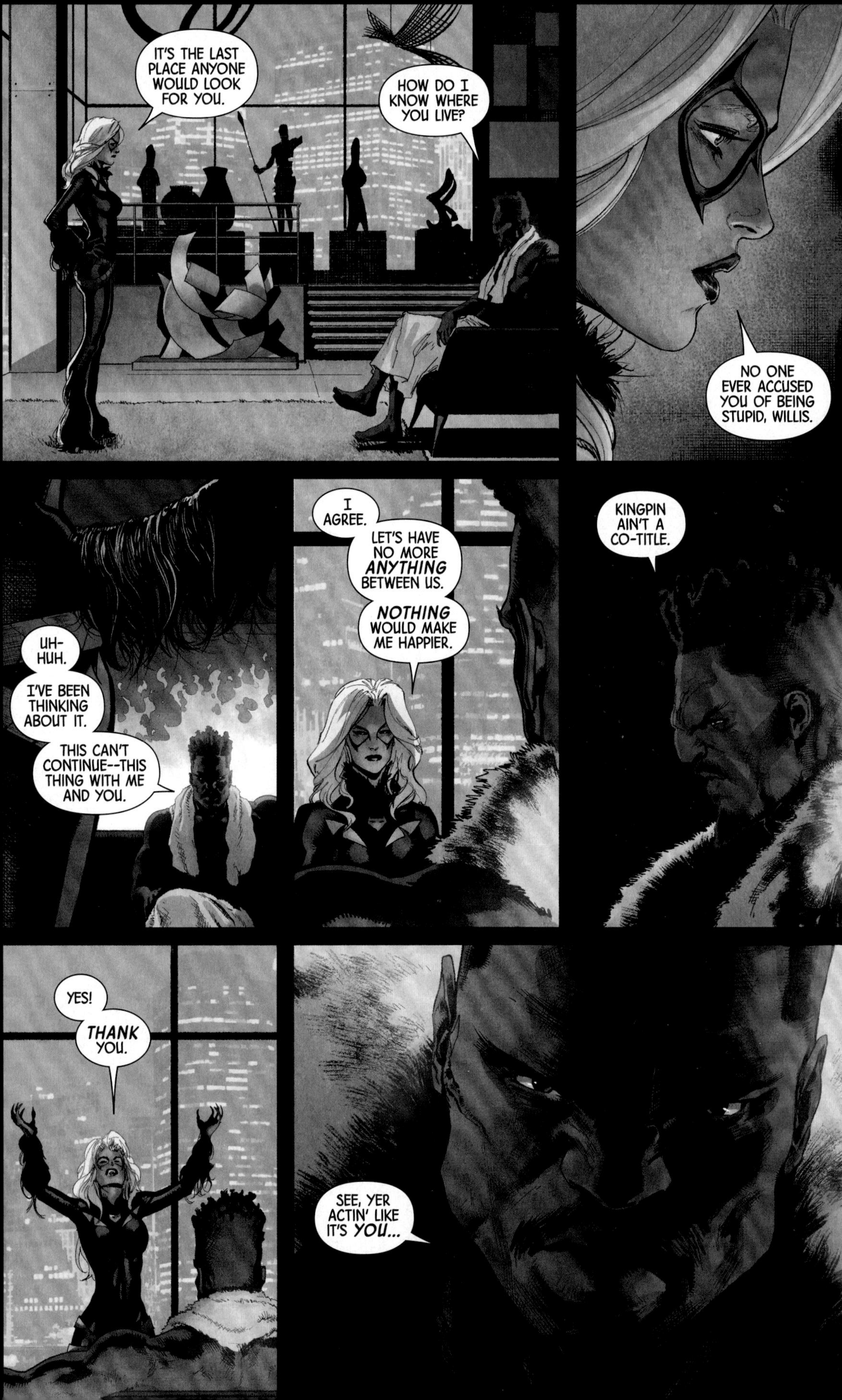
IT'S THE LAST PLACE ANYONE WOULD LOOK FOR YOU.
HOW DO I KNOW WHERE YOU LIVE?
NO ONE EVER ACCUSED YOU OF BEING STUPID, WILLIS.
UH-HUH.
I'VE BEEN THINKING ABOUT IT.
THIS CAN'T CONTINUE--THIS THING WITH ME AND YOU.
I AGREE.
LET'S HAVE NO MORE *ANYTHING* BETWEEN US.
NOTHING WOULD MAKE ME HAPPIER.
KINGPIN AIN'T A CO-TITLE.
YES!
THANK YOU.
SEE, YER ACTIN' LIKE IT'S *YOU*...

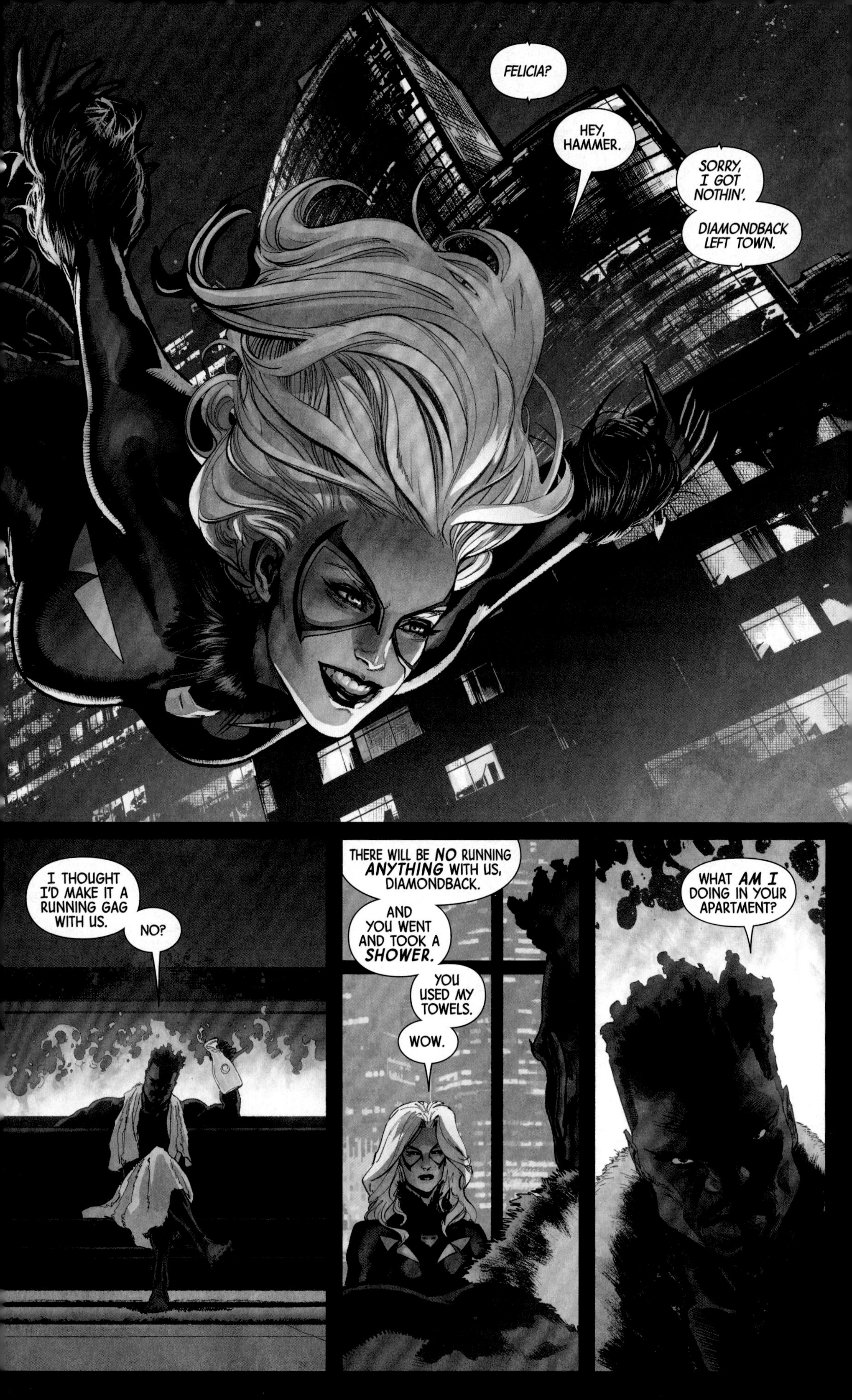
FELICIA?
HEY, HAMMER.
SORRY, I GOT NOTHIN'.
DIAMONDBACK LEFT TOWN.
I THOUGHT I'D MAKE IT A RUNNING GAG WITH US.
NO?
THERE WILL BE NO RUNNING ANYTHING WITH US, DIAMONDBACK.
AND YOU WENT AND TOOK A SHOWER.
YOU USED MY TOWELS.
WOW.
WHAT AM I DOING IN YOUR APARTMENT?

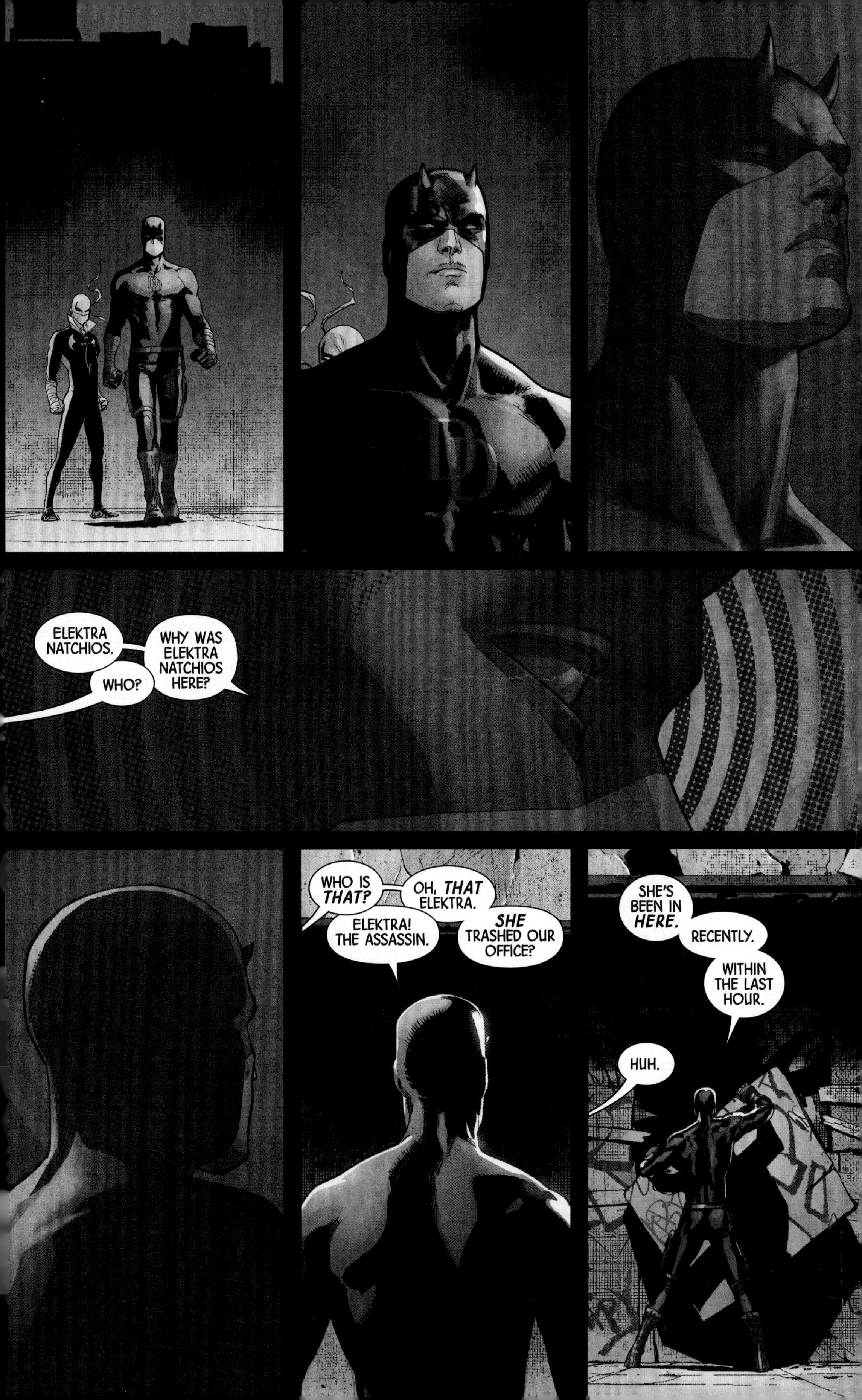
ELEKTRA NATCHIOS.
WHO?
WHY WAS ELEKTRA NATCHIOS HERE?
WHO IS THAT?
OH, THAT ELEKTRA.
ELEKTRA! THE ASSASSIN.
SHE TRASHED OUR OFFICE?
SHE'S BEEN IN HERE.
RECENTLY.
WITHIN THE LAST HOUR.
HUH.

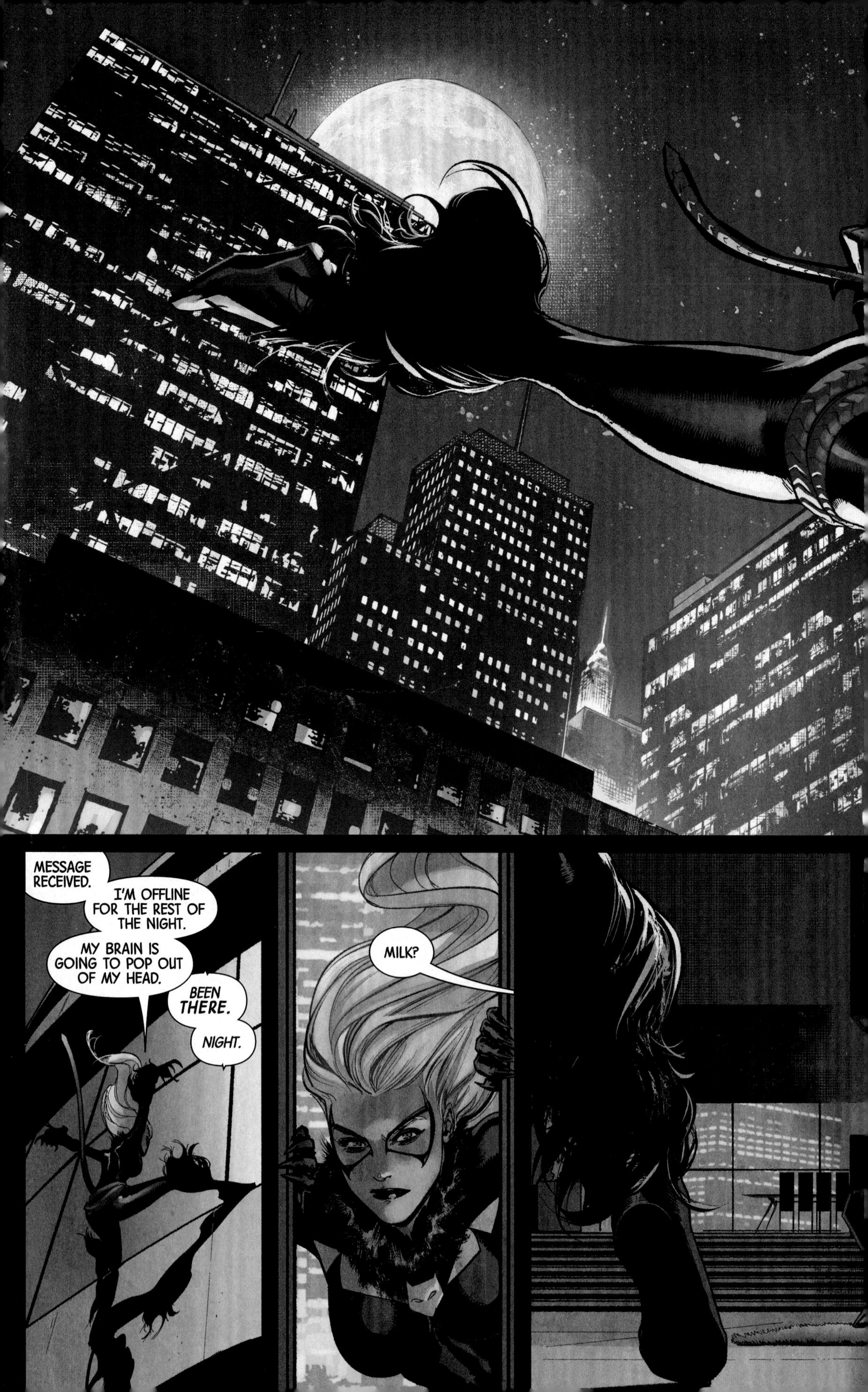
MESSAGE RECEIVED.
I'M OFFLINE FOR THE REST OF THE NIGHT.
MY BRAIN IS GOING TO POP OUT OF MY HEAD.
BEEN *THERE.*
NIGHT.
MILK?

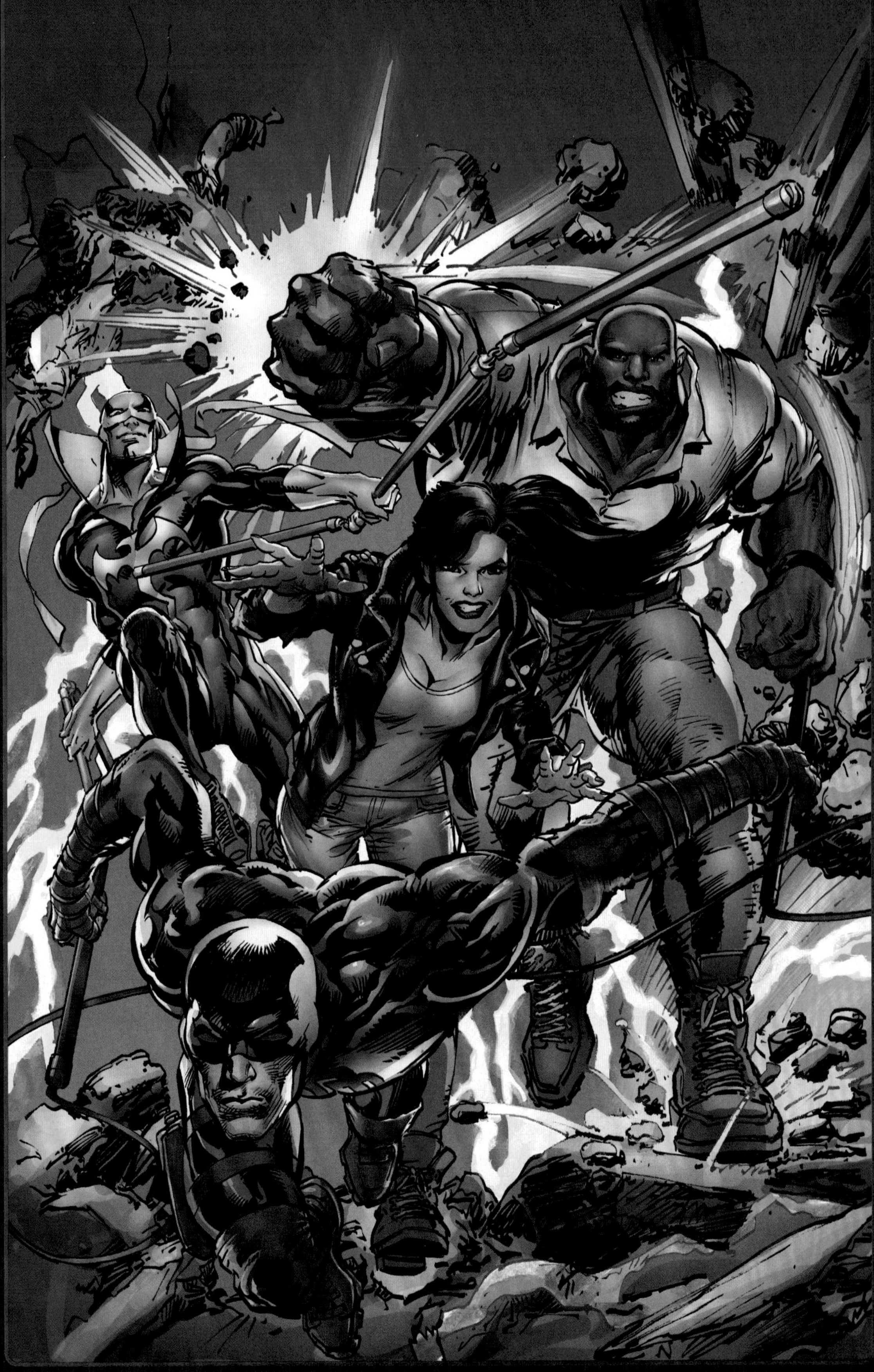

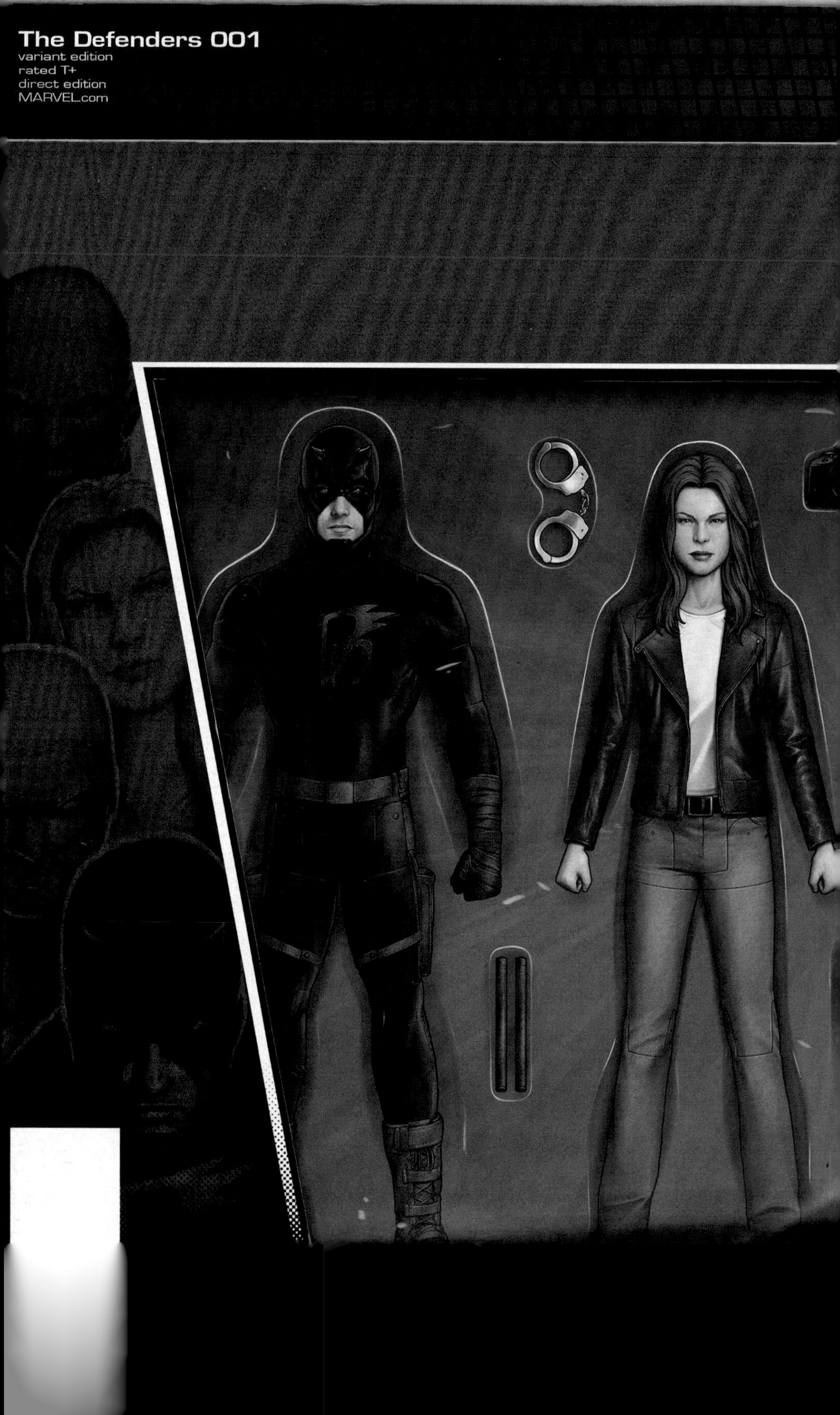
The Defenders 001
variant edition
rated T+
direct edition
MARVEL.com

New York City.

We are lousy with super heroes.

Every day, as editor in chief of one of the largest newspapers in the entire world, I receive voluminous updates on numerous super hero activities throughout the city, the country and the world.

So why can't I stop thinking about Daredevil?

There has been many a night--and I know so many of you will sympathize with this--that I have slept on the couch in my office because I looked outside my window to see the traffic backed up down Fifth Avenue for as far as the eye can see. On the far, far end of the miles-and-miles-long parade of cars, you can clearly see the firefight of super heroes stopping someone from doing something. I remind myself that whatever stopped traffic that bad was probably going to do something far worse if not for our citywide surplus of super-powers. No matter how you look at it, it's better to be sitting alive in your car (or couch) than dead and vaporized by Doctor Doom's death ray you didn't even see coming.

Then there's the little things: I have caught myself worrying about Spider-Man if he doesn't swing by my office at least twice a day.

That is what it's like to live in New York City.

Every kind of super hero you can think of finds their way here. I don't know why. But 99 percent of them are here. The biggest question is why is 99 percent of the super-criminal activity is ALSO located here. Why are you here where all the super heroes live? We'll put a pin in that for another editorial.

But, with all this...why can't I stop thinking about Daredevil?

I keep asking myself: Why is there a man in a devil costume running around the shadows of Hell's Kitchen--even though I believe he is the only one that still calls it Hell's Kitchen? Why does every police blotter and eyewitness report that I have read about him seem go out of its way to point out Daredevil was "badly hurt" doing whatever he was doing?

Police and eyewitnesses all comment about the cuts and bruises and blood. If Daredevil has powers, they are certainly not in the Hulk/Thor/Thing category. He doesn't even seem close to the Spider-Man category. This very well may be an ordinary man dressed

as the devil going out every night doing whatever he can to scare the crap out of the bad people so the good people can get a good night's sleep.

Why do I keep thinking about Daredevil?

Because I wish I was him.

This city is a mess. This country is a mess. We are more divided now than we thought possible. And with that comes insulation. People stop enjoying going out. People stop enjoying interaction. People stay home. People make their own entertainment. We cower in fear and start resenting each other for it.

Except people like this Daredevil.

He goes out and makes the world a better place, and he

doesn't seem to have much to back it up. Nothing but sheer force of will.

I wish that instead of sitting here wondering if I locked all the doors, I had the courage to stand outside my house and guard my neighbors. I wish my next-door neighbor, a fellow I'm quite fond of, had the courage to guard me as well. I wish we all had each other's backs. I wish all of us had the desire to bleed a little bit for our fellow person's well-being.

Arguments about vigilantism will never go away. There have been those who will take the law into their own hands for as long as there has been man and law. I decided to abandon the argument and instead focus my attention on admiring those worth admiring.

I sometimes wonder how many times my life has been saved by people like Daredevil without my ever even knowing. According to Chief of Crime Control Strategies Richard Cheek, criminal activity in that area of the city is at a historic low. Thank you to the police, thank you to the FBI, the agents of S.H.I.E.L.D., the EMTs and security guards, but I think some of us might owe Daredevil more thanks than we think.

Until the streets are safe and the local authorities finally get this city under peaceful control, until we can stand together and protect each other...

Thank you, Daredevil.

I wish I was you.

Follow *The Daily Bugle* Opinion section on Facebook and Twitter @DBUGLEopinion, and sign up for the DB Opinion Today newsletter.

A version of this editorial appears in print on April 20, on Page A22 of *The Daily Bugle*. Today's Paper | Subscribe

LUKE CAGE

THE PULSE *interview*

By Benjamin Urich

Designed By Manny Mederos

Luke Cage.

Of the seemingly endless list of people who have taken on the role of protector of this city, this country, this planet and beyond...Luke Cage, for all of his in-your-face bravado, is actually one of the least controversial and most beloved members of the super-powered community.

According to a recent *Daily Bugle*/Gallup poll, Luke Cage is actually the People's Choice to run for mayor of the City of New York–a role Cage is quick to reject. "Not my world" is all he had to say on the subject.

Maybe it's because Luke Cage's story is, oddly, an American story of survival. Carl Lucas grew up on the mean streets of Harlem, only to find himself in prison for a crime it has since been proven he did not commit. In prison, as part of an illegal experiment, Carl Lucas, against his will, underwent a procedure that gave him what the government labels "omega-event-level super-strength" and his signature unbreakable skin. He left prison a changed man in every conceivable way, and has since dedicated each day of his life to doing everything he can for anyone who needs him. Some people even pay for the privilege. Luke Cage has been an Avenger, a Defender and, of course, a founding member of Heroes for Hire. A man has to eat.

After a handful of recent salacious tabloid headlines, some perpetrated by this very organization, I sat down with Cage to talk about his career and what's next for those of us who live down in the mean streets of the five boroughs.

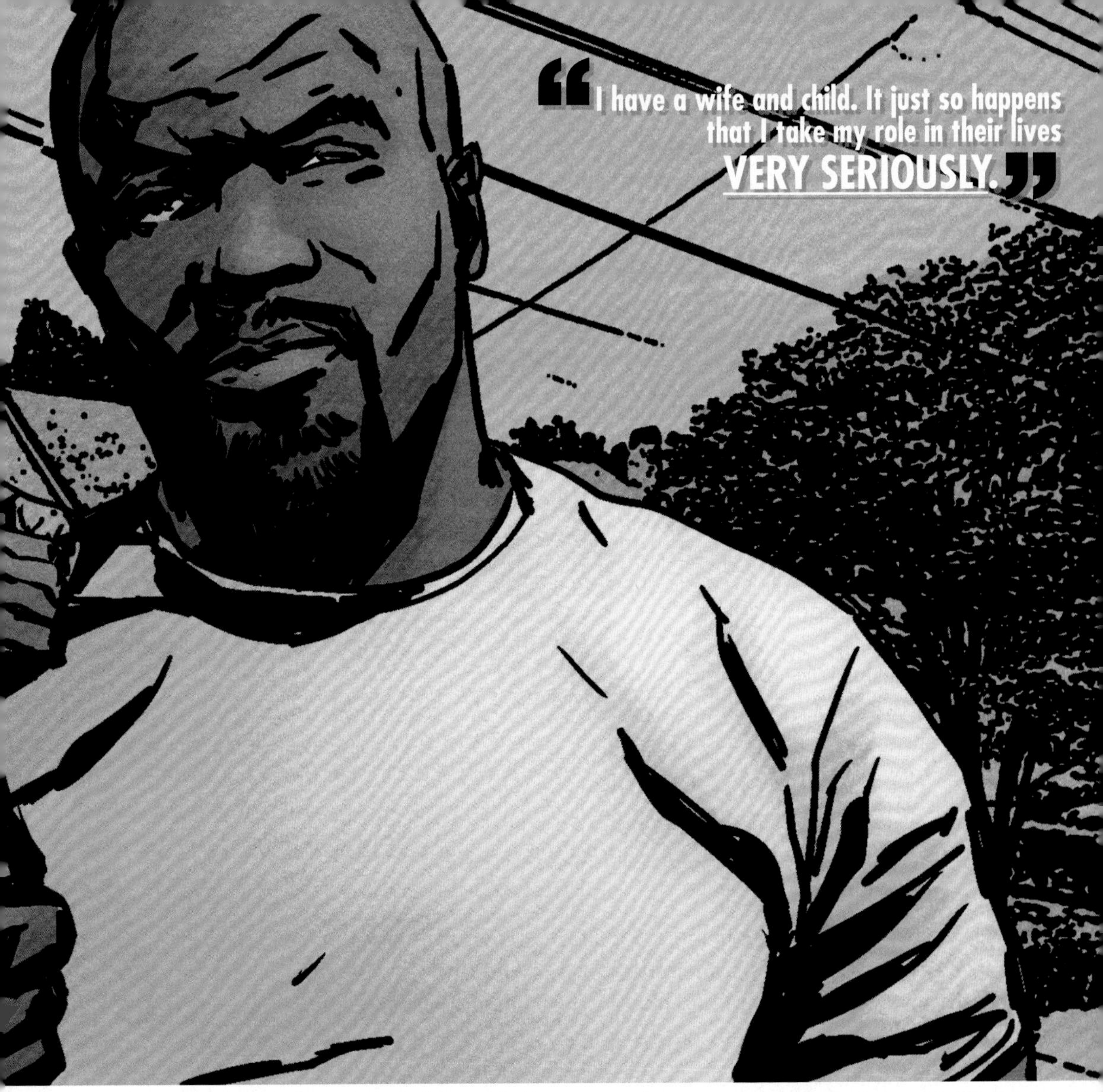
"I have a wife and child. It just so happens that I take my role in their lives VERY SERIOUSLY."

Art by: Michael Gaydos & Matt Hollingsworth

BEN URICH
Luke Cage. According to my research, this is the first sit-down interview you have given in many years...

LUKE CAGE
Yes. I'm not--a lot of people run to the press to ensure they're being heard. I get that. I guess it was the way I was raised--words can be cheap. All that matters is action. You see a lot of politicians saying one thing and doing another, and still, in this day and age where these lies are so obvious, people still fall for them. I can't stand it. I thought the best way was to not participate in the nonsense, allow my actions to speak for themselves. It works most of the time.

BEN URICH
What convinced you to sit down with me today?

LUKE CAGE
Well, a couple of things. Number one is... There have been some headlines about me and my wife, and they were painting a picture that was the direct opposite of the truth. A good friend of mine pointed out that no matter what I think my silence means, it is interpreted by most as non-denial... If I'm not denying it, it must be true. No one knows that I'm choosing to ignore it because it's stupid. So I thought I would come here and tell people that it's stupid.

BEN URICH
So I take it you're here to say you're not having an affair...

LUKE CAGE
Perfect example. I'm out on the street, speaking to a longtime colleague of mine, like a war buddy... we hug goodbye, someone takes a picture of the hug from a distance...and it looks like I'm macking on some lady in broad daylight. What bothers me about this is, of course, it's not true. I have a wife and child. It just so happens that I take my role in their lives very seriously. I take my role as an African-American man in the public eye very seriously. Someone else used me to make money...with a lie. I guess I can put up with people using us to make

Art by: Michael Gaydos & Matt Hollingsworth

money if it's the truth, but this is the opposite. I don't like being painted as something that I find abhorrent. And the flip side is, I know by denying it, I might sound guilty too. I know this. But I have to tell the truth.

BEN URICH
You and Jessica Jones are still together...

LUKE CAGE
Yes.

BEN URICH
You have a lovely daughter.

LUKE CAGE
Yes. Thank you.

BEN URICH
How is fatherhood?

LUKE CAGE
Fatherhood. True story, I once got into a good old-fashioned street fight with Dr. Doom...

BEN URICH
And fatherhood is scarier?

LUKE CAGE
You beat me to the punchline! (laughs)

BEN URICH
How is raising a family, doing what you do?

LUKE CAGE
Ask me in ten years. Is it any different than a cop or a fireman, a federal agent or S.H.I.E.L.D. agent with a family? It's a scary job. But I come home every day, so far, and if I've done it right, I've left the world better than I found it. So does my wife. So does my best friend. My feeling is, if we do that every day, then the world my daughter is going to grow up in will be far better than the one my wife and I grew up in, which, in fact, sucked. I'm not alone in this, but I live by the idea that if everyone woke up one morning and decided to actively be the best version of themselves, or just do their job exceptionally well, the entire world would shift immediately into something–well, frankly, something we all deserve. Right?

BEN URICH
Fair enough. It's just a very unique thing for your community.

LUKE CAGE
What's that now?

BEN URICH
Other than the Fantastic Four, you don't see many public displays of family in the super hero--

LUKE CAGE
Well, that's not true. The Avengers are a family. The Defenders are a family. The X-Men? Most of the super hero community

tends to gravitate toward each other, because we came from broken homes or disappointing homes or just bad homes. While we're pulling ourselves up out of the sludge, we meet other people like us and we end up really bonding with each other and helping each other, lifting each other up–then all of a sudden, you turn around and you have a family. I built my family. Danny Rand is my family. He is my brother. Daredevil is family. Literally, I'd do anything for these people. Anything. It's one of the great surprises of doing this–that you get to meet the other people who inspire you and you get to see how amazing they are in real life. These people understand me on levels that other people might not, because we share a common experience. It's cool to have super-powers, it is. I'm not ever going to be one of those people that complains about my power and the responsibility it brings. But, like everything, it comes with its own problems, and you still want to complain about work to your peers. Especially if that work includes getting punched in the side of the head by a cosmically enhanced Doctor Doom. You're going to want to have a friendly, trustworthy ear. It's nice to have that. I know I sound like one of those billionaires whining about

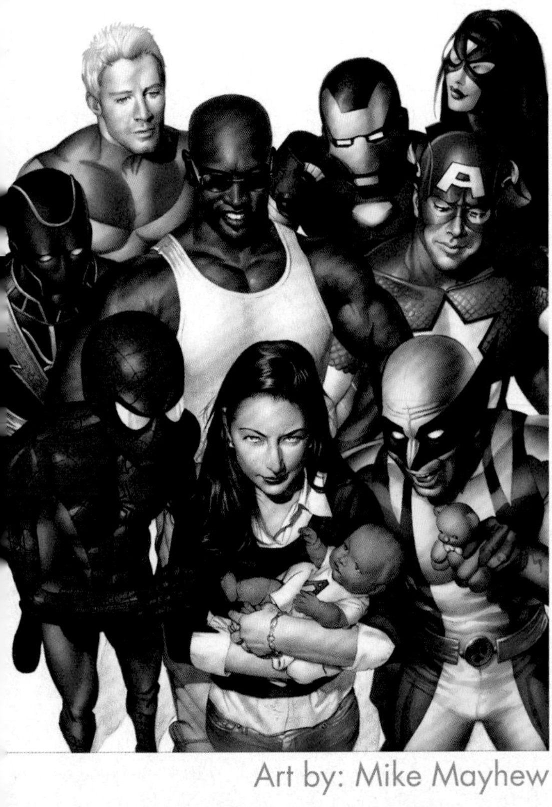

Art by: Mike Mayhew

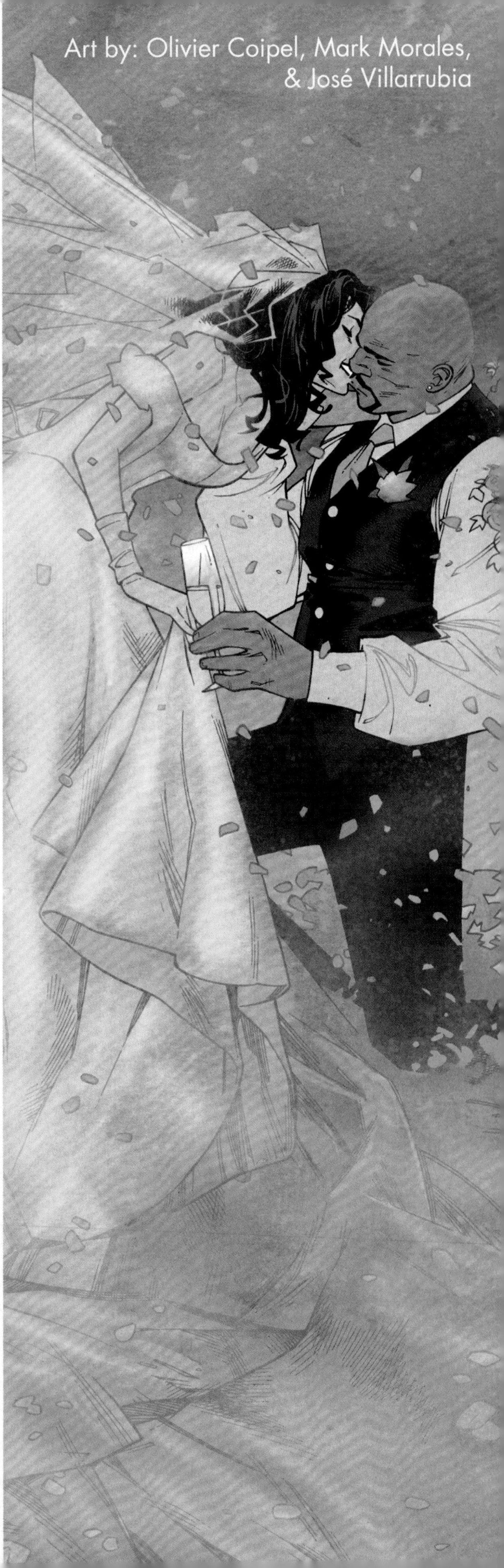

Art by: Olivier Coipel, Mark Morales, & José Villarrubia

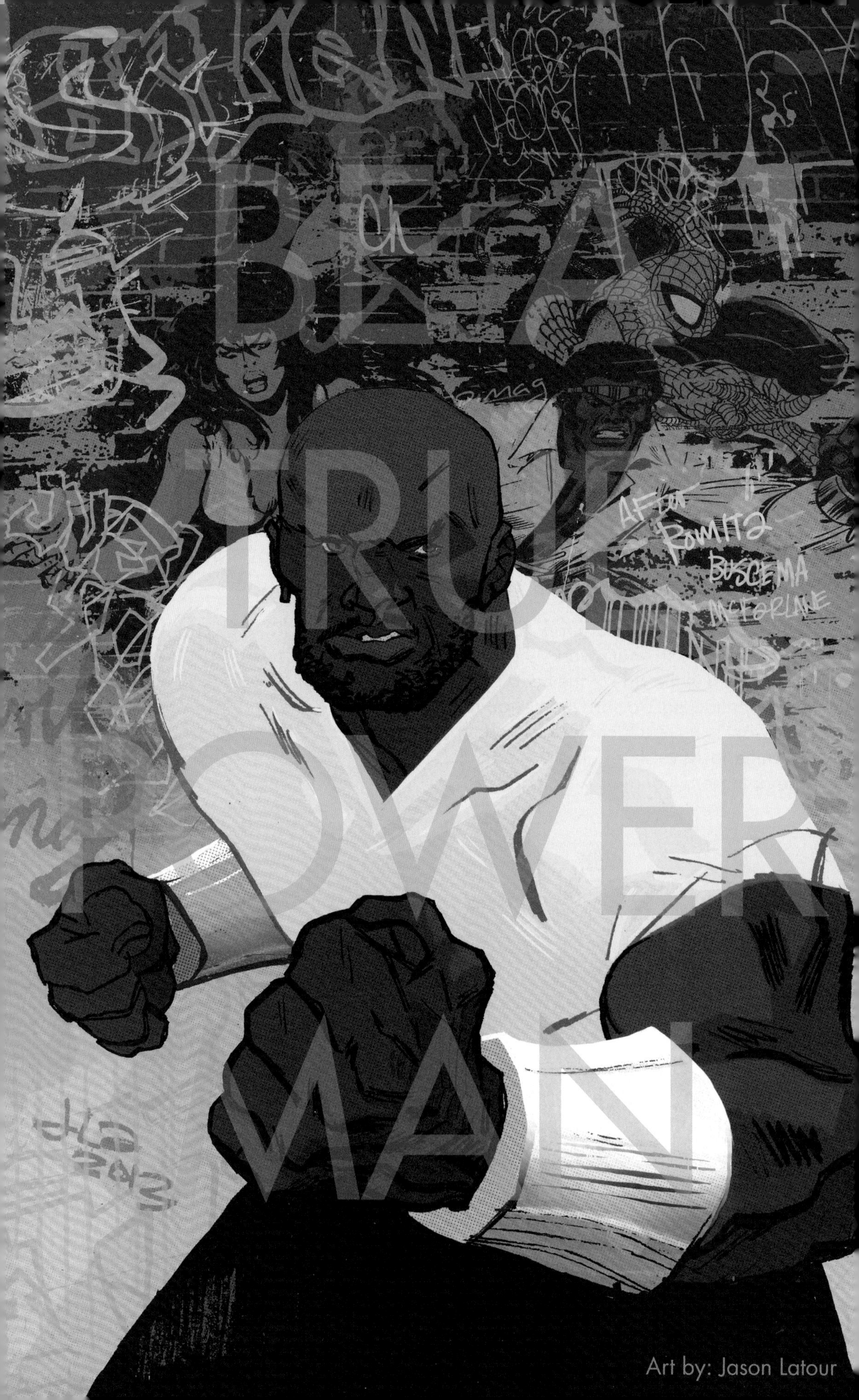
TRUE
POWER
MAN
After Romita
Buscema
McFarlane
Art by: Jason Latour

tax reform, but when you have super-powers, there are still concerns.

BEN URICH
The safety of those around you--

LUKE CAGE
Number one concern.

BEN URICH
There's been a lot of talk recently about vigilantism and the role of the costumed hero--

LUKE CAGE
There always is.

BEN URICH
So if you have something to lose--if you have family--why do it?

LUKE CAGE
We need cops and we need firemen and we need agents of S.H.I.E.L.D. And you know what? We need more of all of them. But we CLEARLY need more than that. There are really dangerous people out there eager to take advantage of everything and anyone because, dammit, they have it coming. I have seen this since I was a baby. I know this. There are people who will do and say anything to get "what's theirs" and they don't follow any kind of code. They run by rules the police cannot work with.

BEN URICH
Sometimes very brazenly.

LUKE CAGE
Right?

BEN URICH
Recently, a character that calls himself Diamondback has been making some bold moves. A blast from your past.

LUKE CAGE
You mind if we don't talk about that?

BEN URICH
Okay.

LUKE CAGE
It's just, I'm inclined not to give that guy press. You know?

BEN URICH
I do. I was more interested in the history between you two.

LUKE CAGE
It's just that.

BEN URICH
What?

LUKE CAGE
It's history.

BEN URICH
Okay, today then. Are you surprised to find yourself "married with children"?

LUKE CAGE
Surprised doesn't quite cover it.

BEN URICH
I'm sure.

LUKE CAGE
I don't talk about it much because it is what it is and I have come to terms with it, but there was a time in my life where I thought I was going to die. First, on the streets. Then I thought I was going to die in jail. And for a long time, even after I got my powers, I thought I was going to just die from having something this unnatural done to my body. So for a good long period of my life I thought I was going of die. It's probably why I appreciate how lucky I am–

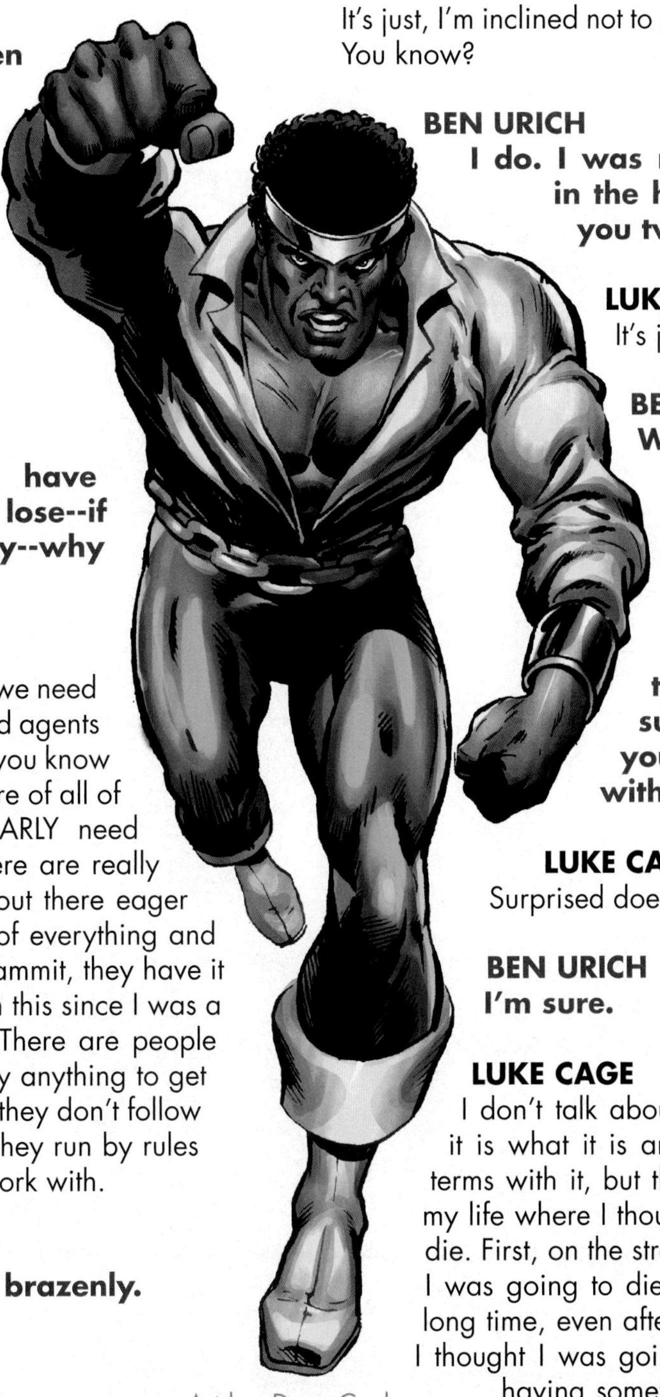

Art by: Dave Cockrum, Rich Buckler, & Paul Mounts

[Luke Cage pauses for over three minutes. In this time he does nothing but actively control his breathing and look out the window. Eventually, composed, he returns to the conversation as if no time has gone by at all.]

LUKE CAGE
What was the question?

BEN URICH
How has fatherhood been treating you?

[Luke Cage laughs. He realizes the question got the best of him. An omega-level super hero done in by the oldest of concerns.]

Obviously, this story is... to be continued.

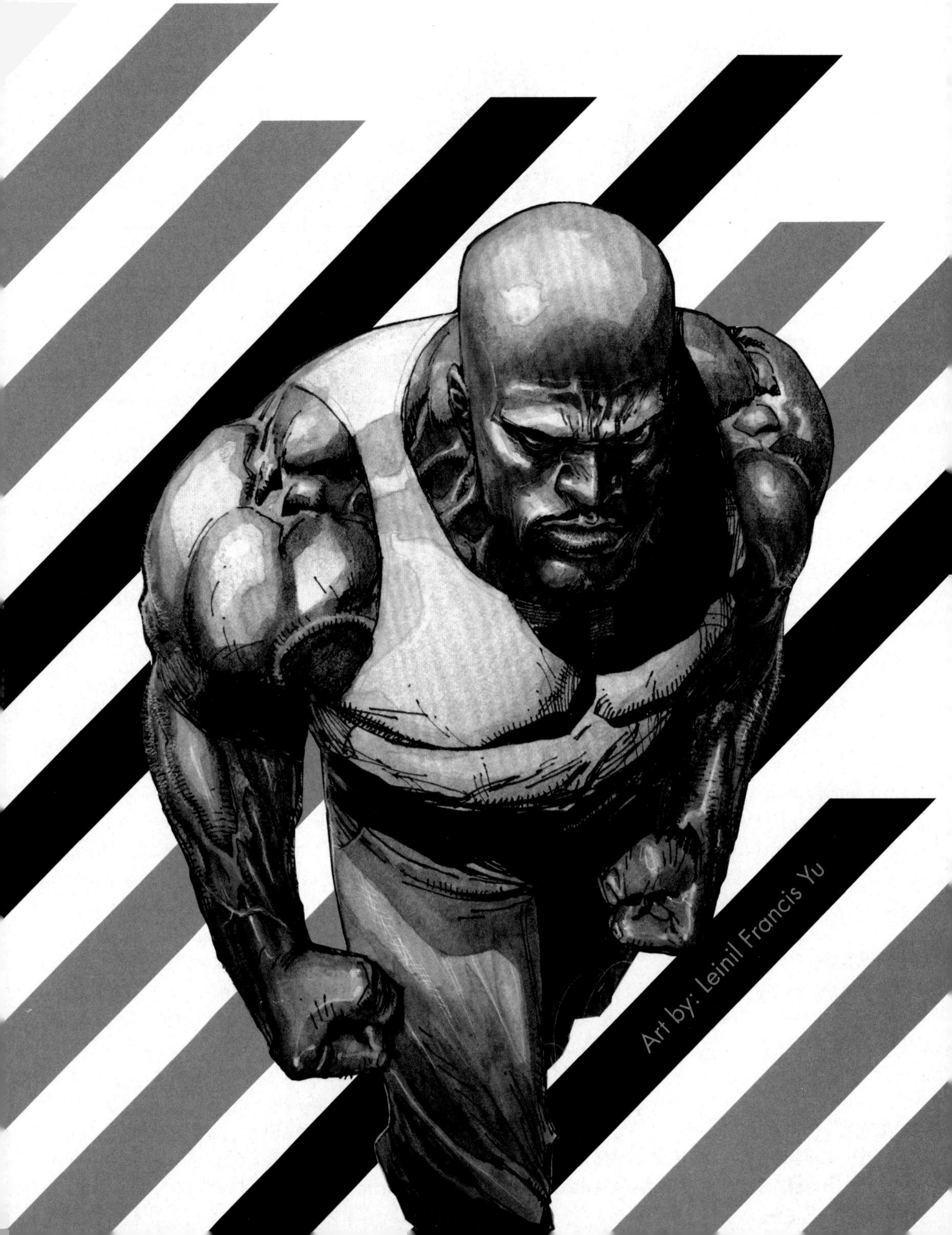
Art by: Leinil Francis Yu